STRANGERS IN OUR OWN LAND

STRANGERS IN OUR OWN LAND

RELIGION IN CONTEMPORARY U.S. LATINA/O LITERATURE

HECTOR AVALOS

Abingdon Press
Nashville

STRANGERS IN OUR OWN LAND
Religion in Contemporary U.S. Latina/o Literature

Library of Congress Cataloging-in-Publication Data

Avalos, Hector.
    Strangers in our own land : religion in contemporary U.S. Latina/o literature / Hector Avalos.
       p. cm.
    Includes bibliographical references.
    ISBN 0-687-33045-9 (binding pbk. : alk. paper)
    1. American literature—Hispanic American authors—History and criticism. 2. Religion and literature—United States. 3. Hispanic Americans—Intellectual life. 4. Hispanic Americans in literature. 5. Hispanic Americans—Religion. 6. Religion in literature. I. Title.

    PS153.H56A94 2005
    813'.509382--dc22

                                                                    2005024142

All scripture quotations unless noted otherwise are taken from the *New Revised Standard Version of the Bible*, copyright 1989, Division of Christian Education of the National Council of the Churches of Christ in the United States of America. Used by permission. All rights reserved.

Quotations from "La Carreta Made a U-Turn" are reprinted with permission from the publisher of *La Carreta Made a U-Turn* by Tato Laviera. Houston: Arte Público Press, University of Houston © 1992.

Quotations from *Borderlands/La Frontera* by Gloria Anzaldúa are printed with permission from the publisher, Aunt Lute Books, San Francisco, California © 1987, 1999.

05 06 07 08 09 10 11 12 13 14—10 9 8 7 6 5 4 3 2 1

MANUFACTURED IN THE UNITED STATES OF AMERICA

Contents

Foreword

All authors are debtors. First and foremost, I am indebted to my wife, Cynthia Avalos, who provided patience, proofreading, and the emotional nutrition on which scholars subsist.

Iowa State University provided a leave of absence in the spring of 2001 in order to help me begin reading the now extensive corpus of U.S. Latina/o literature. Most of the writing was done in the spring and summer of 2002. Diana Carson Boeckmann, Meghan Kershner, Jonathan Meier, Alexis Smith, and Christina Rodriguez gathered materials and/or proofread versions of this manuscript in their capacity as research assistants.

The book was born of the fires of teaching Latina/o literature and religion at Iowa State University. My dialogues with students were central to how this book developed in its approach and overall organization. I am a biblical scholar and scholar of religion by training and still an apprentice in U.S. Latino/a literature. No doubt, I have much to learn in all areas.

A number of authors made time to communicate personally with me about their work, including Alejandro Morales, James Curtis, and Ronald Ruiz.

Ilan Stavans provided some guidance on bibliography. Last but not least, I would like to thank "Rusty," the family squirrel, whose entertaining antics broke the tedium of writing a seemingly endless stream of characters on these pages.

I hereby absolve them all of any transgressions I very likely committed, for I am but human.

Preliminary Notes to the Reader

Ethnic terminology: Where relevant, I have used the terms, Latina/o, Latinas/os, though I also use Latino and Hispanic as an antidote to monotony. Chicana/o is used as virtually equivalent to Mexican American, and especially those that designate themselves by this term.

Orthography: Spelling names of deities and other foreign words are sometimes variable in the sources we have used. I generally follow Murphy (1993) in spelling terms and names found in *santería*. He does not underline the names of deities but does underline terms. He omits accentuation in most cases. I retain the spelling of the original sources when quoting those sources. Examples of such spellings include (see also the glossary): *ota*, Shangó, *santería*, Yemayá.

Pages in parentheses: In order to avoid tedious repetition of the source's name, and unless a source is explicitly mentioned, all page numbers in parentheses should be attributed to the book being featured as a Case Study in the relevant sections. Thus, pages in parentheses appearing after quotes/citations in the section titled Case Study 1: *Bless Me, Ultima* should be attributed to that work.

Introduction

B ehind the pen of every author is a theologian—or so it seems. Indeed, literature and religion have embraced each other since the dawn of writing. From at least 3100 B.C.E. (Bottero 1992; von Soden 1994), we have stories of gods and goddesses in Mesopotamia, the cradle of writing located in what is now Iraq. By the second millennium B.C.E. Mesopotamians had engendered the *Enuma Elish*, one of the earliest creation stories known to humanity (Heidel 1951). Mesopotamians bequeathed to us *The Epic of Gilgamesh*, formed around important religious concerns such as immortality and the purpose of life (Kovacs 1989; George 1999; Abusch 2001).

The Bible, the preeminent collection of religious books of Western civilization, is also considered one of the prime works of literature in human history. In fact, the history of Western thought can be encapsulated in the shift from seeing the Bible as sacred inerrant history to seeing the Bible as a predominantly political and literary expression of the Hebrew people and the sect of Judaism that became known as Christianity (see Frei 1974; Alter and Kermode 1987; Whitelam 1996).

Around the rest of the world, the literature deemed best is often religious in nature. Examples range from the *Mahabharata* in India to the *Popol Vuh* in Mesoamerica (for the latter, see Tedlock 1991). *The Book of the Dead* in Egypt and Dostoyevsky's *The Brothers Karamazov* cannot be understood without some knowledge of the religious traditions with which they are in dialogue. Cervantes, Dante, Milton, and Joyce all integrate or discuss religion to some level.

European literature in the Americas, brought here first by the Spaniards, began as a religious exercise in many ways. Christopher Columbus's *El Libro de las Profecías*, for instance, is little more than a compendium of biblical prophecies into which he has injected himself. He believed that his mission was prophesied in Scripture, and he saw himself as nothing less than the man who would pave the way for the Second Coming of Christ (Avalos 1996). Sor Juana (1648?–1695), the most celebrated woman writer in Mexico, was first and foremost a theologian with a pen, despite complaints that her subject matter was too secular (Paz 1988, 416–424).

Likewise, Anglo-American literature has often mirrored the religious life of its authors. Cotton Mather's *Magnalia Christi Americana* (1702), considered one of the most important books in the first one hundred years of Anglo-American history, is thoroughly religious in its orientation. Mather sees our country as a sort of new promised land. Most, if not all, subsequent American authors cannot be understood without some knowledge of religion.

Some even suggest that "the failure of religion" propelled the rise of English studies in the late nineteenth century (Eagleton 1983, 22). It is no surprise, therefore, that by 1926 important units of the Modern Language Association had already determined that the study of religion was an indispensable part of any advanced degree in American literature (Vanderbilt 1986, 262–263). Books by, among others, Halford Luccock (1934), David H. Hirsch and Nehama Aschkenasy (1984), David Jasper (1989), R. L. Brett (1997), and Michael E. Schiefelbein (2001) have helped relate religion to American and modern European literature.

Given such an intimate relationship between religion and writing, it is not surprising that the literature of U.S. Latinas/os would also bear religion as a dominant theme. There is hardly a single novel or work that does not discuss religion, or even center on it. And while the relationship between Latin American literature and religion has received attention (Brown and Cooper 1980; Díaz-Stevens 1996; Rivera-Pagán 1996, 2000), there is yet no systematic treatment of religion in U.S. Latina/o literature.

We do have many programmatic shorter studies, however. One of the first examples is an article by Dávid Carrasco (1982) on *Bless Me, Ultima*. More recent examples include comments on Cherríe Moraga's adaptation of indigenous traditions (Busto 1998) and a study of John Rechy's *The Miraculous Day of Amalia Gómez* by Luis León (1999). There are studies of U.S. Latina/o literature in anthologies relating to broader topics in religious studies, one example being a study of Judith Ortiz Cofer's *Silent*

Dancing by Elena Olazagasti-Segovia (1996). Note also efforts to integrate religion in a wide-ranging anthology of Latina/o literature compiled by Heyck (1994, 92–152).

On a broader level, the study of religion in U.S. Latina/o literature is important in light of the continuing discussion of what constitutes an "American identity." Samuel P. Huntington (2004), for instance, has argued recently that "Anglo-Protestant" culture is at the core of an American identity that is being threatened by Latinas/os, and, more specifically, by Mexican Americans. Huntington believes that Mexican Americans do not value key elements of the Anglo-Protestant culture, such as individualism and use of English as the primary language. Our study of U.S. Latina/o literature shows that U.S. Latinos are, in fact, following a very common trajectory as its members become educated segments of America. Moreover, any changes to the majority culture are happening in a peaceful manner driven mostly by market and demographic forces rather than through military force or coercion.

My objective is a programmatic monograph on religion and contemporary U.S. Latina/o literature. Within the field of U.S. Latina/o studies, my book represents a natural extension of the recent interest in the religious experiences of Latinos. According to Deck (1994), the "boom" in Latina/o theology began in 1992 (see also Díaz-Stevens and Stevens-Arroyo 1998; De La Torre and Aponte 2001). Among the most notable achievements in the study of the Latina/o religious experience is the multivolume series, *The Notre Dame History of Hispanic Catholics in the U.S.* (Dolan and Hinojosa 1994; Dolan and Vidal 1994; Dolan and Deck 1994), and volumes published by the Program for the Analysis of Religion Among Latinos (Stevens-Arroyo and Diaz-Stevens 1994; Stevens-Arroyo and Cadena 1995). A more comprehensive history of U.S. Latina/o religion by Moisés Sandoval (1990) needs updating. *The Journal of Hispanic/Latino Theology*, first published in 1993, also has many important articles on the religious experience of Latinas/Latinos.

The present study will show that U.S. Latina/o literature represents only partially the religious experience of the broader Latina/o communities. Within this religious experience, the long history of Catholicism dominates the discussion of U.S. Latina/o literature; however, the authors are exploring the Latina/o rediscovery and recovery of indigenous and African traditions. This survey shows that Latina/o authors constitute an elite group representing religious values typical of those held by Anglo-American educated classes. Some Latina/o authors are influenced by Marxist-inspired liberation theologies, which are not the norm for most

Latinas/os in the United States. Still other Latina/o authors have works predicated on stereotypical assumptions about African and indigenous traditions that were probably absorbed from a Eurocentric world. Indeed, a principal result of this study is that U.S. Latina/o writers often perpetuate Anglo-American and Eurocentric religious perspectives even as they purport to create, establish, or reclaim authentic indigenous traditions.

Scope

The definition of "American literature" has been a primary domain of academic institutions and publishing houses (See Shumway 1994; Graff 1987; Vanderbilt 1986). To distill this complex history, all we need to do is compare the views of American literature in Francis Otto Matthiessen's celebrated *American Renaissance* (1941) and anthologies of American literature, especially beginning in the 1980s (e.g., Baym et al. 1989). Matthiessen (1902–1950) saw as paradigms of American literature five white male nineteenth-century New Englanders who were active in the five-year period of 1850–1855 (see also Shumway 1994, 236–260). The five writers are Ralph Waldo Emerson, Henry D. Thoreau, Herman Melville, Nathaniel Hawthorne, and Walt Whitman. In contrast, more recent anthologies show growing interest in Spanish/Hispanic authors from Hernan Cortéz to Alberto Rios.

But Matthiessen was not alone in such biases. We could just as easily consider other milestones in the study of American literature, including Vernon L. Parrington's *Main Currents in American Thought* (1927) or the first edition of the *Cambridge History of American Literature* (1917–1921).

Even today it is not difficult to find a lack of recognition for U.S. Latina/o authors as American authors. In one university with which I am familiar it is still sometimes suggested to place U.S. Latina/o literature in Foreign Languages and Literatures. In any case, our study will argue that insofar as religion is concerned, U.S. Latina/o literature is a subset of American literature that has Latin American roots.

There are hundreds of written works of Latina/o literature, and it is impossible to feature them all in one volume. The focus is on a discrete set that might be used as a point of departure for a truly comprehensive and exhaustive treatment. Being cognizant that all selection is fraught with subjectivity, authors have been chosen, for the most part, by the following criteria, not necessarily in ranked order: (1) religious content and significance; (2) representation of the major Latina/o subgroups; (3) English-inclusiveness; (4) contemporaneous significance and prominence; (5) gender representation; and (6) prose narratives. Each of these deserves some justification.

Obviously, a book about religion in literature seeks works that discuss religion at some significant level. "Religion" here means any mode of life or thought that presupposes a relationship with supernatural beings and/or forces. We have an unabashedly empirico-rationalist definition of "supernatural" as anything that cannot be verified by one or more of the five senses and/or logic. In particular, I treat religions that are relatively well-known, such as Catholicism, Protestantism, and *santería*. I am interested in how U.S. Latina/o authors relate to these religions and how often they attempt to form their own substitutes or gravitate toward terms like "spirituality" or "higher consciousness."

By religious "significance," I refer to discussions that have relevance to recent and current history of religion in America. I attempt to include at least two complementary or contrasting case studies in each chapter that will serve as representatives of broader logical and ideological positions concerning religion among U.S. Latinos. In addition, I place these positions in a context that the modern lay reader and college student can understand without neglecting scholars of literature and religion.

In order to understand more specifically what we mean by U.S. Latina/o literature, we first must understand that "Latina/o" refers here to all groups of people living in the United States who trace their roots to the Spanish-speaking countries of Latin America. As such, literature by Haitians, Brazilians, and Spaniards is not included here. I do not include literature about Latinos written by Anglos—one interesting example being Louisa May Alcott's "M.L." (1863; see Elbert 1997, 3–28), which features a Cuban immigrant at a time when there was no cognizance that this character qualified as "Latino."

We can divide up this definition of "Latina/o" into at least two groups of authors. The first, and smaller, group consists of immigrants who are conscious of living as a Latina/o in America and write substantially in English. Such writers include Cristina García and Ilan Stavans. Adapting categories outlined by William Luis (1997, xi) for Latina/o Caribbean literature, I do not focus on writers who were "raised and educated in their native countries and later emigrated or were forced to live in the United States . . . [who] continued to write in the vernacular, mostly about themes pertaining to their island of provenance." Examples would include José J. Martí (1853–95) and Octavio Paz (1914–1998). As Bruce-Novoa (1990,

26) notes, these writers see themselves more as visitors than as permanent members of an American Latina/o community struggling with an Anglo majority.

The second and larger group consists of Latinos who were born and raised in the United States and who write principally in English (Luis 1997, xi). These writers are conscious of being part of a community of other Latinos (or their subgroups) living in the United States who struggle with their majority culture as well as with their own. Associated with the second group is the criterion of English-inclusiveness. Since this book is aimed primarily at American college students, I select Latina/o books that they can read. Thus, we differ little from preferences expressed for English inclusiveness by, among others, Marc Zimmerman (1992, 5). Where a Spanish-language book or passage is deemed necessary to our discussion, I include a translation.

Representation of the major Latina/o subgroups is more difficult to achieve. We have strictly followed a population approach. Mexican Americans form the largest group and have the longest continuous history in the United States. The bulk of Puerto Ricans and Cubans form smaller groups with shorter histories in the United States. We have included only one Dominican American, Julia Alvarez, who has described herself as a "Vermont writer" (Alvarez 1999, 195). We probably have not done justice to a growing number of Central American-Americans who will become an even more important part of U.S. Latina/o literature in the near future.

There is an intimate link between chronology and our criterion of contemporaneous significance. I focus on the period after 1959 for Mexican Americans because of the widespread opinion that this is when the first Chicano novel, *Pocho*, was written (Augenbraum and Stavans 1993, xvii; Leal 1985, 49; Paredes 1993, 41). Second, most works in this period manifest developments right before and after Vatican II, the most recent of the general Catholic councils that are instrumental in setting Catholic policy. I also believe that works written since 1959 form the bulk of the Latina/o literature that is well known and read by most college students today. Finally, it makes a book like this of manageable size.

We realize that there are objections to this focus. Luis Leal (1985, 44–62; 1997, 113) argues, for example, that Mexican American literature can be traced back to the sixteenth century. He identifies five periods: (1) The Hispanic period (to 1821); (2) The Mexican period (1821–1848); (3) The Transition period (1848–1910); (4) The Interaction period (1910–1942); and (5) the Chicano period (1942–present). If we follow Leal's periodization, then our book falls within the Chicano period.

For Cuban Americans, I focus on literature written after 1959, when a substantive Cuban American community formed. This means that Cristina García and Oscar Hijuelos are represented here, but José Martí (again) is not, despite recent attention to his theological ideas (see Arce-Valentín 1996). Puerto Rican literature here is mostly post-World War II, when there was a large influx of Puerto Ricans to the mainland, and particularly into New York. As such, we are often discussing what is sometimes called the "Nuyorican" stage of Puerto Rican literature (see Flores 1993, 64). The influence of important pre-World War II island writers such as Luis Llorens Torres (1878–1944), although it should be acknowledged, will not form a central focus of our study.

I acknowledge that gender affects reading and the themes chosen (Flynn and Schweickart 1986; Rebolledo 1995). There are now significant anthologies of Latina literature (Goméz, Moraga, and Romo-Carmona 1983; Rebolledo and Rivero 1993), as well as collections of studies of Latina literature (Sánchez 1985). I have not included enough women's perspectives. Protestantism was very difficult to represent from a gender perspective, as there are very few Protestant Latina writers who comment extensively on Protestantism. My admittedly male perspective, despite my pretense in reading feminist criticism, can profit from what I hope will be more voices of female scholars.

The ascendance of female scholars of religion is also changing the ways in which we think about the role of women in U.S. Latina/o religions. Various studies accent the manner in which women feel oppressed by religious structures (see Isasi-Díaz and Tarango 1992). There has been a multiplication of feminist/*"mujerista"* ("womanist") theologies (see Isasi-Díaz and Segovia 1996; I. García 2001). There are renewed studies of figures, such as Sor Juana, from a feminist perspective (Kirk 1998; Vuola 2001). Such interest in Latinas is, of course, part of efforts in America to raise the status of women in various religious bodies and study the role of women in American religion (see James 1980; Ohanneson 1980).

Genre forms yet another issue in selection. I have bestowed primary importance to prose narratives—novels. Most well-known literature by Latinos is narrative rather than poetry per se. We do include poetry that bears religious content and is exceptional in some other characteristic. A prime example is *La Carreta Made a U-Turn* (1979) by Tato Laviera, who is hailed as the bestselling Latina/o poet. I generally have avoided works intended as nonfiction, such as those written by Richard Rodriguez (1982, 1992). And I have not included genres that have been of historical significance in helping to create at least parts of U.S. Latina/o literature, including the *corridos* and the popular theater movement (A. Paredes 1958; Trejo 1979, 205–209; Leal 1997). In sum, aside from exceptional cases, the focus is on prose fictional or semifictional narratives.

Since I focus on religion, my "canon" can never be absolutely coterminous with the selections of an anthology chosen on other criteria. Other anthologies, as inclusive as their philosophy might be, also are cognizant of subjectivity in all selection and organization (see Warhol and Herndl 1991, xvi; Tweed 2002). For comparative purposes, my "canon" treats four out of the five main texts in the sample course syllabus of Augenbraum and Fernández Olmos (2000, 201). Twelve of our authors are represented in the anthology of twenty-five authors compiled by Augenbraum and Stavans (1993; see further our appendices 2 and 3). Chronologically, our selection roughly corresponds to that of chapter 7 "Contemporary Reflections of Identity" in *Herencia*, the recent anthology published by Nicolás Kanellos (2002).

General approach

The primary approach is *attitudinal*. This study is interested in how specific novels express attitudes toward particular religious traditions and/or religion in general. One principal reason for selecting this approach is pedagogical. This book was born out of the fires of teaching the subject of religion and Latina/o literature at Iowa State University. The audience was mostly Euroamerican, and none had advanced training in either religion or in literary criticism. I suspect the same is true for most students in most universities. The simple dichotomies of "positive attitudes" versus "negative attitudes" toward particular religious traditions proved very fruitful *as points of departure* for more sophisticated analyses by students. Sometimes we saw the ambiguity of authors who did not have purely negative or positive attitudes. Complexity arose out of the search for simplicity.

Having received rigorous philological training in ancient Near Eastern languages and literature, I also see the wisdom of centering all interpretations on references to the text. I attempt as much as possible to avoid theoretical literary speculation that cannot be supported by the text. I regard some literary theory as much too speculative, jargon-laden, and ethereal when applied to subjects that are relatively clear—namely, evaluation of whether attitudes toward religious traditions are positive or negative and whatever else we might infer about religion from direct reference to the text.

In some ways, I represent the reverse of Harold Bloom, a literary critic who may be mistaken for a scholar of religion after the publication of his *The American Religion* (1992). I am a scholar of religion pretending to be a literary critic. Needless to say, I do not engage in advocacy for a particular religious or nonreligious viewpoint in this book, even if my own viewpoint is that of a secular humanist. Rather, I am interested in how Latina/o authors view particular religious traditions and ideas. I talk about what authors believe and not what authors should believe. I attempt to gauge beliefs and draw sociological conclusions on the basis of statistical surveys when possible, even as I am aware of how statistics can be abused in the study of religious behavior (see Peña 1997). This is consonant with the manner in which religious studies ideally has been taught in major American universities (Capps 1995; Ramsey and Wilson 1970; Roberts and Turner 2000; Sizer 1967), even if some scholars think universities are still much too uncritical toward religion (Wiebe 1999; McCutcheon 2001).

Organization

One could construct a book on religion and literature in a number of ways. Ramón Gutiérrez (1991), for instance, sees the institution of marriage as a useful lens to study various aspects of society and religion in New Mexico. We could have studied a particular religious institution in literature as well, but I thought it too restrictive for my purposes. Another possible approach is as a "systematic theology," which follows traditional subjects of Christian theology. It might begin with views about God, then proceed to anthropology, Christology, hamartiology (the doctrines pertaining to sin), soteriology (the study of salvation), and eschatology (doctrines about the end of the world). Although Latina/o authors discuss these topics, such discussions are never so detailed as to warrant separate chapters that would be symmetrical in length and scope. A systematic theology approach would result in a very imbalanced treatment.

Since the fundamental approach adopted here is *attitudinal*, I have organized the book under the guiding theme of "attitudes toward" different larger socio-religious units such as Catholicism, Protestantism, and indigenous religions, among others. These units are much more understandable and meaningful for readers. The authors themselves think in this manner, as we can gather from interviews. But "attitudes" are simply a point of departure for our discussions, which additionally treat the narrative techniques and symbolism used by authors to express these attitudes. I aim for a happy medium between theology and literary issues.

I feature works that would be more representative than others when it comes to particular religious traditions. For example, Tato Laviera's *La Carreta Made a U-Turn* could have been featured (and is mentioned) in the chapter about attitudes toward Catholicism. However, as there are plenty of other works that can exemplify attitudes toward Catholicism, *La Carreta* is best featured in the chapter on attitudes toward African traditions, where representatives are more difficult to find, relatively speaking. Gloria Anzaldúa's *Borderlands* certainly could be featured in the chapter on Catholicism, but with plenty of other good candidates in that chapter, *Borderlands* is featured in the chapter highlighting attitudes toward indigenous religions. Anzaldúa provides a good juxtaposition to the male point of view found in Anaya in that chapter.

Each chapter begins with a "socio-historical overview," which aims to provide only enough information about the social history of the religious tradition at issue to appreciate the books that are featured. I cannot provide a comprehensive treatise on any particular religious tradition. This book includes statistical studies of Latina/o and American religious behavior published in the 1970s, 1980s, and early 1990s (e.g., González and La Velle 1985; de la Garza et al. 1992), when most of the books we feature were written.

As of this writing, we are also awaiting the final results of the massive survey called "Hispanic Churches in American Public Life" (hereafter HCAPL) under the direction of Dr. Gastón Espinosa. Sponsored by the Alianza de Ministerios Evangélicos Nacionales (AMEN) and the Mexican American Cultural Center (MACC), the survey may provide some of the most important statistics about the status and development of the U.S. Latina/o religious experience. We rely on the HCAPL preliminary report, published in 2003 (Espinosa et al.) for the most recent statistics on Latina/o religion. In all cases, statistics are to be used with caution, and only for the most general comparisons.

The main section of each chapter consists of "case studies" in which specific books will be discussed in some detail from the perspective of religion, even if there are other aspects that might be of interest, as well. The "critical discussion" section which follows each "case study" aims to place the author's work within the larger context of the attitudes toward religion. I also use this section as an opportunity to analyze critically where an author's work fits within the larger scope of religious research.

The length of the critical discussion depends on the depth of the religious content of the book. For example, *Borderlands* raises a host of religious issues that merit attention, while a book such as *Down These Mean Streets* may not raise as many. Finally, each chapter offers a "comparative summary," which briefly relates the works discussed in a chapter to: (1) other works in the same chapter; and (2) other books in our study and in the larger corpus of U.S. Latina/o literature.

Summary

Thomas Carlyle (1831/1937, 338), the famous Scottish author, noted that "literature is but a branch of religion and always participates in its character." The study of religion in U.S. Latina/o literature is a continuation of the study of religion in the literature of the world (see Kevane 2003). We see U.S. Latina/o literature as continuation of both Latin American and American literature. Some pedagogical handbooks of U.S. Latina/o studies (and of various subgroups) still overlook religion (e.g., Keller, Magallán, and García 1989). But, given the rise in academic interest in U.S. Latina/o religious experience, such an oversight is even less justifiable now. This book is meant to be programmatic, not exhaustive or even thoroughly representative of all views of religion that can be found in U.S. Latina/o literature. Mine is not the only way to study religion in Latina/o literature, or in any body of literature. I will count myself successful if I stimulate further research and expansion of the Latina/o corpus that will be analyzed for its religious content.

Chapter 1

Indigenous Religions

M ost Latinas/os see their roots as a mixture, a *mestizaje*, of indigenous and European blood. But while most Latinas/os are aware
that the predominant European heritage is specifically Spanish,
there is almost no symmetrical knowledge of the indigenous side.
Nonetheless, some U.S. Latina/o authors and scholars purport to be recovering authentic or representative indigenous religious traditions. But how
authentic and representative are those "indigenous" religious traditions?
In order to answer this question, we concentrate part of our discussion on
the concept of the "indigenous" among U.S. Latina/o authors, and particularly Mexican American authors, since the 1960s. Otherwise, we concentrate on attitudes toward indigenous traditions exemplified by two
well-known authors.

Socio-historical overview

European literary images of the "indigenous" peoples of the Americas
began with the first encounters (Alvar 1976; Jara and Spadaccini 1992).
Later, Hernán Cortés, Bernal Díaz del Castillo, Diego Durán, Bernardino
de Sahagún, and other explorers also produced influential and authoritative accounts of native cultures that guided imperialistic policies. Despite
the writings of Bartolomé de las Casas and a few other defenders of the
Indians, the majority of Europeans saw themselves as civilizing and

Christianizing superstitious and otherwise "savage" people (see Greenleaf 1994; Niezen 2000,12–67). The fact that Indians were truly men (*veri homines*) was not officially acknowledged until 1537 in the bull *Sublimi Deus* (Poliakov 1974, 135). And, as Dussel (1995) has amply demonstrated, many "modern" Latin American efforts to elevate Mesoamerican peoples entail repressive and ethnocentric agendas toward Indians and other groups (see also Russell 1994, 172–174).

At the same time, efforts to validate indigenous identities have not been universally welcomed by many Native Americans themselves. In a recent commentary on Native American history, Ronald Niezen discusses the concerns with "indigenism" expressed by members of the Circle of Elders of the Indigenous Nations of North America and the American Indian movement. Niezen (2000, 195) notes that "A radical shift has taken place from selective or universal prohibition of native spiritual practices to their celebration as a solution to individualism, alienation, rampant technology—all the perceived ills of postindustrial society." Niezen observes that the very zeal for reclaiming indigenous roots has compromised the integrity of Native American spirituality. Niezen (195) includes the critical comments of Vine Deloria Jr. (1994, vii):

> Bookshelves today are filled with pap—written many times by Indians who have kicked over the traces and no longer feel they are responsible to any living or historic community, but more often by wholly sincere and utterly ignorant non-Indians who fancy themselves masters of the vision quest and sweat lodge. Lying beneath this mass of sentimental slop is the unchallenged assumption that personal sincerity is the equivalent of insight and that cosmic secrets can be not only shared by non-Indians but given out in weekend workshops as easily as diet plans.

It is difficult to assess to what extent Niezen or Deloria would fault Latina/o authors with contributing to this compromise of integrity. Native American identity is contested, and various groups vie for the authority to define the indigenous. However, I argue here that many Latina/o portrayals of "indigenous" religions sometimes owe more to Eurocentric and Anglo-American viewpoints than they do to any substantiated indigenous tradition.

Indeed, already by the beginning of the twentieth century, most Latin American *mestizos* (people of mixed European and Native American ancestry) would be unable to trace their genealogy to any particular Indian group. Yet, some Latin American thinkers saw the glorification of *mestizaje* as tacit evidence that the indigenous was also valued. One famous example of the glorification of *mestizaje* is found in *La Raza Cósmica* (1925), by José Vasconcelos (1882–1959). Called an anti-intellectualist by Octavio Paz (1986, 126, "Vasconcelos era anti-intelectualista"), Vasconcelos was an education minister under Álvaro Obregón (1920–24). Vasconcelos believed that there were four races in the world: white, red, black, and yellow. A new fifth race, comprising all the previous races, was born in Latin America.

According to Vasconcelos (1948, 52–53), this "cosmic race" would be the final race ("*la raza final*") and a superior ethnic group ("*tipo étnico superior*"). Additionally, Vasconcelos (1948, 37) believed that humanity was deterministically divided into three periods of social history—"*tres estados sociales*" (1) material or warrior ("*material o guerrero*"); (2) intellectual or political ("*el intelectual o político*"); and (3) spiritual or aesthetic ("*el espiritual o estético*"). The last stage of social history, which Vasconcelos (51) saw in terms of a "spiritual plan" ("*plan del espíritu*"), would result in a loving and peaceful utopia. The reason is that five (the number of the fifth race) + three (the number of the third period) equals eight, which in Pythagorean numerology was the ideal number of equality for all humanity. The United States would be the last bastion of the unmixed white race.

Despite the outdated mixture of racism and occult mysticism espoused by Vasconcelos (see Bruce-Novoa 1990, 35–36; Goizueta 1994), many Mexican and U.S. Latina/o thinkers and scientists still refer to his ideas for inspiration at varying levels (Flores 1983; Guerrero 1987, 122). Some U.S. Latina/o authors have continued or modified the ideas exemplified by Vasconcelos and other "indigenistas" active in Latin America (see Carmack, Gasco, and Gossen 1996, 266–288). For our purposes, the most vociferous movement to reclaim an indigenous past manifested itself among Mexican American writers in the late 1960s and early 1970s. Important discussions of this phenomenon have been offered, *inter alia*, by Mario Barrera (1988), Egla Morales Blouin (1979), Jane Hedley (1996), and Luis Leal (1997). Rebolledo (1995, 98–100) notes some of the feminist twists that have been applied to Vasconcelos's ideas, as well.

Perhaps the pivotal moment of this "indigenismo," as the movement was sometimes dubbed by scholars, came with Rodolfo "Corky" González's promulgation of the so-called Spiritual Plan of Aztlán (*el plan espiritual de Aztlán*) at the National Chicano Youth Liberation Conference convened in Denver in March of 1969. *El plan espiritual de Aztlán* had rhetorical links to Vasconcelos's idea of a "*plan del espíritu.*" *The Plan* advocated a sort of neo-Aztec nationalism intent on retaking power from

Euroamerican colonialists. González incorporated this ideology in his famous poem first published in 1967, "Yo Soy Joaquin" (2001; see also Trejo 1979, 188–200).

Alberto Baltazar Urista (1947–), a founder of M.E.C.H.A. (*Movimiento estudiantil Chicano de Aztlán*/Chicano Student Movement of Aztlán), was present at the Denver conference. He became widely known for his powerful poetry (e.g., Alurista, *Floricanto en Aztlán*, 1971), replete with references to the Aztec past. Ricardo Sánchez, another celebrated poet, promoted Aztlán in his poem, "Denver" (1995, 93–94). Important presses, such as Quinto Sol and Tonatiuh, bore names that alluded to an Aztec past. A principal journal, *Aztlán: A Journal of Chicano Studies*, can also be traced to an indigenist ideology. The celebration of *mestizaje* has its echoes in Mexican American theologians, the works of Virgilio Elizondo (1978, 1988) being primary examples.

But the militant and separatist indigenism advocated by many literati did not take deep roots among Mexican Americans. For example, a survey published in the 1980s showed that third-generation Mexican Americans selected the more assimilationist term "Mexican American," rather than "Chicano," to describe themselves (Keefe and Padilla 1987, 38). A survey published by De La Garza et al. (1992, 63) showed only one Mexican American (born in the U.S.) who used the term, "la raza" ("the race," "the [Chicano] people"), as a self-identification, and "Mexican American" was the overwhelming favorite self-designation.

Despite the apparent rejection of separatism by most Mexican Americans, the idea of an indigenous past is still found among the literati and scholars (see Lux and Vigil 1979). Luis Leal (1997, 110) notes: "As late as 1992, the Chicano poet Francisco X. Alarcón joined the indigenistas in his book *Snake Poems: An Aztec Invocation*, a translation of 194 Aztec beliefs collected by Hernando Ruiz de Alarcón in 1629." In short, the extreme forms of neo-Aztec identity are more at home among elite Mexican Americans than among the general population of Mexican Americans.

But the definition of "indigenismo" supported by Latina/o literary elite could itself be deemed Eurocentric. First, there are thousands of individual tribes in the Americas, but not all of them have been equally represented in Latina/o literature. It is true that, among other examples, we find a Yaqui Indian featured in Miguel Méndez's (Miguel Méndez M.) *Peregrinos de Aztlán* (1974), and we find Pueblo Indians mentioned in Castillo's *So Far From God* (1993). However, as Eloise Quiñones Keber (1992, 132) notes, one indigenous group seems to have garnered more attention than others from the beginning:

> Eyewitness narratives like those of Díaz and Cortés . . . are invaluable records of contact and conquest. These and a wealth of other sixteenth-century ethnohistorical sources written by Spanish, Indian and *mestizo* authors have made the Aztecs the best documented indigenous people of the New World.

Although the Mayas certainly rank a close second, the Aztecs are actually what many Mexican American authors regard as the prime example of their "indigenous" roots.

To understand why the Aztecs were so privileged, some familiarity with this culture is necessary. According to Michael Smith (1996), from whom we compile most of the following historical narrative, the Nahuatl-speaking group known as the Aztecs is believed to have arrived in the Valley of Mexico around the year 1200 and after the fall of the powerful city of Tollan (Tula), capital of the Toltecs. The Aztecs' own tradition claims origin in a place called Aztlán, which many Chicano writers place in the U.S. Southwest. But Aztec references to Aztlán, like Aztec references to Tula, may blend myth with actual geography (on Tula, see Carrasco 1992, 72–73).

Tenochtitlán, which became the capital of the Aztecs, was founded around 1325. After defeating a number of rivals in the Valley of Mexico and beyond, the Aztecs established a powerful empire by around 1428. It was at its zenith at the time of the Spanish conquest by Hernán Cortés in 1521. The city was impressive, with perhaps two hundred thousand residents inhabiting about 13.5 square miles of a well-planned urban isle (Smith 1996, 196). Tenochtitlán was the Manhattan of Mexico. And to maintain its glory, it preyed on a periphery of peoples with a brutality that would equal that of the Europeans (see Carrasco 1999; Conrad and Demarest 1984).

Aside from the urban nature of Aztec culture, this group also had a form of writing—a feature that Bartolomé de las Casas and Jose de Acosta, among other European graphocentric chroniclers, saw as measure of "civilization" (see Mignolo 1992, 312–313). Commenting on the recovery of authentic indigenous religious traditions from Aztec documents, Prem (1997, 186) warns, "The sources reflect the official religion of the elite, while the concepts and activities of the majority of the population cannot be found at all." Indeed, Mexican American authors have shown very little interest in groups who left no written records or who otherwise did not match European standards of "civilization." Here we may mention groups like the Afumes, Babun, Hio, and Obaya, among other groups listed by Barnes, Naylor, and Polzer (1981). The obsession of scholars with indigenous literate cultures is even noted by Elizabeth Fox-Genovese (1995,

137), a conservative scholar, who asks, "And what about the claims of cultures that have produced little or no literate culture? Are we entitled to dismiss them as unworthy of our attention?"

The complexity of Aztec religion seemingly could rival anything that the Catholic host of gods, angels, and saints could offer. There appear to be enough gods and goddesses with which individual Mexican American male and female writers can identify. These range from *Huitzilopochtli*, a war god invoked by Oscar Zeta Acosta, to Coatlicue, the goddess who becomes a favorite of Anzaldúa. Female figures, such as La Virgen de Guadalupe, La Malinche, and La Llorona, also are given Aztec/Nahuatl genealogies by some Latina writers (see Rebolledo 1995, 49–81). In reality, of course, there were many Aztec deities whose mutual relationships and roles within the pantheon still elude complete description (for one attempt, see Nicholson 1971).

Just like Christians, the Aztecs also had myths of creation. The creation myth of the five suns was a primary narrative for the Aztecs (see Elzey 1976). In the beginning, according to the myth, a high god, who existed in androgynous form, gave birth to Tezcalipoca, Xipe Totec, Quetzalcoatl, and *Huitzilopochtli*. These younger gods initiated a cycle of four ages, called "suns," each populated by a distinct set of people and controlled by a particular god. The first age, for example, was controlled by Tezcalipoca, and populated by roaming giants. Each age was destroyed cataclysmically. The current age, the fifth sun, will also end in destruction. Such a destruction can come only at the end of a fifty-two-year cycle, though which particular future cycle will bring destruction is unknown. At the start of each cycle, priests must perform rituals to ensure that the new period will be favorable.

Parallels between Christianity and the Aztecs can also be found in the notion of sacrifice. The relationship between religion, sacrifice, and Aztec imperialism has been studied extensively by Dávid Carrasco (1992, 1999), among others. Carrasco (1999) links the spatial organization of the sacred center of Tenochtitlán and its spectacular Templo Mayor ("The Main Temple") with Aztec views of cosmology and imperial policy (see also Broda, Carrasco, and Moctezuma 1987; Moctezuma 1988). Although Anawalt (1982) believes that tales of human sacrifice have been exaggerated by Spaniards, most scholars find evidence that sacrifice formed an important part of Aztec religion and politics. Motives for sacrifice have been attributed to terroristic demonstrations of power and protein deficiencies (a widely repudiated view), as well as more subtle and complex interactions with other aspects of the Aztec symbolic world (see Carrasco 1999, 167–168).

Just as Christianity espouses a belief that Jesus will return, Spanish chronicles tell of the return of an Aztec god, Quetzalcoatl. Susan Gillespie (1989, 228–230), among other scholars, believes that the story of Quetzalcoatl's return is a post-conquest invention meant to excuse Montezuma's inaction. However, Carrasco (1992, 48) believes that it has pre-Columbian roots. According to Carrasco, the myth of Qutezalcoatl's return, which was originally meant to legitimize the Aztec king's authority, served eventually to undermine it with the appearance of Hernán Cortés, who was mistaken for Quetzalcoatl (Carrasco 1992, 151).

Given this very brief synopsis, why would the Aztecs become the paradigm of the "indigenous" for Mexican American authors? As mentioned above, there are thousands of Mexican tribes. So why are the Tepecans of Jalisco (see Shadow 1987) or the Hohokam of Arizona not regarded as paradigms of the "indigenous" by most Mexican American authors? The Hohokam, for example, thrived in the very place where many Chicanos place Aztlán, the American Southwest (see Acuña 1994, 17–18; Gumerman 1991; Vélez-Ibáñez 1996). If we speculated enough, we could just as well posit that the Hohokam are the ultimate progenitors of the Aztecs.

I suggest that the Aztecs became the paradigm of the indigenous culture because they exhibit so much of what Europeans consider "civilization." As Rey Chow (1995, 109) comments, "Of all the prominent features of Eurocentrism, the one that stands out in the context of the university is the conception of culture as based on the modern European notion of the nation-state." The Aztecs were indeed a culture that most resembled European nation states. The Europeans valued writing, and the Aztecs had writing. The Europeans were a highly urbanized culture, and so were the Aztecs. The Europeans were imperialistic, and so were the Aztecs. The Europeans even had a soteriology based on the sacrifice of a god, and the Aztecs were no strangers to this idea. The Aztecs may also have had apocalyptic myths of returning deities. In short, the selection of the Aztecs as the paradigm of the "indigenous" still betrays Eurocentric yardsticks for validating a culture (see also essays in Jara and Spadaccini 1992). With this argument in mind, let us now turn to a couple of examples of attitudes toward "indigenous" religions in U.S. Latina/o literature.

Case Study 1: *Bless Me, Ultima* (1972)

One of the most celebrated Mexican American novels of all time is also one of the most extensive meditations on the nature and the value of indigenous religions as compared to Christianity. Anaya, himself, confirms the religious nature of this work, "The novel has to do with the meaning of good and evil and the nature of God, our purpose in life and the whole idea of the sacred. What is the sacred and how can we respond to it in a spiritual way? So yes, those are questions that I have always asked myself and have had to resolve for myself" (Dick and Sirias 1998, 172).

Rudolfo Anaya won almost instant acclaim when he published *Bless Me, Ultima* (henceforth, BMU) in 1972. The novel won the prestigious Premio Quinto Sol National Chicano Literary Award in the same year. Anaya was born in Pastura, New Mexico, in 1937. Soon thereafter, his family, which included three older brothers and six sisters, moved to Santa Rosa, where he grew up. In 1952, the family moved to Albuquerque, where he attended high school. At the University of New Mexico, Anaya earned an undergraduate degree in English in 1963, and a master of arts degree in English in 1968. Anaya also had a long teaching career at the University of New Mexico. Aside from numerous short stories, poems, and novellas, his main works include *Heart of Aztlán* (1976), *Tortuga* (1979) and *Jalamanta: A Message from the Desert* (1996).

The role of religion in BMU has been the subject of analysis by various scholars (Ray 1978; Lattin 1979; Cantú 1979; Portillo-Orozco 1981). The most notable scholar of religion to have analyzed BMU is Davíd Carrasco, who focused on the "the sacrality of the landscape and the shamanic relationship between Antonio and Ultima" (1982, 219). Furthermore, Anaya has granted extensive interviews that provide some insight into the role of religion in BMU (for example, Dick and Sirias 1998).

BMU is narrated by an adult named Antonio Márez y Luna (henceforth, Tony/Antonio) who tells of his experiences as a seven-year-old boy. His family has moved from Las Pasturas, a sort of wilderness area of New Mexico, to a town named Guadalupe. Tony experiences a growing awareness of the end of his world when Ultima, an elderly folk healer, comes to live with his family one fateful summer. Tony's family, which includes three older brothers and three older sisters, brings Ultima (also known as *La Grande*, "the grand one") to live with them so that she will not be left alone in the last days of her life.

"Ultima" means "the last one," and in the first page we are told about "the beginning that came with Ultima," thus juxtaposing "beginning" and "last" in the plot. In fact, the book has an apocalyptic theme as well as a notion of the cyclical nature of time. Ultima is a *curandera*, a folk healer, who can heal as well as harm those who wreak evil. In fact, she was often considered to be an evil witch herself (4). She was trained by the flying man of Las Pasturas, a sort of shamanic figure (80). Ultima's constant companion is an owl (11). She had acted as a midwife for the Márez family and others in the Llano (the range), and she had helped to deliver Tony himself.

Her connection to the indigenous peoples of the Americas is indicated by Tony, "She spoke of the ancient medicines of other tribes, the Aztecas, Mayas . . . " (39). Tony, himself, represents the "indigenous person," according to Anaya (Dick and Sirias 1998, 134).

Tony's family name is laden with religious symbolism. His last name, Márez, alludes to "seas." In a dream, the cowboys of the range liken his father's family to the restless seas (6). The wind is seen as the brother of the Márez people. They are *conquistadores* (conquerors), and so linked with the masculine aspect of life. The Márez men are also linked with the sun (25). The father is not very religious, and his clan is full of freethinkers.

The mother, who bears the last name of "Luna," is clearly associated with the moon. She is also associated with a more sedentary and edaphic life of the farmer, rather than the restless men of the range. A devout Catholic, the mother expects Tony, her youngest son, to become a priest (4). She is distressed whenever her sons show any inclination to follow the Márez way of life (7).

El Puerto is the community to which the mother's family had ties. The family of Tony's mother had colonized the land around El Puerto, and the colonization was led by a priest (27). The place is called el Puerto de la Luna because it is the gate through which the moon passes each month on its journey from east to west. The Luna clan wants Tony to spend a summer with them "before he is lost" (47). In sum, the mother and father clearly symbolize different aspects of Tony's world that are often in religious conflict. Ultima resolves these opposing tendencies symbolized by the different branches of Tony's family.

The story's first dramatic moment bears repercussions that eventually end Ultima's life. The town sheriff, named Chávez, has been killed by Lupito (Guadalupe), a demented veteran of World War II. Lupito flees to the nearby river, which is also sacred to an ancient indigenous deity. At around midnight, near a bridge over the river, some of the men from the town catch up with Lupito, who fires his gun to draw their fire, and so commits suicide by proxy (20). His blood spills into the sacred river. The connection between Lupito's World War II experiences in the Pacific and his death in a New Mexico river also shows the interconnectedness of the planet.

Tony, who has been hiding on the bank of the river, witnesses the whole incident. This murder triggers questions that are almost wholly within the Catholic worldview that Tony has accepted. Tony recites the Act of Contrition as a last prayer before Lupito's death (20). But he also hears the owl, Ultima's emblem. The performance of a Catholic ritual and the hearing of the owl seem to prefigure yet another conflict that will ensue in Tony's life—i.e., the conflict between Catholicism and indigenous traditions.

Tony wonders what happened to Lupito's soul, and he wonders whether his own father participated in Lupito's death. Ultima counsels Tony to let God determine who deserves forgiveness and discourages any thought that his father took part in Lupito's death (31). Tony also sees humans as born in sin, and the sacraments only begin to wash that sin away. He sees Communion as the final removal of human sin (43) and as an instrument through which one understands good and evil (66). Furthermore, eschatology figures in the mind of Tony (Cantú 1979). In fact, he and his friends expect the end of the world to come soon, based on their reading of the Bible (70).

Tony's exposure to an indigenous religion, encapsulated in the story of the golden carp, provides yet another moment of crisis. The story is first told to Tony by his friend Samuel, who heard the story from another boy named Jasón, who, in turn, received it from an Indian. This chain shows the centrality of oral tradition in the transmission of this religion. It also shows the ultimate indigenous origin ("the Indian") of the tradition.

According to Jasón's Indian informant, when the earth was young, a tribe of strange people had been sent by the gods to the area where Tony now lives. These people had wandered the land for many years, but had never given up faith in their gods. Thus, they were rewarded with a fertile promised land (73). Only one thing was withheld from them—a fish called the carp. However, after a drought of some forty years, the tribe ate the carp when faced with starvation.

The gods were angry and wished to kill them. However, one of the gods argued against destruction, and so it was decided to turn *the people* into the carp that now populate the river. The golden carp was the god who had argued against the destruction of humanity. He requested to be turned into this fish so that he could take care of his people (75). The golden carp had only a black carp as its principal nemesis (104). Both the black and the golden carp live in the same waters.

This story makes Tony wonder if he is worshiping the right god (75). He had been taught that there is only one God, and now he hears that this may not be true. The story of the golden carp also raises other questions, "If the golden carp was a god, who was the man on the cross? The Virgin? Was my mother praying to the wrong God?" (75). He despaired at his inability to verify which story was true.

Soon, other events begin to erode further his faith in his own Catholic tradition. Lucas, Tony's uncle on his mother's side, becomes ill. Lucas lives in El Puerto, the traditional home of the Luna clan. Lucas believes his illness is somehow caused by the daughters of Tenorio Trementina, the town barber and saloonkeeper (86). Tenorio's wife is thought to make dolls used to place curses on people, and eventually she gave birth to three evil witches. Lucas thinks that those witches are punishing him for discovering their secret ceremonies. Everyone thinks Lucas has no hope of recovery, and the Luna clan goes to Ultima for help.

Ultima goes to El Puerto, taking Tony with her. Her first task is to confront Tenorio at the saloon. Tenorio attempts to repel her by making the sign of the cross in front of Ultima, but Ultima does not retreat. He and his friends inferred that she was either not a witch or she was using the Devil's own powers against them (87). Ultima responds that she is a *curandera*, and that she comes to lift the curse wrought by Tenorio's daughter. Tenorio will not listen, and Ultima threatens to use her eternal and transcendent magic (88). Ultima and Tony then return to see Lucas.

Lucas, however, nearly dies, and Tony begins to lose his faith in the power of doctors and the Church (92). Ultima performs an effective ritual, using magic dolls she made. Lucas coughs up what appears to be a hairball, which is interpreted to be evil coming out of him. This hairball is burned where the witches dance, and Lucas revives in about three days (97).

Some family members wonder how Ultima performed the cure. Some say she is a witch, and others say that she is sinless. The episode shows Tony that Ultima's indigenous magic may be even more powerful than the magic of organized religion. In fact, Ultima herself notes that the Church, fearing her powers, would not let her use her powers (90). The narrative implies that the Catholic Church wishes to monopolize all power, but cannot.

In the next episode, Tony goes down by the river and encounters Cico, who moves about barefooted. Cico, who seems to function as the priest of the golden carp, offers Tony the opportunity to see the fabulous creature, but Tony remembers the commandment, "Thou shalt have no other gods before me" (99). He tells Cico that he is a Catholic and he is only allowed to believe in one God. Cico respects Tony's honesty but consents to show

Tony the golden carp if Tony swears not to try to kill it. Before he knows it, Tony is beholding the golden carp. It was a fish larger than even Tony himself. He feels he is in the presence of a real deity. Cico exclaims, "The golden carp is my god, Tony" (111).

Cico, then, begins to relate how the whole area was once covered by a sea. Cico says that the golden carp will come to rule again. The sins of the land would one day grow so heavy that the whole town would collapse into the sea. Tony wonders when this will happen, but Cico does not know. When Tony asks what he can do, Cico responds, "Sin against no one" (111).

As Tony departs from the scene, he laments that beholding the beauty of the carp had now imposed a responsibility upon him (111). When he arrives at home, he asks Ultima whether the story of the golden carp is true. She seems to already know the story, but she encourages Tony to seek the truth for himself (111–112).

Later that night, Tony has a dream in which his mother argues that he was baptized in the holy water of the Church. The father counters that this is a lie because Tony was actually baptized with the salty seawater (112). Ultima, however, represents a compromising position, which argues that "The waters are one" (113). Again, Ultima seems to function as the synthesis of a thesis and antithesis. It is the indigenous religions that hold a balanced view between the orthodox oppressive Church, represented by the mother, and the unbelief, represented by the father.

Not long after Tony's dream, a family friend named Narciso bursts into the house to announce that one of Tenorio's daughters has died. Tenorio blames Ultima for the death because he found Ultima's pouch, which she wears around her neck, under his daughter's bed. Now Tenorio and his men approach Tony's house and want his family to hand over Ultima. They place two needles at the top of the door frame and dare Ultima to walk out through the threshold. According to their belief, an evil witch will not be able to walk through, but Ultima walks through effortlessly. Moreover, Ultima's shrieking owl comes and gouges out Tenorio's eye (127). Tenorio and his men disappear into the night, still vowing to kill Ultima.

As chapter 13 opens, we learn that the priest of El Puerto will not allow Tenorio's daughter, believed to be a witch, to be buried on sacred ground. Tenorio attempts to bring his daughter's casket into the church, but the priest stands firm at the door with his refusal. At about the same time, Tony and his family are headed for El Puerto, where his mother's family is centered. Tony's thoughts turn to religious questions as he passes some familiar landmarks. As he passes by Rosie's house (the local brothel), Tony thinks about the sins of the town and how the golden carp would punish sinners. As he passes the church, Tony thinks about how the Christian God punishes people in a fiery hell and suggests that perhaps the best sort of deity should be a woman because only women know how to forgive (130). Indeed, he reasons that God is too much like a man to forgive.

When Tony arrives in El Puerto, he has a dream about the witches' Black Mass for the departed Trementina sister. But as he peeks into the coffin, he sees Ultima instead. The dream seems to prefigure the death of Ultima and shows that she also can be thought of as a witch. As he awakes, Tony sees Tenorio's funeral procession. After failing to bring his daughter's casket into the church, Tenorio turns his mournful procession back and is resigned to bury his daughter in unconsecrated ground.

As the summer ends, Tony enters the third grade. He arrives in school and tells Samuel that he has seen the golden carp. Other children tell Tony that they heard what happened between Ultima and Tenorio, and the discussion then turns to whether hell is real. A boy, named Horse, argues that another boy, named Red, is going to hell because Red is not Catholic (140). Another claims that Ultima is an evil witch, and Tony defends her. In a subsequent discussion about the approaching Christmas play, another character argues that the Virgin Birth is a myth (145).

At the start of the Christmas break, Tony walks home in a blinding snowstorm and soon finds himself witnessing a savage fight between Tenorio and Narciso at the door of the Longhorn Saloon. The fight brings more threats from Tenorio, who is shouting that a second daughter is ill. He expects her to die, and he holds Ultima responsible. Tony follows Narciso, who is desperately trying to find Andrew (Tony's brother) to warn Ultima of Tenorio's impending actions. Narciso ends up at Rosie's brothel, and Tony finally learns that Andrew is a regular customer there. Tony wonders whether he has lost his innocence in seeing so many crucial events, ranging from Lupito's murder to the marvellous golden carp (156). Andrew refuses to leave the brothel, and now Narciso sets off to the Márez house. Along the way, Tony concludes that the waters of the golden carp, not the sacraments of the Church, will wash away the sins of the town (158).

Then, near the bridge that separates the town from the Llano, Tony witnesses another fight between Tenorio and Narciso. This time, there is a gun involved, and Narciso is shot. As he is dying, Narciso looks at Tony to fulfill the role of the priest. Tony does his best to administer the Act of Contrition. Narciso begs for God's forgiveness. He dies in the Llano. Narciso's blood is literally on Tony's hands (163).

Tony rushes home to tell his family what has happened. As he arrives, he becomes ill and begins to go into a sort of dream world that includes a lengthy theological meditation. He encounters God, who tells him that his brothers have sinned. God threatens to take revenge for what has happened (165–166). Tony begs God to forgive Andrew, but God says, "I am not a God of forgiveness!" (165). Tony promises God that he will become his priest, but God responds that he "can have no priest who has golden idols" (165). Then the Virgin promises to forgive everyone, but Tony tells her to forgive only Narciso, and punish Tenorio. But God scolds Tony for wanting a God of forgiveness, except when that does not suit Tony's own vengeful desires (165–166).

The theological reflection continues as Tony sees the blood of Narciso mix with the blood of Lupito in the river. A mob gathers to taste the blood that they believe has curative powers. They want Ultima's blood to be part of the river as well. Then Tony sees that his three brothers are crying in anguish because they have lost their way. They lament the fact that they have not followed the Christian God, nor the golden carp, nor paid heed to the magic of Ultima (166).

As the dream continues, the Trementina sisters seize Tony, cut off his hair and mix it with the blood of bats and toad guts. They drink the repulsive mixture. Tony begins to die without the benefit of the Eucharist. He seeks the face of God but cannot find God. The Trementina sisters lead a mob of wicked people who kill Tony's family. They also kill Ultima and drink her blood. Finally, they kill the golden carp. A natural cataclysm ensues, with the sun turning blood red and the wicked people withering in their skin. But the golden carp sees what is happening and decides to swallow everything. He swims into the sky and becomes a new sun in the heavens that shines upon a new earth. Apocalypse accomplished.

The brothers eventually go to Santa Fe (178), leaving their father, with Tony as the only other male presence in the house. On his way home from school, Tony encounters Tenorio, who is wearing a long black coat, and a wide-brimmed hat pulled low. Tony accuses Tenorio of being a murderer, and Tenorio says that Tony's curse is too much knowledge (181). In fact, Tony does not feel that he knows enough (184).

As spring approaches, Tony is involved in catechism lessons in preparation for his First Communion. The atomic bomb has just been exploded in the desert of New Mexico, and people are blaming it for harsh storms. Old ladies complain that the atomic bomb is an example of humanity trying to know more than God. But as the catechism lesson focuses on God's omniscience, Tony dwells on his lack of knowledge

(184): "Why does He allow evil to exist? I wondered if the knowledge I sought would destroy me. But it couldn't, it was God's knowledge—Did we ask too much when we asked to share His knowledge?"

A theological discussion then ensues with Florence, a character representing an atheistic position. Tony explains that sins are forgiven after confession. Florence wonders if this is a fair system, as one can sin as much as one wants, and then just confess. Such a theology would be an incentive to sin, according to Florence (185). Horse repeats the charge that Florence will go to hell for not believing in God. Florence replies that his atheism means also that there is no hell (187). Florence asks Tony questions about why God would allow evil. Tony replies that it is a good way to become better Catholics. Florence says that a smart God would not need to know such things. Despite his inability to answer Florence's questions, Tony does not think that he can live a godless life (189). But Tony allows for the possibility that other gods might rule instead of the Christian God (190).

As Ash Wednesday arrives, Tony encounters even more theological conundrums. Tony is horrified at the thought that God would forever torture his soul in a fiery hell for making one mistake (196). Tony hates the thought that God's omnipresence means that he is also in bed with the Trementina sisters. On Good Friday, Tony is inside the church along with Ultima and his mother. Tony is plunged into despair as he hears one of the last words that Christ spoke on the cross, "My God, my God, why hast Thou forsaken me?" (199). Tony believes that he could say the same thing, as he feels alone in a dying universe.

On Saturday, as Tony goes to church for his first confession, some of Tony's friends want him to play the role of the priest in a game of mock confession (200). Each child tries to outdo the others with a greater sin to confess. When Florence's turn comes to confess his sins, he defiantly states that he has no sins. Some of the other children tell him that he is going to hell. Florence, exasperated by the inquisition, finally thunders, "It is God who has sinned against me!" (204). This angers those who want Florence punished. They urge Tony not to forgive his sins. They want to punish Florence for not believing in God, but Tony forgives Florence's sins. Consequently, the kids beat up and desert Tony. Florence says, "You could never be their priest" (206).

Easter Sunday arrives, and Tony is filled with anticipation about his First Communion. He believes that it is his opportunity to have his questions answered as now God will be in him. At the same time, he sees the correlation between the blood he will be asked to drink and the blood that has been spilled in the river. Tony finds no satisfaction in this ritual. He leaves somewhat dejected and complains, "The God I so eagerly sought was not there" (212).

As another summer nears, a man named Tellez comes to seek Ultima's help. He is from a ranch called Agua Negra (black water), and he is frightened of stones that have been falling from the sky and pelting his house. A Catholic priest had come to bless the house, but it did not help. Now Ultima is asked to remove a curse, which originated when Tellez's grandfather hanged three Comanche Indians who had been raiding the family's flocks. The bodies were left hanging from a tree, and thus did not receive a proper burial. Now the souls of those Indians are being used by witches to wreak evil. When asked if this evil can be stopped, Ultima says, "All evil can be stopped" (216).

Ultima's ritual consists of burning a platform supported by four posts. The fact that the ritual works only makes Tony wonder why the Church's magic does not work. That night he dreams that his brothers ask him for help. He replies that he has no magic left, but they insist, "You have the power of the church, you are the boy-priest! . . . Or choose from the power of the golden carp or the magic of your Ultima. Grant us rest" (225). Clearly, the dream suggests there are three religious systems that are somehow linked.

As chapter 21 opens, Tony is still wondering why God is silent. He has a conversation with Cico, the priest of the golden carp. Tony no longer seems certain of why he worships the Christian God. He tells Cico that he goes to church only to please his mother. Then he asks Cico why he does not tell everyone about the golden carp. Cico responds, "They would kill him . . . The god of the church is a jealous god, he cannot live in peace with the other gods" (227). Unlike the Christian God, the golden carp accepts all magic that is good. Cico tells Tony that he must choose between the God of the Church and the "beauty that is here and now" (227).

Tony manages to convince Cico to reveal the secret to Florence. On their way to tell Florence, they notice that some of the children are near the lake and shouting an alarm. Florence is in the lake and has not come up. They see Florence's golden hair as his dead body floats up to the surface. He has a red mark on his forehead and some black barbed wire wrapped around one arm. Thus Florence seems to parallel the golden carp. The black bass seeks to kill the golden carp in the river, and now some black barbed wire has helped to kill the golden-haired boy in the river.

16

The final chapter begins with a dream in which Tony sees the three people he has seen die—-Lupito, Narciso, and Florence. He asks Florence if there is a God in heaven. Florence points to the church where the priest is desecrating the altar by using the blood of pigeons on the holy chalice. Florence adds that "The old gods are dying" (233). Tony asks Florence if there is a heaven or hell, and Florence curtly replies, "Nothing." Tony asks about Ultima's magic, and Florence points to Ultima's owl, which is being murdered by Tenorio. Tony cries that his beliefs are destroyed. He repeats Jesus' words "My God, my God, why have you forsaken me!" (233).

As he wakes from his dream, his mother comes to him to wish him well before his trip to El Puerto. She tells him to accept change, as change is difficult but necessary. She blesses him in the name of the Holy Trinity. Ultima too comes by and blesses him, but without using the name of the Trinity. Yet, "her blessing was Holy" (234). Tony does something he has never done before—he kisses Ultima good-bye.

Tony, then, rides to El Puerto with his father, who tells him about the conflict between the masculine Márez wind and the feminine Luna-earth associations. Tony wonders if he has to be either a Márez or a Luna, and ventures that he can be both. His father tells him that a man can make something new out of his past. At this point, Tony asks his father if a new religion can be made, "A religion different from the religion of the Lunas" (236). His father replies that if the old religion could no longer answer the questions of the children then perhaps it was time to change it (236).

At this point, Tony also wants to know how his father would answer theological questions, including "why is there evil in the world?" (236). His father replies that "most of the things we call evil are not evil at all; it is just that we don't understand those things and so we call them evil. And we fear evil only because we do not understand it" (236). His father adds that understanding does not come from God, but from life. Tony's father asserts that Ultima's magic resides in that she "has sympathy for people, and it is so complete that with it she can touch their souls and cure them—That is her magic" (237). Indeed, Ultima personifies goodness (243).

Tony's stay with the Márez clan seems to agree with him. He feels he has grown in wisdom and strength. His bad dreams have disappeared. Just when things seem to be going well, one of his uncles announces the death of another of Tenorio's daughters. Tenorio has even stretched out her corpse in the bar of his saloon. Following his uncle's instructions, Tony goes to his grandfather's house to await the outcome of events. On the way, he again encounters Tenorio, who is riding a large, black, murderous horse that Tony manages to outmaneuver as he seeks shelter in an embankment. Tenorio tells Tony that he has discovered that the owl is Ultima's soul itself. Tenorio now intends to kill the owl. Tony decides to run the ten miles it takes to reach Guadalupe to warn Ultima.

Tony arrives just as Tenorio himself has reached Tony's father's house. Before Tony knows it, Tenorio shoots the owl. Tony's uncle Pedro shoots Tenorio dead. Tony enters the house and finds Ultima on the bed. He lays the owl beside her and tells her the owl is dead. Ultima says that the owl is not dead but that it is going to a new place and a new time. She tells him that the owl was given to her by a wise old man who told her it was her spirit and her "bond to the time and harmony of the universe" (247). She tells Tony to bury the owl by a forked juniper tree in the western hills. Her last words are also a blessing: "I bless you in the name of all that is good and strong and beautiful, Antonio. Always have the strength to live. Love life, and if despair enters your heart, look for me in the evenings when the wind is gentle and owls sing in the hills, I shall be with you" (247).

Tony's last action in the book is to officiate at the burial of the owl. And Tony knows that while Ultima will receive a Christian burial of her body, her soul is really resting in the western hills.

Critical discussion

Anaya has structured his characters, places, and events to represent conflicting aspects of a religious spectrum. Indeed, when asked by an interviewer whether the pagan religion of the golden carp and Catholicism in *Bless Me, Ultima* conflict, Anaya answers, "Yes, they do in the sense that the Catholic religion in *Bless Me, Ultima* is very dogmatic. It has a dogma that must be adhered to and followed. The golden carp that Tony sees as the alternative doesn't have that dogma, and, of course, they're going to be in conflict" (Dick and Sirias 1998, 171).

At least three religious systems can be identified in *BMU*. These systems are outlined by the brothers, when they ask Tony for help: "You have the power of the church . . . Or choose from the power of the golden carp or the magic of your Ultima" (225). Florence represents a complete lack of any religious system, and so we can make a case that at least four worldviews are represented.

The most dominant religious system is orthodox Catholicism, represented principally by Tony's mother and the Church. It is dogmatic. Its

God is vengeful. God's unforgiving nature is linked directly to his masculinity. This God does not seem just either, as the same punishment is meted out to the person who commits one sin or to the person who commits one thousand sins.

We may describe the essence of the second religion, which has the golden carp as its main deity, as "nondogmatic aestheticism." The undogmatic element is seen not only in the contrastive descriptions offered by the carp-priest Cico, but also in Anaya's own words quoted above. The aesthetic element is seen in repeated allusions to the beauty of the golden carp. Thus, after seeing the fish, Tony exclaims, "I had seen beauty, but the beauty had burdened me with responsibility" (111). Tony also tells us, "I had seen and reveled in the beauty of the golden carp!" (156). When Cico asks Tony to choose religions, the choice is between the Christian God and the "beauty that is here and now" (227). We may also note the rhetorical link with Vasconcelos's social stage (1948), which he calls "aesthetic" (see also Mejido 2001).

The religion of the golden carp has other dissimilarities with Christianity. First, it is a minority religion, and its practitioners must be secretive. While Catholicism celebrates the intake of the transubstantiated body of Christ, the golden carp is not to be eaten (74). While the religion of Catholicism is highly centered on written traditions, the religion of the golden carp is centered on oral traditions. Unlike the Christian God, the golden carp accepts all magic that is good. Catholicism is graphocentric and nomocentric, while the religion of the golden carp is highly contemplative.

But the golden carp also bears many similarities with Christ. Both Christ and the golden carp are said to be gods who had incarnated themselves in order to save their people. Both are masculine gods. Both are associated with water—baptism for Christians and bathing in the river for the golden-carp religion. They both threaten to destroy people for sins. Both have a nemesis, the devil being the enemy of Christ, and the black bass being the enemy of the golden carp. Finally, both Christ and the golden carp are expected to return and rule a renovated world.

Between the orthodoxy of Catholicism and the nondogmatic aestheticism of the golden carp, we find the compromise represented by Ultima. Following Anaya's own description, we may describe this religious tradition as "holistic." Indeed, Anaya says that Ultima teaches Tony "the holistic nature of the universe, to see beyond the dualities that at first are very apparent to him and those people he comes in contact with" (Dick and Sirias 1998, 52). Thus, Ultima does seem to function as the synthesis of a thesis-antithesis structure.

There are some very pointed examples of this synthesis. Note the dream in which the mother wants Tony baptized with the water of the Church while the father wants him immersed in the salt water of the seas. It is Ultima who argues, "The waters are one" (113). Ultima does not accept the duality of salt water and holy water, but reaches beyond to the more basic essence of all water. Her blessing of Tony is also meant to be as inclusive as possible: "I bless you in the name of all that is good and strong and beautiful, Antonio." (247). This contrasts with the Christian Trinity's "the Father, the Son and the Holy Ghost," which is very deity-specific and more restrictive. Ultima both attends church and practices her non-Catholic magic. She presumably accepts or acknowledges the power of the golden carp.

So how fair and representative is Anaya's portrayal of these different religious systems? On one hand, an argument can be made that Anaya is representing elements that are found in indigenous Mesoamerican traditions. Thus, the story of the golden carp is reminiscent of the story of the founding of Tenochtitlan, which is also a city surrounded by water. Like *Huitzilopochtli*, the solar deity who led his people to Tenochtitlan in Old Mexico, the golden carp seems to be a solar deity that leads his people to a land in New Mexico. The Nahuatl legend of the five suns, despite its various versions, also includes the idea of the end of a succession of four eras, called suns, which end in a cataclysm. At least some of the inhabitants of these eras are destroyed or turned into aquatic animals (Elzey 1976, 117–118).

Ultima's folk religion derives from a genuine tradition of the *curandera* and the holy woman. These traditions have been documented by, among others, Trotter (1991) and Sánchez Mayers (1989). Like Ultima, many of these *curanderas* are more accepting of the Church than the Church is accepting of them. They too have rituals that are based on sympathetic magic. Most of these women are very tied to the earth, with an extensive knowledge of herbs and galenicals. *La Llorona*, the mythical woman who eternally wails her murder of her children, is also mentioned in *BMU*. This figure been traced to indigenous traditions, though Rogers (1977) also notes parallels in Greek mythology.

On the other hand, it can be argued that Anaya's vision is not very representative of indigenous religions. After all, the myth of *Huitzilopochtli* does not represent all of the indigenous people who lived here. Anaya also has not shown that Tony's search for the *self* is a very predominant part of indigenous cultures. Indeed, one should note that Anaya seems to favor a sort of individualistic approach to religion. When asked whether his books were directing readers to search for a religion based on myths and nature, Anaya responds, in part (Dick and Sirias 1998, 87–88; emphases mine):

> I didn't think that the church was providing me everything that *I needed*. I also think that in many respects the church has been an institution that to be quite blunt, has been repressive in the lives of people. I meet people who talk about having a sense of this institution, that is very important and intricately tied in with faith, being a force that, rather than liberating *self*, represses *self*. And since I think that's part of my job as a writer—to liberate *myself* and to search out what it is the most authentic to me—I did have years of questioning the basis of this very fixed and dogmatic religion and then embarked on *my own path*. But I don't really proselytize for everybody to do that because religion is, I think, a question bound up with what you believe with faith.

Anaya's search for an individual's own path, in turn, is mirrored by Tony, who is Anaya's sort of alter ego. Note what Anaya concedes, "I think that in a sense the novel is autobiographical. I identified very strongly with Antonio while I was writing the novel" (171–172). And Tony, if anything, desires to find or develop a religion to fit his own needs. He is encouraged to find his own path.

So, instead of being an "indigenous" person, Tony reflects a very old Anglo-American tradition of individualism, especially when it comes to religion. This search for one's own path is precisely the attitude described by Robert Bellah in his celebrated *Habits of the Heart: Individualism and Commitment in American Life* (1985, 62–63):

> The self-reliant American is required not only to leave home but to 'leave church' as well. This may not literally happen. One may continue to belong to the church of one's parents. But the expectation is that at some point in adolescence or early youth, one will decide on one's own that that is the church to belong to. One cannot defend one's views by saying that they are simply the views of one's parents. On the contrary, they must be particularly and peculiarly one's own.

According to a poll conducted in 1978, not long after *BMU* was published, 80 percent of Americans agreed "an individual should arrive at his or her own religious beliefs independent of any churches or synagogues" (Hoge et al. 1981, 167). In fact, this Anglo-American idea of finding one's own path is found at least as far back as Emerson's essay on "Self Reliance," in which he says, "Trust thyself: every heart vibrates to that iron string" (Emerson [1983], 259). And, of course, we find it in Walt Whitman's *Leaves of Grass* ([1986], 22), where he prophesied that, in America, "every man shall be his own priest."

Yet no theologian is completely consistent. Anaya would probably admit that *BMU* is more about questions than answers. He does not purport to give a definitive answer in this book. But it is clear that he does not like the organized Catholic Church. And while it is clear that Anaya does favor noninstitutional religions, his notion of individuality is more Anglo-American than indigenous. His notion of "indigenous" is also highly indebted to Aztec elite sources, which formed only a small proportion of the indigenous traditions of the Americas.

Case Study 2: *Borderlands/La Frontera* (1987)

Described in one of her short biographies (Anzaldúa 1999, 252) as a "Chicana tejana-lesbian-feminist poet and fiction writer from South Texas," Gloria Anzaldúa is certainly one of the most provocative writers on the subject of U.S. Latina/o religion. She provides us, *inter alia*, with a woman's perspective on indigenous religions. Fortunately, we have access to her extensive interviews on the subject of religion, most notably in a volume edited by AnaLouise Keating (2000). Otherwise, Anzaldúa's religious views have been studied by only a few academic scholars of religion (see Maldonado 1995).

Anzaldúa was born in 1942 in the Rio Grande Valley of South Texas. At age eleven she moved to the city of Hargill, Texas, on the border between the United States and Mexico, where she became a field worker. Her father, who died when she was fourteen, decided that education was more important than the migrant worker lifestyle that he had adopted. The demise of Anzaldúa's father meant that she bore much of the burden for the family's income.

Reminiscent of the educational pattern seen in Rudolfo Anaya, Anzaldúa received her B.A. in English, Art, and Secondary Education from Pan American University in 1969. She earned an M.A. in English and Education from the University of Texas in 1972, and then enrolled in Ph.D. studies in literature at the University of California, Santa Cruz (Ramos 1993, 19). She also taught courses in feminism, Chicano studies, and creative writing at (among other places) the University of Texas at Austin, Vermont College of Norwich University, and San Francisco State University. Her awards include the Small Book Press Award for *Making Face* (1990), an NEA

22

Fiction Award, the Before Columbus Foundation American Book Award for *This Bridge Called My Back* (1981), and the Sappho Award of Distinction. Anzaldúa died in 2004 after years of chronic illnesses.

Regarding her religious background, Anzaldúa says, "My family was not religious at all . . . My grandmother was more pagan than Catholic . . . my father never stepped into a church unless someone died and when his corpse was taken into a church" (Keating, 2000, 94–95). In general, the term "religion" has a negative connotation for Anzaldúa, and she proclaims that "Religion eliminates all kinds of growth, development and change, and that's why I think any kind of formalized religion is really bad" (Keating, 2000, 98).

One of her most extensive works on religion is *Borderlands/La Frontera: The New Mestiza* (1987; second edition 1999; henceforth *Borderlands*), which was selected by *Literary Journal* as one of the thirty-eight best books of 1987.[1] The book essentially describes in prose and poetry Anzaldúa's struggle to forge a new identity. What appears to be a hodgepodge of theological ramblings, literary genres, and historical lessons is part of the intentional literary artifice of Anzaldúa. The mixture of dialects of Spanish, for instance, mirrors the linguistic mixture one sees in the borderlands, though analogous blendings are found in European works (see Erickson 1988; Winner 1988). Ian Barnard (1997, 44) deems her use of English, Spanish, and "smatterings of Nahuatl" as reflecting her anti-Eurocentrism. The merging of genres, including scholarly essays and poetry, mirrors her poetic sensibility combined with academic interests.

Borderlands is divided into two main parts. The first part consists predominantly of essays and scholarly inquiries. The footnotes attest to the range of religious and philosophical interests which intersect in Anzaldúa. We find references to the *I Ching*, Friedrich Nietzsche, Carl Jung, and Andrés G. Guerrero, author of *A Chicano Theology* (1987). Though not a trained scholar of religion, Anzaldúa has thought long about how religion impacts her life. The second part, titled *Un Agitado Viento/Ehecatl, The Wind*, is devoted primarily to poems permeated with religious meaning. These poems, like the prose essays, move between English and Spanish, and have other allusions to Anzaldúa's love of amalgamation.

What is most relevant for our purposes is that Anzaldúa consciously attempts to integrate indigenous traditions into her own religious framework. As she declared in an interview (Anzaldúa 1999, 239), "The grounding of my spiritual reality is based on indigenous Mexican spirituality, which is Nahualismo, which loosely translates as 'shamanism.'" The role of Native Americans in her vision of the U.S.-Mexico borderlands is also clear when she says, "This land was Mexican once / was Indian always

23

/ and is. / And will be again" (91). The last sentence also seems to express a sort of futuristic or apocalyptic vision shared with Anaya's *BMU*.

Like Rudolfo Anaya, Anzaldúa rejects her Catholic upbringing. She says the Catholic Church fails to give meaning to her daily acts. Indeed, she rejects both major branches of Christianity: "The Catholic and Protestant religions encourage fear and distrust of life and of the body; they encourage a split between the body and the spirit and totally ignore the soul; they encourage us to kill off parts of ourselves" (37). She thinks that Christianity and most major religions see Woman as "carnal, animal, and closer to the undivine, she must be protected. Protected from herself. Woman is the stranger, the other" (17). Anzaldúa, in fact, accuses "culture" and "the Church" of keeping women subservient to men (17):

> The culture expects women to show greater acceptance of, and commitment to, the values system than men. The culture and the Church insist that women are subservient to males. If a woman rebels she is a mujer mala . . . For a woman of my culture there used to be only three directions she could turn: to the Church as a nun, to the streets as a prostitute, or to the home as a mother. Today some of us have a fourth choice: entering the world by way of education and career and becoming self-autonomous persons.

Note that being "self-autonomous persons" seems to be a preferred choice. And Anzaldúa specifically wishes to reclaim the goddesses and female symbols of Mesoamerica as her icons of self-autonomy. One of these emblems, which is contraposed to Christianity, is the serpent. In Christianity, the serpent is a prime symbol of evil. It is the instigator of the fall of humankind in Genesis 3. In fact, Genesis 3:15 declares the serpent to be the permanent enemy of woman. The serpent is the embodiment of Satan himself, and the paragon of chaos that will be vanquished in a lake of fire in the end of time (Rev. 20). Christian iconography also paints this Edenic serpent as a woman, one example being in Michelangelo's frescoes in the Sistine Chapel (see Schuyler 1990).

Anzaldúa's view of the serpent in Mesoamerican religion is quite the opposite. For her, the serpent is Woman herself. Anzaldúa (34) says, "In pre-Columbian America the most notable symbol was the serpent." As she sees it, the Olmecs saw the serpent's mouth as a toothed vagina. She identifies the earth with a coiled serpent. Her journey involves entering the Serpent itself, something that involves acknowledging that she has a body, is a body, and wishes to adopt an animal body and soul (26). She proclaims that the wound caused by the serpent should be cured by the serpent. Indeed, for Anzaldúa, the serpent can be a benign symbol.

Coatlalopeuh, the mistress of serpents, is a principal deity to which Anzaldúa appeals (27). This deity is a later form of another goddess named *Coatlicue*, ("serpent skirt"). Anzaldúa describes *Coatlicue* as an archetype that passes through her mind, and "the symbol of the underground aspects of the psyche" (46). Coatlicue symbolizes the fusion of opposites, including life and death, beauty and horror. She adds, "I've always been aware that there is a greater power than the conscious I. That power is my inner self, the entity that is the sum total of all my reincarnations, the god-woman in me I call *Antigua, mi Diosa* [The Ancient, my Goddess], the divine within, *Coatlicue-Cihuacoatl-Tlazolteotl-Tonantzin-Coatlalopeuh-Guadalupe*—they are one" (50).

Exploring the characteristics of these goddesses, then, becomes a major part of Anzaldúa's connection with her indigenous religious traditions. She portrays the general history of the female deities thus: "The male-dominated Azteca-Mexica culture drove the powerful female deities underground by giving them monstrous attributes and by substituting male deities in their place, thus splitting the female Self and the female deities" (27). Apparently, Anzaldúa believes that female deities who had been prominent in earlier times were banished to a lower echelon of the pantheon by a patriarchal religion. Matrilineality, she opines, character-ized the Toltecs (33). As we shall see following, this idea of female deities being supplanted by patriarchal ones has many important parallels with Euroamerican traditions about a golden age of goddesses.

The Virgin of Guadalupe has been a predominant Mexican American symbol in much of Mexican American literature. Guadalupe is seen as a New World version of the Virgin Mary. Anzaldúa continues a long tradition of associating the Virgin of Guadalupe with a supposed Aztec goddess named Tonantzin. This tradition is echoed in the classic 1967 poem "I Am Joaquín" (Rodolfo González 2001, 22), as well as in more prosaic feminist anthologies such as *The Goddess of the Americas*, edited by Ana Castillo (1996). Anzaldúa's description (27–29) of what she regards as the goddess named *Tonantsi* bears extensive repetition:

Tonantsi—split from her dark guises, *Coatlicue, Tlazolteotl,* and **Cihuacoatl**—became the good mother . . . After the Conquest, the Spaniards and their Church continued to split *Tonantsi/Guadalupe* . . . *Guadalupe* appeared on December 9, 1531, on the spot where the Aztec goddess, *Tonantsi* ("Our Lady Mother"), had been worshipped by the Nahuas and where a temple to her had stood. Speaking Nahua, she told Juan Diego, a poor Indian crossing Tepeyac Hill, whose Indian name was *Cuautlaohuac* and who belonged to the *mazehual* class, the humblest within the Chichimeca tribe, that her name was *María Coatlalopeuh* . . . .

Because *Coatlalopeuh* was homophonous to the Spanish *Guadalupe*, the Spanish identified her with the dark Virgin, Guadalupe, patroness of West Central Spain. From that meeting, Juan Diego walked away with the image of La Virgen painted on his cloak. Soon after, Mexico ceased to belong to Spain, and la Virgen de Guadalupe began to eclipse all the other male and female religious figures in Mexico . . . Since then for the Mexican to be a Guadalupano is something essential.

Anzaldúa (30) also claims that Guadalupe unites people of different races, including Chicano Protestants—something also argued in Andrés Guerrero's *A Chicano Theology* (1987, 143).

Aside from these largely prose meditations on how an Aztec female pantheon can help Anzaldúa survive, the poetic part of her book becomes a sort of indigenous liturgical exercise. She reinterprets Christian symbols and sacraments in indigenous garb. For example, in the poem titled, "The Canibal's Canción" [The Cannibal's song], Anzaldúa transforms cannibalism, a despicable practice from the ortho-dox Christian viewpoint, into a normal part of the new Mestiza's culture, "It is our custom / to consume / the person we love./ Taboo flesh: swollen / genitalia, nipples / the scrotum, the vulva / the soles of the feet / the palms of the hand / heart and liver taste best / Cannibalism is blessed" (143). The obvious identification of cannibalism with sexual acts would be further anathemized by Christianity. Insofar as Anzaldúa is concerned, sexual intimacies have just as much right to be seen as sacred rituals as the Eucharist.

> I'll wear your jawbone
> round my neck
> listen to your vertebrae
> bone tapping bone in my wrists.
> I'll string your fingers round my waist—
> what a rigorous embrace.
> Over my heart I'll wear
> a brooch with a lock of your hair.
> Nights I'll sleep cradling
> your skull sharpening
> my teeth on your toothless grin.
> Sundays there's Mass and communion
> and I'll put your relics to rest.

Toward the end of the book, Anzaldúa presents us with a poem that features Teresa de Avila (1515–1582), who, in 1970, became the first woman named a "Doctor of the Church" (see further, Slade 1995). She indeed had served the Catholic Church in many capacities, but she is perhaps best known for founding the Discalced (Barefoot) Carmelites, despite numerous obstacles posed by her immediate male superiors. De Avila is also known for her claims of extraordinary visions and experiences, including the persistent feeling that an angel was literally piercing her heart with a lance. This particular experience is captured in a masterful sculpture completed in 1646 by Gian Lorenzo Bernini, and located in the church of Santa Maria della Vittoria in Rome.

In Anzaldúa's poem, Teresa's bones repeat the lament, "We are the holy relics, the scattered bones of a saint, the best loved bones in Spain. We seek each other" (154). The refrain is repeated because priests keep pieces of her body each out of the five times that they disentomb her. De Avila wishes for all the pieces of her body to be reunited and left alone. Her body symbolizes the disintegration of the self and the disintegration of women in the Catholic Church. And here Teresa de Avila symbolizes the fragmented *mestiza* identity Anzaldúa experiences.

Critical discussion

Anzaldúa seeks in her indigenous past what she cannot find in today's Eurocentric and patriarchal Christianity. Her very survival depends on finding her indigenous *mestiza* self, which she compares to corn, a Mesoamerican plant also generated by crossbreeding (81). She has created her own religion out of the deities of the Aztecs, in particular. The adoption of the serpent as her emblem signifies, for her, a rejection of Christianity and an acceptance of indigenous traditions.

Anzaldúa's views certainly can be considered antithetical to orthodox Christianity. First, Christians usually speak of the "greater power" being a male God, not themselves. Orthodox Christianity does not believe in reincarnation. The Christian God is primarily depicted as a male, not a *Diosa* (a goddess). Finally, the idea that Anzaldúa's Mesoamerican goddesses "are one" is reminiscent of, and perhaps contraposed to, the controversial text of 1 John 5:7, which declares that the Father, Son, and Holy Ghost "are one."

Anzaldúa says, "I want to take these figures and rewrite their stories. These figures we're given have been written from the male patriarchal perspective" (Keating 2000, 219). A similar perspective may be seen in the anthology, *Goddess of the Americas*, edited by Ana Castillo (1996). At the same time, Anzaldúa purports to represent authentic indigenous traditions. In fact, Anzaldúa goes much farther than Anaya by documenting her assertions with footnotes. She wants her religious traditions to be grounded as much in historical fact as in her imagination.

And indeed, the goddesses and symbols she has chosen are indigenous. But Anzaldúa also is creating or accepting myths of Mexico's indigenous past from very patriarchal Spanish sources that she otherwise rejects. Despite the assurances of León-Portilla (1992), there is still much skepticism about how much we know about authentic Aztec traditions. Indeed, one can argue that much of what Anzaldúa claims to be an "indigenous" religious tradition is actually more the product of post-conquest Eurocentric and patriarchal inventions of tradition (Burkhart 1993; 2001; Poole 1995).

As mentioned above, Anzaldúa's preference for Aztec culture bespeaks a Eurocentric stance, even as she is often seen as disputing the monolithic vision of Aztecs in Mexican culture (Anzaldúa 1999, 6). More importantly, there is no credible evidence that Guadalupe replaced an Aztec goddess named Tonantzin. Bernardino de Sahagún (ca. 1500–1590) is apparently the first author to report this story. He does so in an appendix to his *Historia General* (1576). He was apparently afraid that the worship of Guadalupe was being contaminated by the worship of a deity named *Tonantzin*.

But as far as can be determined, *Tonantzin* is not the name of a specific Aztec goddess, but rather an honorific title derived from *To-* ("our"), *nan* (mother). The element *-tzin* is a reverential/honorific "compounding element," as described by the Nahuatl lexicographer Frances Karttunen (1983, 314). This element was applied to the Church itself, and it could be applied to deities of either sex (Burkhart 1993, 207–208). The story of Tonantzin, then, was born of Sahagún's hatred of the indigenous. And Anzaldúa has uncritically accepted the story of Sahagún, one of the most Eurocentric and patriarchal of Spanish writers.

Despite Anzaldúa's claim, there is no credible evidence that any Aztec goddess was worshipped at Tepeyac, which supposedly became the first Guadalupan shrine. Louise Burkhart (1993, 208) says, "The Indians were not perpetuating memories of pre-Columbian goddesses but were projecting elements of their Christian worship into their pre-Christian past, conceptualizing their worship in terms of Mary." Burkhart adds that there "is no evidence that Tepeyac held any special meaning for sixteenth century Indians" (209).

Likewise, a thorough historical analysis by Stafford Poole (1995) shows that the story of Juan Diego cannot be traced back much before 1648, when the Oratorian priest Miguel Sánchez published a famous version of the story. In 1649, it appears that Luis Laso de Vega published another account (sometimes attributed to Antonio Valeriano) called the *Nican mopohua*, for a Native American audience. The story of Guadalupe, moreover, was intended more for a *criollo* (Mexican-born Spaniards) audience, and they were the first significant devotees (Taylor 1987; Burkhart 2001, 2–7; Poole 1995). Guadalupe worship by the oppressed classes and Indians began to be prominent primarily in the eighteenth century (Poole 1995, 2–3). Therefore, the most ardent defenders of the antiquity of the Guadalupe traditions reflected by Anzaldúa are ironically the same conservative patriarchal Catholic priests whom she so fervently criticizes.

The Eurocentricity of Anzaldúa's ideology may also be seen in her selection of Carl Jung (1875-1961) as a guide to her own "thealogy." Jung was a Swiss psychologist who promoted the idea that human beings share a collective unconscious that consists of primordial images and themes called archetypes. These archetypes are expressed in myths, fairy tales, and dreams. Jung believed that connecting with these unconscious images was the key to reclaiming the wholeness of the self. Jung's famous works include the *Psychology of the Unconscious* (1912) and *Psychological Types* (1921).

Jung has indeed attracted many Latina/o authors and even scholars of Latina/o religion. For instance, the book by David T. Abalos (1986) on the sacred and the political aspects of Latinas/os is thoroughly Jungian in its approach. Many feminists also have adopted Jungian literary interpretations (see Pratt 1981). It is not certain why Jung has proved to be such an attraction for U.S. Latina/o authors, but one reason for Jung's appeal has been proposed by Richard M. Ryckman (1982, 87), "It is not too surprising, then, that Jung has enjoyed popular success among many idealistic, middle-class students surfeited with material possessions and shaken by a crisis of faith with authority figures." One can only speculate that such attraction was due to desire for a spirituality not based on institutionalized religion.

Far from being a flag-bearer for any new feminist or multicultural theologies, Jung now is seen by many scholars as a bearer of old-fashioned European ethnocentrism, especially in his discussions of the "Aryan unconscious" and "oriental mind" (Morris 1987, 171; Ryckman 1982, 69). Richard Noll (1994, 1997), perhaps Jung's most vociferous critic, has even accused Jung of initiating a sort of Aryan cult, though Noll's idea has been vigorously contested by other scholars (Shamdasani 1998). Given Jung's ideology, Anzaldúa's use of this psychologist is ironic.

Anzaldúa's notion of a patriarchal banishment of matriarchal goddesses in Aztec society also parallels ideas about European prehistory seen in the work of Marija Gimbutas (1982), among others. Usually, these writers posit a prehistoric era in Europe that was women-centered and goddess-worshiping. These theories have now inspired searches for goddess-centered cultures in China (e.g., Riane Eisler 1987) and other areas of the world.

But Cynthia Eller (2000, 7), who has written a pointed critique of matriarchal golden age theories, comments, "Indeed, the myth of matriarchal prehistory is not a feminist creation, in spite of the aggressively feminist spin it has carried over the past twenty-five years." Eller argues that the modern incarnation of this myth was initiated by Johann Jakob Backhofen (1815–1887), who regarded the replacement of matriarchies as an evolutionary advance. More balanced treatments of the place of women in Aztec society may be found in the work of Susan D. Gillespie (1989; for a critique of Eller, see Coleman 2001). In any event, sometimes Anzaldúa seems unaware of the patriarchal origins of some of these feminist ideas about religion.

One could note that Anzaldúa has also absorbed what some might call very pernicious Christian stereotypes. For example, in describing the God of the Mexicans as benign, Anzaldúa (Keating 2000, 95) uses the following contrast, "It wasn't this God of the Old Testament—judgment, hellfire, brimstone, and punishment." However, "hellfire" is not an Old Testament concept, but a New Testament Christian concept. The Old Testament God usually punished people during their lifetime. Christianity in the New Testament extended punishment into an eternal hell in the afterlife (see Matt. 10:28, Rev. 20). Thus, punishment was actually much harsher in the New Testament.

Jews have usually contested this Christian contrast of an angry God of the "Old Testament," with the benign loving God of the New Testament. In addition, Jews would see the term "Old Testament" as one that denies and erases the right of the Hebrew Bible to claim continuance. To use the term "Old Testament" is to succumb, from a Jewish viewpoint, to a very imperialistic and supercessionist Christian term in itself (Weiss-Rosmarin 1993, 108–109).

Finally, one may note that Anzaldúa has been criticized for a sort of "dualistic thinking" that divides the self from the larger community (Gagnier 1991, 138). Criticism of "essentialist" thinking—which sees particular characteritistics of an entity as inherent rather than as changeable components—has also been launched against Anzaldúa, but denied by Blom (1997, 300-301). Anzaldúa, of course, evolved in her religious viewpoint and did not prefer the term "religion" for what she practiced just prior to her death. Her practices may be characterized as a conglomeration of New Age ideas, beliefs in psychic phenomena, neo-Aztec mythology, and other elements that are not associated with institutionalized religions. It is her antipathy toward institutionalized religions that renders Anzaldúa more a member of an Anglo-American individualistic type of religion than a member of a communitarian and highly stratified Aztec religious tradition.

Comparative summary

Both Rudolfo Anaya and Gloria Anzaldúa consciously look toward indigenous traditions to replace or oppose orthodox Catholicism. Anaya focuses on folk healers as a way to provide an alternative form of religion. At the same time he includes legends (the golden carp) that integrate male divine images into an acceptable alternative for him. Anzaldúa looks almost exclusively toward Aztec goddesses for her inspiration (see Branche 1995, 42). And while Anaya focuses on the divinity of the soul, Anzaldúa focuses on the divinity of the body (see also Hall 1999). Although Anzaldúa complains about the patriarchy of Aztec traditions, both Anaya and Anzaldúa generally see indigenous traditions favorably. In fact, it is difficult to find a U.S. Latina/o author that is hostile toward indigenous traditions, the exceptions being evangelical Christian writers like Nicky Cruz.

While Anaya and Anzaldúa do allude to some authentic traditions and deities, they cannot escape the very Eurocentric ideas that they purport to strive against. The sort of New Age mysticism that both Anzaldúa and Anaya espouse has as many European roots as indigenous ones (see Stuckrad 2002). Their emphasis on the self, the uncritical acceptance of traditions invented by Eurocentric writers, and the selection of the Aztecs as representative of "indigenous" can be traced to Eurocentric notions of what constitutes a worthy "civilization." We rarely see any Latina/o author attempt to reclaim the indigenous voices and cultures that have no writing or complex urbanism, or were not bent on military conquest and imperialism (see Shea 1993). It is these now-silent Amerindian voices that perhaps constitute the majority of the authentic indigenous traditions of the Americas. And, if Christianity deserves to be abandoned for its impe-rialistic dogmatism, as Anaya and Anzaldúa argue, then why not do the same with Aztec religious traditions?

For comparative purposes, we suggest Agnes Sam's *Jesus Is Indian* (1989), where a South African author of subcontinental Indian descent addresses her view of "indigenous" religious traditions. Graciela Limón provides yet another Aztec-centered novel in *Song of the Hummingbird* (1996). Robert Maldonado (1995, 25) sees the non-Christian Anzaldúa paralleling the ideas found in the works of Virgilio Elizondo, the cele-brated Chicano theologian, insofar as they both see "*mestizaje* as a locus for healing a racially divided world" (see also Debra Castillo 1995). The importance of the "borderlands" as a useful trope for the study of Mexican American religion is exemplified by Luis D. León's insightful work, *La Llorona's Children: Religion, Life, and Death in the U.S.-Mexican Borderlands* (2004).

Note

1. Unless otherwise noted, all quotes are from the 1987 edition.

Chapter 2

African Religions

L
ike the indigenous traditions, African religions in the Americas were much more numerous than what is represented in U.S Latina/o literature. Indeed, the slave trade brought to the Americas various African groups, from Senegal to Madagascar. Even within relatively small areas of Africa, there were different groups with a large variety of religious traditions. Nigeria alone, for example, has nearly four hundred language groups within it (Sow and Abdulaziz 1999, 543). Yet, the most prominent African religious tradition represented in U.S. Latina/o literature derived from the Yoruba-speaking peoples, and it is commonly known as *santería*. We are fortunate to have some insightful studies already of the relationship of *santería* and literature (Brathwaite 1974; Matibag 1996; Marrero 1997; see also De La Torre, 2004).

Socio-historical overview

Santería is the name given to the specific religious syncretism that resulted from the interaction of principally Yoruba religious traditions with Catholicism in the Caribbean, and particularly in Cuba.[1] Some scholars and practitioners prefer the term "orisha religion" or "orisha tradition" (see Sanchez Cárdenas 1993). However, "*santería*" is sufficiently common to merit standard usage in our treatment. Accordingly, the focus here is on how this syncretism is mirrored in U.S. Latina/o literature and how the attitudes about this syncretism are reflected in the relevant literature.

It is important to realize that almost all religions are syncretistic, insofar as most result from mixtures to some degree. Christianity mixes Judaism and Hellenistic concepts, among others. Judaism blends Near Eastern traditions that can be traced from Greece to Mesopotamia. Thus, the term "syncretism" is not meaningful unless one specifies the particular religious traditions that are being mixed. "Syncretism" itself has a long history in the study of religion (see Pérez y Mena 1991, 33). Sometimes "syncretism" is used pejoratively (see Tamez 1997, 18). So again, the mixture in focus here is that of Yoruba religious traditions and Catholicism, for the most part.

The Yoruba people had a highly organized urban culture that can be traced back at least one thousand years in Nigeria (Murphy 1993, 7). In the standard historiography, the royal house of Oyo formed one of the most important political entities of the Yoruba, and its principal deity was Shangó, the god of thunder, lightning, and war. Conflicts with the Muslim Fulani tribes to the north, as well as conflicts with the Fon kingdom to the west, helped bring about the collapse of the Oyo empire in the early 1800s. Hundreds of thousands of Yoruba peoples were enslaved in the aftermath of the Oyo collapse.

The slave trade, then, explains why Cuba formed the most important cauldron for the mixture of Yoruba and Catholic traditions. Estimates of the number of African slaves brought to Cuba range from 526,828 to 702,000 (Murphy 1993, 23). Most of these were presumed to be Yoruba- and Bantu-speaking peoples. Many of these Yoruba slaves ended up in Cuba working on sugar plantations. In Cuba, the Yorubas became known as "Lucumí," the meaning of which has been traced to a Yoruba greeting meaning "my friend" (Murphy 1993, 27) and/or to the name of a port in Nigeria (Barnet 1997, 83).

Spanish law required that the Yoruba be baptized as Christians. However, the Lucumí did not abandon totally their African gods. The African pantheon was flexible, and the Lucumí could worship their African deities under the guise of Catholic saints (Spanish, "*santos*"). It is important here to remember that practitioners could also say that they were not hiding anything, but simply worshiping another aspect of the same deity.

Many of these Lucumí were also forced by the Spanish to join ethnic organizations called *cabildos*. The purpose of the *cabildos* was to separate ethnic groups from one another in order to avoid cooperative insurrections and to facilitate Christianization. However, these organizations had also the opposite effect of helping to preserve African traditions. They also helped to promote syncretism, as some of these *cabildos* were ostensibly sponsored by Catholic saints such as Santa Barbara, whose feast day is on the fourth of December.

The regulations of *cabildo* life gave rise to "*reglas,*" or forms of worship, which consequently became a principal name for particular forms of *santería* following independence and the separation of church and state. Thus, *santería* is also called "*Regla de Ocha*" and "*Regla Lucumí.*"

The form of worship became more important than the specific ethnic derivation of the worshipers. In any event, this worship of Catholic saints by the Lucumí resulted in the word "*santería*" being applied to the newly emerging religious tradition.

It is too simple to call the Yoruba religion polytheistic, as eventually all of the *orishas* (a general name for African spirits or deities) are but an aspect of the supreme god, named Olodumare ("the Lord of all destinies"). But, as in Africa, the *orishas* had a primary manifestation in stones (*otá*). These stones were believed to be the remnant of *orishas* after their descent from a sort of heavenly primordial place called *Ile-Ifá*. These stones are considered living entities that must be, among other things, bathed and fed the blood of animals. These stones, like the *orishas* and human beings, are imbued with the *aché*, the force or power that permits the *orishas* and human beings to perform all sorts of miracles and solve human problems (Sánchez Cardenas 1993, 484–485).

A community of practitioners is called an *ile*. One joins the community by being initiated by a *babalawo*, a priest who might have years of training, particularly in the complex art of divination, poetry, and other rituals associated with a particular *orisha*. An *ile* is also the name for a shrine, and often the shrine is dedicated to a specific *orisha*. Passage into Cuba also apparently attenuated the pantheon. While hundreds of divinities are known in Nigeria, we usually find no more than about thirty in Cuba (Barnet 1997, 87).

The year 1959 marked a turning point for *santería*. Although Cubans had been coming to America already in the nineteenth century, it was the Cuban revolution that resulted in hundreds of thousands of new Cuban immigrants to the United States, and particularly to South Florida (see Curtis 1980). *Santería* thereby entered a new phase in a relatively new environment. As noted by Sánchez Cardenas (1993, 478), "practice of the Orisha religion, prior to 1959, was limited primarily to Cuba." In America, *santería* was "desyncretized," meaning that it sought to reclaim

its African origins (Curry 2001, 86). The number of practitioners is difficult to estimate, but Drinan and Huffman (1993, 21) accept an estimate
of some sixty thousand believers in the Miami-Dade area.

Santería attracted much public attention in 1987 when Ernesto
Pichardo, a priest of the order of Shangó (divinity of thunder and fire)
announced his intentions to establish the Church of Lukumí Babalú Ayé
(CLBA) in Hialeah, Florida. The CLBA was the first significant estab-
lishment of a santería "church" in the United States. The city council
responded by banning animal sacrifice within city limits, and Pichardo's
group challenged the ordinance in court (Drinan and Huffman 1993).
After a lengthy legal battle, the Supreme Court ruled in 1993 that the
City of Hialeah was in violation of the "free exercise" of religion of CLBA.
In short, the Supreme Court accepted the premise that CLBA was part of
a legitimate religious tradition protected by the United States
Constitution.

Perhaps the most important public gateway to the world of *santería* in
the United States is the *botánica*, a sort of *santería* supermarket, which usually stocks the herbs and paraphernalia needed by practitioners. One may
find cans of aerosol sprays marketed for their efficacy in love or other
aspects important to everyday life. As such, the *botánica* represents the use
of capitalistic marketing techniques by *santería* (Curtis 1982, 348). The
multiplication of *botánicas* in Miami reflects a more accessible attitude
toward *santería* in the United States.

Divination is probably one of the most recurrent services that a *babalawo* performs for his family of practitioners. As Eugenio Matibag (1997,
151) notes, "Divination mediates between earth (*aiye*) and heaven (*orun*).
It proffers counsel and guidance to believers at all critical junctures and
transitional experiences of the life cycle." *Ifá*, which relies on the casting
of palm nuts or the reading of a necklace, is perhaps the most prominent
form of divination. Other divinatory systems rely on *obi*, a coconut parted
into four parts, or on reading shells. The procedures of *Ifá* aim to create a
dialogue between the various configurations of the divining instruments
and the client. Matibag notes that *Ifá* constitutes a complex narrative system that, among other things, helps to transmit extensive bodies of
knowledge, and its practice requires extensive skills of memorization, as
well as creativity.

Also from Africa is a religion known as Mayombe or Palo Mayombe.
This is mostly associated with Bantu-speaking people who were brought to
Cuba as far back as the sixteenth century (Cabrera 1986, 1). Mayombe is
deemed more "minimalist" in its practices than the *orisha* traditions. The

rituals are simpler and less festive, sometimes eschewing even the use of loud instruments (123–124). There is less emphasis on colorful costumes and caring for their deities in shrines. Nonetheless, Mayombe is concerned with worshiping ancestors and with divination.

The practitioners of *santería* often labeled their own practices as "religion" and those of Mayombe as *"brujería"* ("witchcraft"), thus reflecting European values. Cabrera (211) acknowledges that Mayombe may include elements intended to harm others, but otherwise she thinks that the label of "witchcraft" is unjust ("To the Congos . . . was assigned the role of sorcerers, and unjustly so . . . ").[2] Since most religions can include practitioners who wish ill on others, Mayombe is not very different in this respect.

Aside from *santería* and Mayombe, we also find other syncretisms in the Afro-Caribbean world. Perhaps one of the most important is Spiritism, which is prominent in Puerto Rico and among Puerto Ricans in the U.S. mainland, particularly in New York City. One of the foremost scholars of Spiritism, Andrés Isidoro Pérez y Mena, distinguishes between "Spiritualism" and "Spiritism." The former "is mostly concerned with a medium's psychic power and her ability to communicate with the dead for the benefit of her clients, for a price" (Pérez y Mena 1991, xiii). Spiritism is "an actual movement" that syncretizes Spiritualism, African, and Catholic traditions with the work of a Frenchman named Alan Kardec (xiii).

Dr. Hippolyte Leon Denizard Rivail (1804–1865) became better known as Alan Kardec, a name that appears on his epitaph at Père Lachaise cemetery in Paris. Rivail believed himself to be a reincarnation of a Celtic poet by the name of Alan Kardec. Although raised in a Catholic family, Kardec became interested in Protestantism, and eventually he sought to unify all religions. He believed that the spirits of the dead still communicated with the living. He published his theory in *The Book of Spirits* (1857), *The Book of Mediums* (1861), *The Gospel According to Spiritism* (1864), *Heaven and Hell* (1865), which talks about the justice of God according to Spiritism, and *The Genesis, the Miracles and the Predictions* (1868), which speaks about the end of the world.

Kardec's philosophy, which was brought to Puerto Rico by the 1890s, resonated at first with the white upper-income stratum in Puerto Rico. As Pérez y Mena notes, "Paradoxically, the upper classes turned to the French Spiritist beliefs, not wanting to identify themselves with the African and *Jíbaro* elements within their society. Yet the upper classes, by practicing Spiritism, provided legitimation of the ancestor worship already flourishing in Puerto Rico" (25). Indeed, the idea of communicating with the dead existed among the indigenous *Taino* and in traditions brought from Africa.

In New York, Puerto Rican Spiritism began to mix with Cuban *santería*. Much of the mixing took place through the interaction of Puerto Rican and Cuban musicians (48). Spiritism now provides a serious alternative to Protestant and Catholic traditions among New York Puerto Ricans. In New York City there are *centros* ("centers") where practitioners gather. Sometimes these *centros* become the target of protests by other Puerto Rican evangelicals who see them as centers for witchcraft. In any event, literature offers us a lens to examine how these Afro-Caribbean religions have evolved in the United States.

Case Study 1: *La Carreta Made a U-Turn* (1979)

While our book concentrates on novels, our first case study in this chapter features the poetry of Tato Laviera because he is reputed to be the best selling Latina/o poet in the United States (Kanellos 1993, 3.452). Moreover, few other Latina/o authors grant as much prominence to African religious traditions. Born in Santurce, Puerto Rico in 1951, Laviera came to live in New York City in 1960. He attended Catholic high schools and briefly attended Cornell University and Brooklyn College. Arte Público Press has published all of his major works, including *La Carreta Made a U-Turn* (1979), *Enclave* (1981), *AmeRícan*, and *Mainstream Ethics* (1989). Laviera sees himself as "Nuyorican," a term that reflects his Puerto Rican and New York heritage. Artistically, he sees himself as the heir to Puerto Rican poets such as Luis Pales Matos (Hernández 1997, 79; see also Flores, Attinasi, and Pedraza 1981).

Perhaps Laviera's most famous work is *La Carreta Made a U-Turn* (1979; all citations are from the edition of 1992), which is a response to those who claim that Puerto Ricans living in the U.S. mainland should return to their island (see also Flores, Attinasia, and Pedraza 1981). Laviera is a spokesperson for the right of Nuyoricans to have, and to celebrate, their own culture. At the same time, *La Carreta* is replete with condemnations of any Eurocentric and Catholic religious traditions, and he concurrently extols African traditions. Accordingly, *La Carreta* is a good example of how African traditions are treated positively among U.S. Latina/o authors.

In general, Laviera is very cognizant of his African heritage. In "the africa in pedro morejón," Laviera says (57), "Yes, we have preserved what was originally african / or have we expanded it? i wonder if we have / committed the sin of blending?"

The poem immediately turns to the subject of religion (57). "I had a dream that i was in Africa / it took me a long time / to find the gods inside / so many moslems and christians, / but when I did, they were the origin of everything! / then i discovered bigger things / the american dollar symbol, / that's african." Clearly, the poet touts the preeminence and priority of the African deities over Christian gods.

Despite wondering whether his people have committed the sin of blending, the poet is adept at blending traditional Catholic liturgy with expressions of African religiosity. One example is "Excommunication Gossip," a title with obvious religious allusions. The poem is ostensibly about the disparity between the Eurocentric church hierarchy and the Puerto Rican laity. Note the beginning of this sort of "counterliturgy" (23): "If it is dreams you seek / after your body is cremated / inside the grave of roofless / cemeteries. / if it is an everlasting life / heaven or infinite salvation / you seek, don't cry in heaven / when you find out the lord / discriminated against minorities." He adds later (23): "and the bishops / and the archbishops / and the cardinals / and the pope / slept in golden beds / i provided the good income / yes, I live on welfare but those so-called princes / live on welfare of the people."

The poet complains that heaven, at least as envisioned by the Catholic hierarchy, is not a place for minorities. Moreover, the poet sees the Catholic Church as living well at the expense of the poor. In short, the Church has de facto excommunicated the poor, and "gossip" appears to be an allusion to the idea that this excommunication is not official, but is still well-known among the members.

In lines 37–53, the poem moves from this complaint about the Church toward a remembrance of his father. The poet resents that he confessed his father's sins to the priest, and yet he never spoke to his own father so well. His own father was self-destructing (24), "porque el estaba rechazando estas maldiciones / estas contradicciones inconcientemente" ("Because he was rejecting these curses / these contradictions unconsciously"). The contradictions apparently are those between a merciful god and the sufferings of people. The segment focusing on his father may parallel African rituals that center on remembering the ancestors. At the same time, this segment functions as a criticism of the Church, insofar as the only "Father" that the poet remembers is his earthly one, not the Church's heavenly one.

The poet now continues his counterliturgy in lines 54–62, which blend a series of nine complaints with the traditional "Kyrie/Christe eleison," a Greek expression meaning "Lord/Christ, have mercy."

LAVIERA		ENGLISH TRANSLATION	
muchas basuras	kyrie eleison	Much garbage	Lord, have mercy
muchos robos	kyrie eleison	Many robberies	Lord, have mercy
mucho frio	kyrie eleison	Much cold	Lord, have mercy
sin educacion	christe eleison	Without education	Christ, have mercy
sin viviendas	christe eleison	Without housing	Christ, have mercy
sin patria	christe eleison	Without homeland	Christ, have mercy
orando	kyrie eleison	praying	Lord, have mercy
con hambre	kyrie eleison	while hungry	Lord, have mercy
sin nada	kyrie eleison	with nothing	Lord, have mercy

The apparent implication is that if God were merciful, these sufferings would not exist. The ninefold repetition of Kyrie/Christe eleison, found commonly in Catholic liturgies, also serves ostensibly to underscore how often the Christian Lord does not have mercy. Each part of the traditional Catholic liturgy is juxtaposed with a complaint. Alternatively, the poet may be praying to God for something the Church is not providing.

After the Kyrie eleison litany, Laviera reminisces about the canorous popular music he loves (lines 63–71). This parallels the musical interlude that often is part of a traditional liturgy. In lines 72–90, he alludes to the letters of Saint Paul that he remembers hearing. He thinks these biblical epistles were "fabulous," but then notes that (25):

> the only letters\ we received were dispossess \ notes from the bolitero to the landlord \ and everybody in between. i read a letter discharging me from school \ i read a letter announcing the arrival of pedro's \ coffin from nam \ i read a letter dated by mr. angel ruiz \ commissioner of holy bible payments claiming my mother's favorite passage \ from her rented holy bible. \ i read a letter in which installment payments \ were after our family \ i read a letter to subpoena my younger \ brother to court because he stole one \ lousy egg from the next door neighbor \ who had stole it in la marketa.

So again, Laviera juxtaposes normal parts of the Catholic liturgy, in this case scriptural readings, with the types of "epistles" that he received in the real world that he inhabited outside the Church.

"Excommunication Gossip" continues with a section titled, in Latin, "Oremus" ("let us pray"), in lines 91–104:

may the sentiments
of the people rise
and become espiritistas
to take care of our religious
necessities

y echar brujos de fufú y   [and to cast sorcerers of fufú and
espiritus malos a los que   evil spirits upon those who
nos tratan como naborías   treat us as peasants and
y esclavos . . .   slaves]
and sentence them to hang
desnudos tres dias en orchard   [naked three days in Orchard
beach, pa que yemayá le saque   Beach, so that Yemayá can remove
sus maldades.   their evils]

This is a clear statement that Puerto Rican religious needs are not to be sought in the organized Catholic Church, but rather in "Spiritism." It is uncertain if Laviera is using the term "Spiritism" in the same manner as Pérez y Mena, but a non-Catholic and African-based tradition seems clear.

The poet follows this complaint against the Church with a desire to have the oppressors punished. He threatens to turn those who enslave his people over to the sorcerers of witchcraft ("*brujos de fufú*") and to the evil spirits ("*espiritus malos*"). Note that the judgment is to take place at Orchard Beach, an area of the Bronx that may be a suitable place for *Yemayá*, the mistress of the sea, who protects her children. Finally, he wishes that *Yemayá* sentence these evildoers to hang for three days in Orchard Beach, a number of days that is reminiscent of Christ's death.

Far from being a disorganized series of complaints, "Excommunication Gossip" blends African traditions with Christian formal liturgical elements to enact a counterliturgy and judgment upon the Church. Note the following formal elements:

1. an introductory exhortation critical of the church (lines 1–36);

2. a remembrance of his ancestor (lines 37–53);

3. a litany that juxtaposes traditional Catholic Kyrie eleison with complaints about the suffering of the people (lines 54–62);

4. an interlude focusing on music;

5. an allusion to scriptural readings; and

6. a final prayer focusing on judgment against the oppressors.

Laviera's reproach to the Church also expresses a clear preference for his African roots. At the same time, his blending of Catholic and African traditions reflects the very syncretism that has long been a part of Afro-Caribbean cultures.

Another poem in *La Carreta*, "Orchard beach y la virgen del carmen," uses Yoruba religions as a juxtaposition to Catholicism. The poem is again set in Orchard Beach, and the scene is a sort of feast, which includes an invocation (70):

> Yemayá, Yemayá . . . oh, oh, oh!
> Agua que va caer . . . ["rain that is about to fall"]
> the congas were laid and reached their climax!
> tru cu tú pacutú . . .
> and nobody said it was inspired by
> LA VIRGEN DEL CARMEN
> coming out of the sun.

Note, again, how the poet desires that African rituals be recognized for what they are. The poet apparently suggests that *La Virgen del Carmen* ought not even be mentioned, as the ritual should be recognized as purely African. In fact, the African sounds themselves might be meant to violate the Catholic Virgin—"the sounds raped all the virgins that were left" (70).

In yet another poem, "Santa Barbara," Laviera focuses on the Yoruba deity, Shangó, who is often worshiped as Santa Barbara. The poem depicts a feast for Shangó in which the poet becomes possessed by Santa Barbara. The feast causes the indigenous peoples to rise from their genocide ("*de su genocidio*"), and the spirits to stir within black peoples. As the devotee becomes possessed, he stops breathing, and then he begins dancing and moving with great skill. He believes that his possessor is "HER" (ELLA), or Santa Barbara.

Critical discussion

Laviera exemplifies a Latina/o writer who yearns for a religion based on his African roots, rather than one based on orthodox Catholicism, which he believes has done his people more harm than good. The author weaves Christian liturgical forms with poetic expressions of his desire to reclaim his African roots. Poetry, a major aspect of African rituals, becomes an expression of revolution meant to overthrow the Christian hegemony. Yet, the very liturgical mixture he accepts mirrors the liturgical mixture that occurs in *santería*, in Spiritism, and in other Afro-Caribbean religious traditions. His counterliturgical exercises can be compared to those at Catholic shrines in Miami, where devotees of *santería* contest the authority and orthodoxy of the Catholic Church through alternative rituals (Tweed 1996). We can conclude that Laviera, perhaps more than most U.S. Latina/o authors, is quite conscious of using literary structure itself to contest the powers of the Catholic Church.

Case Study 2: *Dreaming in Cuban* (1992)

A Cuban American woman's perspective on *santería* may be found in Cristina García's *Dreaming in Cuban*. According to the biographical sketch in *Dreaming in Cuban*, García was born in Havana, Cuba, in 1958. She and her family came to the United States in 1960 in the aftermath of the Cuban Revolution. She attended an Ivy League undergraduate college, Barnard College, where she received a bachelor's degree in 1979. She earned a master's degree in international studies at Johns Hopkins. A one-time reporter for *Time* magazine and author of *The Aguero Sisters* (1997), among other works, García has made a name for herself in creative writing.

Dreaming in Cuban tells the story of three generations (from the 1930s to the 1980s) of the del Pino family. The story mirrors the fate of many Cuban families separated by the Cuban Revolution. The first generation is represented by Jorge del Pino (b. 1897) and Celia del Pino (b. 1909). Jorge leaves Celia in Cuba shortly after the revolution and settles in the United States. The second generation consists of Lourdes, Felicia, and Javier. The main characters of the third generation include Pilar (daughter of Lourdes, and born in 1959), and Felicia's children: Luz and Milagro (twins born in 1962) and Ivanito, born in 1967.

Lourdes moved to the United States, where she builds up a bakery business. She represents the more conservative, capitalist, and anticommunist side of most Cubans who fled Castro's revolution. She remembers going to High Mass with her father when they lived in Cuba (68). She bears some anti-Jewish prejudice, which surfaces when she tells Pilar that the Jews "killed Christ" (58). She has regular conversations with her deceased father, beginning forty days after she buries him (64).

Pilar is Lourdes's daughter, and the alter ego of the author, Cristina García. Pilar, who was born in the very year of the Cuban Revolution (1959), has been separated from her grandmother Celia since she was very young. While living a very secular and materialistic life in the United States, Pilar feels a yearning to return to Cuba and visit her grandmother. She has explicitly sworn off Catholicism and is "disdainful . . . of religion" (168). She is particularly critical of Zaida, her paternal grandmother, who is "the most fakely pious person I know" (61). Zaida had eight children out of wedlock, but calls any woman who wears lipstick a whore. Pilar, on the other hand, seems attracted to *santería*. Pilar is not afraid to learn about philosophies and religions that might not be approved by her mother. She reads pro-communist books, to her mother's chagrin. She learns a bit about Eastern religions from her father, who is an intellectually curious man.

García's portrayal of *santería* is particularly outlined in connection with the miserable life of Felicia, whose name ironically means "happy." Felicia identifies strongly with San Sebastian, the saint who had suffered a double death—first by arrows and then by beating (77). She is so unhappy with her first husband that she burns his face. When her son, Ivanito, is born, Felicia pins an onyx ring to his diaper to ward off Evil Eye and then burns votive candles in the nursery until a doctor threatens to expel her.

When Felicia receives notice of her father's death, she recalls that her last visit with him ended badly. Now, she fears that her father's spirit has come back to haunt her and her mother. So, Felicia goes to visit Herminia, her best friend and daughter of a *babalawo*. Herminia diagnoses the problem, and advises Felicia to make peace with her departed father (12). Herminia insists that Felicia must perform rituals for Santa Bárbara/Shangó lest she endanger Lourdes's soul. The *babalawo's* daughter also says that "there's always new hope for the dead" (12). Although Felicia "believes in the gods' benevolent powers, she just can't stand the blood" (12). She requests that no goat be used for sacrifice.

In any event, Felicia is told to be ready at 10:00 p.m., but she arrives an hour late. Herminia, who is wearing a "cream-yellow blouse with a collar the luster of the absent moon," warns that her tardiness might anger the gods (13). Herminia guides Felicia down a corridor lit with red votive candles on one side. Shells collected in a strand hang in the arched doorway at the end of the corridor.

44

La Madrina ("godmother"), who is helping with the ceremony, wears a white turban and layers of gauze skirts. Santa Barbara is positioned at the back wall, with apples and bananas at her feet. There are also offerings for Saint Lazarus, and the African deities, Obatalá and Ogun. Eleggua, the *orisha* who guards entrances, is positioned at the front of the room, and "inhabits the clay eggs in nine rustic bowls of varying sizes" (14). Four mulattas are also in the room praying in front of the shrines. *La Madrina* speaks, "Herminia has told us of your dystopia." The narrator adds, "*La Madrina* is fond of melodious words, although she doesn't always know what they mean" (14).

A *santero* (a *santería* ritual specialist) who has traveled "many hours from the south, from the mangroves," is the principal officiant (14). He announces that "Elleguá wants a goat" (14). Felicia reiterates that Herminia has promised that no goat would be needed, but Herminia then warns that Eleggúa requires fresh blood to be effective. The other participants gather around Felicia and "wrap her in garlands of beads and stroke her face and eyelids with branches of rosemary" (14). Felicia takes some shredded coconut in her mouth and spits it in the goat's face and then kisses its ears. After this, she rubs her breasts on the goat's muzzle while the women sing "*Kosí, ikú, kosí arun, kosí araye*" (15), part of a common prayer to Eleggúa. The *santero* rapidly plunges a knife into the goat's neck, draining the blood onto some clay eggs (15). After witnessing the scene and inhaling the atmosphere, Felicia faints.

In January of 1978, Felicia consults a *santero* again. This time she wants another husband. The *santero* reads cowry shells and predicts only misfortune. He recommends that she "perform a rubbing ritual to cleanse herself of negative influences" (148). However, she falls in love before she completes the ritual. Felicia meets and marries a man named Ernesto Brito, who dies in a fire at a seaside motel about four days after losing his virginity to her. Felicia, who works as a hairdresser, then uses a mixture of lye and menstrual blood to burn the scalp of Graciela Moreira, a regular client who Felicia believes is somehow responsible for Ernesto's demise. Afterward, Felicia disappears until summer, having lost her memory for some six months. When we next encounter her, she has married a third husband named Otto. Felicia apparently hurls him to his death as he tried to have sex with her in a roller-coaster.

García also provides us with the point of view of Herminia, the *babala-wo's* daughter. Herminia recalls that she met Felicia while the latter was searching for shells at the beach. They were both six years old. Herminia, who is very dark, loved Felicia because the latter did not see color.

Herminia told Felicia that the shells belonged to Yemayá, goddess of the sea, and could help divine the future. Felicia responds, "Will you save me?" (183). Herminia also notes that the local people "told evil lies about my father. They said he used to rip the heads off goats with his teeth" (184). She got into fights in school because of her religion.

Herminia also remarks that "Felicia returned to our religion with great eagerness after her disappearance in 1978" (185). Herminia credits *santería* with keeping Felicia stable and happy. However, when Felicia sees that her family does not accept her religion, she becomes depressed. The *santeros* try rituals, but are interrupted by Celia, Felicia's mother, who expels them from her house and overturns the image of Obatalá, Felicia's patron deity. The narrator implies that Celia's actions against Obatalá eventually cause the death of Felicia a short time afterwards.

Luz and Milagro, Felicia's twins, have been taught about *santería* by their mother. In one conversation, Felicia tells Milagro that shells are good luck because they represent the jewels of the goddess of the sea. Felicia compares Milagro to a one of those jewels (120). However, Luz still seems to confuse *santería* with voodoo, and sometimes refers to her mother's rituals as "voodoo meetings" (123). In fact, the girls are never as enthusiastic as their mother about this religion.

Celia has a more ambivalent attitude toward *santería*. Felicia suspects her mother of being an atheist, with "an instinctive distrust of the ecclesiastical" (76). The narrator adds, "Although Celia was not a believer, she was wary of powers she didn't understand" (76). For example, Celia locks her children in the house on December 4, the feast day for Shangó, and warns them that they might "be kidnapped and sacrificed to the black people's god if they wandered the streets alone" (76). She forbids Felicia to visit Herminia because her father was a *santero*, "black as the blackest Africans" (163). Herminia's father erroneously predicted that it was no use fighting Fulgencio Batista (the Cuban dictator ousted by Castro) because he "was under the protection of Changó, god of fire and lightning" (163).

Yet, Celia also "dabbles in *santería's* harmless superstitions" (90–91). She encounters Herminia occasionally and seems to recognize many of the herbs used by *santeros*. Celia is ambivalent in regard to these ingredients because she "fears that both good and evil may be borne in the same seed" (90). Celia was reared by a great-aunt who was familiar with *santería*, and did not like those who attended church (92). In general, Celia's god is Castro, and she "worships him" (110).

In 1934, while still unmarried, Celia had fallen in love with a married Spanish lawyer named Gustavo Sierra. When Gustavo decides to return to his wife in Spain, Celia falls into a deep depression, staying in bed for some eight months. Her great-aunt calls a "*santera* from Regla, who draped Celia with beaded necklaces and tossed shells to divine the will of the gods" (37). The *santera* says, "Miss Celia, I see a wet landscape in your palm." She then addresses Celia's great-aunt, "She will survive the hard flames" (37). Celia did seem to survive by writing undispatched letters to Gustavo. The correspondence begins at the insistence of her then future husband Jorge, who begins courting her while she is housebound. She marries him shortly thereafter.

Some forty years later, when Felicia turns up missing, Celia consults the same *santera*. The *santera* enters a trance that ends in a physical incineration that leaves nothing but a "fringed cotton shawl" (160). This odd turn of events is met with almost casual aplomb by Celia, who picks up the shawl and goes home. She discovers that her son Javier has disappeared and that a lump in her breast has appeared. She later has her breast removed.

It is 1989 when the book returns to Pilar, and we find her as a college student visiting a *botánica* located on Upper Park Avenue, which seems to imply that *santería* is now found at the center of cosmopolitan New York (199). Pilar explains her interest in *santería*: "I'm not religious but I get the feeling that it's the simplest rituals, the ones that are integrated with the earth and its seasons, that are the most profound. It makes more sense to me than the more abstract forms of worship" (199). Pilar selects a red and white beaded necklace and places it over her head. The shop attendant sees her actions and exclaims, "Ah, a daughter of Changó" (200). He recommends that she continue her relationship with Shangó by bathing for nine consecutive nights in an herbal bath.

Before she reaches her dormitory room, however, Pilar is accosted by some youths who sexually assault her in a park. They also take some of the herbs and smoke them. She closes her eyes, and when she next opens them, the boys are gone. She runs back to the university, where she does begin her ritual baths. She buys apples and bananas in the cafeteria for her rituals. She begins to have visions. Then, at midnight, she gets up to paint a canvas in flaming red and white colors. She does this for eight more nights, and on the ninth day of her ritual baths, she finally makes the decision to call her mother to tell her they're going to Cuba (203).

Pilar remembers her nannies in Cuba telling Lourdes that they feared Pilar because they thought she had special abilities; Lourdes fires those nannies. One night lightning hits a palm tree outside of Pilar's window; however, the new nanny is not frightened, and she explains to Pilar that

Shangó once sent a lizard to take a gift to a lover. The lizard accidentally stumbled and swallowed the trinket. The muted lizard then hides in a palm tree to avoid Shangó's wrath, and Shangó henceforth strikes palm trees out of revenge.

In Cuba, Pilar becomes even more interested in *santería*. She looks up Herminia to hear more about her religion. She seems to develop a special connection to her grandmother Celia. Pilar, however, realizes that she belongs in New York, not Cuba. Lourdes and Pilar eventually help Ivanito, Felicia's son, escape Cuba. Celia loses her will to live after learning of Ivanito's escape. She sees this escape as a further death of her family. Celia commits suicide by walking into the sea, the province of Yemayá. Ironically, the whole book began with Celia looking north through binoculars for some sort of military attack from the United States. But the danger from the north came, instead, from her daughter and granddaughter, who helped to separate the family forever.

Critical discussion

Cristina García provides a multiple viewpoint approach to *santería*. Celia is ambivalent about *santería*. Whereas Felicia embraces it as a means to salvation, her girls have only a passing acquaintance with the religion. Herminia was born into it. Pilar becomes fascinated by *santería* even as she lives a secular life in America. *Santería* exists both in communist Cuba and in the heart of capitalist New York City. In short, García appears to strive for a variety of viewpoints about *santería* that is hardly found in any other U.S. Latina/o work.

Color symbolism is extremely important in telling the religious aspects of this story. Thus, blue is the color of Yemayá, the sea goddess, and Celia is said to be an expert on every shade of blue. Celia lives by the sea and dies in the sea. Red and white figure repeatedly in stories associated with Shangó, as when Pilar paints her canvas in red during her ritual baths. Herminia, daughter of Shangó, lives in a house painted red and white. Mishaps involving fire are all under the domain of Shangó (Cabrera 1971, 48), and Felicia burns her first husband and the scalp of Moreira. Felicia's second husband dies in a fire and there is fire in her house. Pilar buys bananas and apples, favorite foods of Shangó.

Cristina García most resembles Pilar. She has come to research *santería*. She must acquaint herself, as an adult, with *santería*, which is also part of her lost Cuban heritage. She emphasizes the persecution that occurs in

Cuba against *santería*, though there is more tolerance reported today (see Pérez y Mena 2000). The narrator even implies that there is some truth to *santería*, as Felicia dies when Celia destroys the image of Obatalá. In general, this book's attitude toward *santería* is rather sympathetic.

García seems concerned about providing authenticity to her descriptions of *santería*. For example, a version of the story about the lizard and the palm tree is discussed by Cabrera (1971, 227). Likewise, the prayer to Eleggúa may be found in Cabrera's work (91). Yet, Marrero (1997, 154) notes that "Felicia is the construction of an American-educated imagination. The values and consequences of her choices are the values of U.S. literary conventions and not necessarily those of post-revolutionary Cuban perspectives." Indeed, García's notion of *santería* is perhaps constructed out of the compendia that she has consulted rather than from firsthand experience. García's sympathy for Cuba and her agnosticism may not be representative of the larger Cuban community that has defined Cuban American identity.

Case Study 3: *Shangó* (1996)

Whereas Laviera and García express positive sentiments concerning the *orishas*, we find a more ambiguous and even negative portrayal of some African traditions in *Shangó*—a detective murder mystery that explores *santería* in Miami. The author, James Roberto Curtis, combines didactics and entertainment, including explanatory boxes about, among other things, *santería*, Santa Barbara, the Seven African powers, Oyá, and Mayombe. While some of the information may be authentic, some of it is clearly for effect.

Curtis is an associate professor of geography at California State University at Long Beach. *Shangó* is his first novel. Curtis says that he first became acquainted with *santería* while researching a book on Cuban Americans (Curtis, per. comm. 2002). He adds:

It didn't take long to discover that *santería* was a significant aspect of Cuban religious expression. In addition to standard library research, I attended several *santería* ceremonies in Miami. The power and drama of those experiences convinced me that I would not likely be able to convey much about my gut reaction to the religion in the professional literature (although I did publish a couple of academic articles on *santería*). So I decided, after many delays and abortive starts, to attempt a novel that would evolve around the cult.

The plot centers on a series of murders in the Miami area that are linked to rituals surrounding Shangó. As mentioned previously, Shangó/Santa Barbara controls passion and enemies, and his colors are red and white. His accoutrements include the sword (or axe) and the golden cup. One of his deuteragonists is Ogun, the god of metal, for they both desire the love of Oshun, the *orisha* associated with rivers and fresh water.

The story begins when Osvaldo Gutiérrez, a Miami police lieutenant near retirement, comes upon a patrol car with a flashing red beacon. Waiting by the patrol car are two other Latino officers who have been flagged down by a man. They are led to a body, and the unusual death has caused a patrolman to be almost "pasty white" with fear (8). The body, we learn later, belongs to Xavier "Candy" Cuevas, an ex-prisoner who wanted to be initiated into the cult of *santería* in order to gain extraordinary powers and wealth. Candy was to be initiated by Rosa García-Mesa, who insists that Candy be initiated into the cult before they can be lovers. Candy pays fifty thousand dollars for the initiation, but he thinks he will reap much more than that after he acquires the special powers he seeks. The next day he is found dead.

The death scene includes a headless black rooster crumpled on the threshold, an altar in the middle of the room, and a goat lying across a cauldron. At the base of the altar lies Candy, naked from the waist up. Aside from the double-headed axe buried in his chest, there are red carnations and white chrysanthemums around his neck. Flies hover around the gaping wound. The handle of the axe is covered by alternating stripes of red and white tape. Watermelons, a cantaloupe (a favorite of Yemayá), and several bananas strung together with a red and white ribbon also decorate the gruesome scene. A reddish hue bathes the room. About fourteen days before, a boy named Billy had reported seeing "A ghost. And a giant. And a dwarf, a little colored dwarf" (12). He is an unwitting witness to the robbery of the skull of Elizabeth Mary Rolle from her grave. The detective suspects that this skull is connected to the murder of Candy.

Another character is Miguel Calderón, a twenty-three-year-old man, born in Cuba. We first encounter him on a beach pouring lotion over Vicki, his blond American girlfriend. After reading about the *santería*-related murder in the local newspaper, Miguel and Vicki go to the Botánica Yemayá for *santería* supplies. As Miguel ponders a statue of Santa Barbara in his hand, he wonders if he appears "superstitious" to Vicki. A very large man, perhaps six feet eight inches and weighing around three hundred pounds, is in this store. Miguel's questions prompt the man, later identified as Hernan, to ask, "You're *cubano* and you don't know about the *orishas*, the African gods . . . ?" (29). The man thinks that Miguel is making fun of this tradition and so warns him, "I wouldn't take the *orishas* so lightly if I were you, *cubano*" (30).

In the store is Ileana Acosta, a dark, beautiful girl. She addresses the giant as "Father," a purely honorific title used within *santería*, akin to the Catholic use of "Father" for a priest. After they leave the *botánica*, Miguel and Vicki proceed to his house, which reeks of garlic. His grandmother believes in *santería*, so he queries her about the Yoruba deities. He asks his grandmother about why Ileana wears a necklace with yellow and green beads, and the grandmother replies that this makes her a daughter of Oshun. Eventually, Miguel leaves Vicki, and Ileana becomes his fiancée.

Miguel's anthropology professor is Henry Krajewski, who had gone to Cuba in the late 1950s to research political economy. While there he became interested in *santería* and also met and fell in love with Rosa García-Mesa. He left her while she was pregnant, and she eventually tells him that the child died. Rosa later migrates to the United States. However, after the story of the skull robbery, Rosa calls up her old flame (76). She has now become a professor herself, and Krajewski sends Miguel to her for help with his research. When Miguel arrives at her house, he learns that her bedroom is an *ilé*, a *Santería* shrine.

Gutiérrez has been suspicious of Rosa García-Mesa for some time. He has also kept tabs on Hernan Gerrero and on Dagoberto Villalobos, who lives in New Jersey. The latter is the "dwarf" spotted at the grave robberies. Gutiérrez surmises that Dagoberto was asked to come from so far because he is considered an expert in wielding Ogun's knife. Ogun participates in Shangó ceremonies, where he plays his rival and fights ceremoniously with him for the love of Oshun. So when another skull is stolen, Gutiérrez decides to set a trap. He sees that December 4th will mark fourteen days after the skull was stolen, and that date is well known as Shangó's feast day. Gutiérrez asks Miguel, Ileana, and Krajewski to be part of this trap. Ileana, Miguel, and Krajewski are soon invited by Rosa to the feast to be held on December 4th. Hernan and Dagoberto are to be unwitting participants in Rosa's ceremony.

As they approach the site of the feast, Miguel sees Rosa's car blocking their path. She orders Miguel, Krajewski, and Ileana to park in a clearing and to get into her car. They end up at a detached wooden garage behind a Victorian house. Inside is a cauldron with a human skull, along with other paraphernalia. Hernan and Dagoberto, who had been waiting inside, seemed absolutely surprised by the appearance of Miguel, Ileana, and Krajewski.

Rosa insists that Shangó is about to appear, but Hernan and Dagoberto see that the ceremony is unusual, as there is no music or offerings. As they attempt to leave, Rosa attacks them. She flings the gigantic Hernan like a rag doll. As Dagoberto attempts to flee, she enters into a fight with him. Dago tries to plunge Ogun's knife into her belly, but she sidesteps him. He lands on his own knife, and Rosa smashes his head with her foot. Hernan charges her again, but to no avail. Miguel now enters the fight, but Rosa transmutes into "the unmistakable form of a black male" and then reverts to her normal shape (190–191). She manages to fling both Ileana and Miguel to the floor. Krajewski next attacks her unsuccessfully. Rosa is Shangó. She mocks them (191-192):

> How dare they dishonor Shangó! That *santero* . . . the way he used Ogun's knife . . . thought he was an *orisha* . . . An *orisha*! And that fat bastard child of Yemayá, the old sea hag herself, calls himself a *babalao* . . . He deserves what's coming. They all deserve what's coming! That includes you, too, learned professor, expert on *santería* . . . You who abandoned my faithful, loving servant Rosa . . . Happy feast day, Shangó! Happy feast day!

Rosa tries to burn the place with gasoline, but Gutiérrez shoots the gas can, creating an explosion that engulfs Rosa. Then he pumps four bullets into her, rendering her lifeless. The story ends with the survivors enjoying newfound friendships and material benefits.

Critical discussion

Curtis's plot is predicated on the assumption that "true" *santería* is benign, but Mayombe may be evil. The narrator seems to accept derogatory views about Mayombe, much as Christians historically have espoused derogatory views of *santería*. In fact, according to Pérez y Mena (217), the leaders of the Spiritism group in New York have the following practice, "Individuals must be informed during consultations that Spiritism (Spiritualism) works for 'the good,' while practices like *santería* are used to do evil." We may also note that the Nation of Islam has been described as a "Voodoo cult," even if it did not even practice voodoo (Turner 1997, 163). So Curtis, who otherwise seems to struggle to fight prejudices against *santería*, uses a plot that may promote them.

Curtis's plot is particularly driven by the following assumption about Mayombe found in the fictional source titled, *The Congo: A Basin of*

Christian Challenge (The Catholic Mission Press 1889) by the quasi-fictional Fray Francisco Delgado Arreola.[3] According to Arreola (170):

> Among the more pagan of the native practices that substitute for the True Religion is one called *mayombe*, found in the western region where several Bantu-speaking tribes hold sway. Followers of this heathen cult, known as *mayombes*, worship an innumerable host of deities and idols. Yet the focus of their misguided devotions is on the dead, especially the skulls of the deceased, which are considered to be sacred sources of undying power.

Arreola adds that, in Mayombe, the skull is disinterred and kept for exactly fourteen days. The skull is placed in a large ceremonial kettle called a *prenda*, the instrument for Shangó's rejuvenation, which can only take place if the warm blood of an exsanguinated human being anoints the skull. This is precisely the procedure used by Rosa.

In another episode, Krajewski comments that he knows of no ritual "in *santería* that calls for murder" (67). He adds, however, that "the cult's changing, being influenced by a variety of other beliefs, voodoo for example" (67). The implication is that voodoo might advocate murderous rituals that could influence *santería*. But practitioners of voodoo might object that Krajewski is merely repeating misconceptions about their religion. Previously, Miguel had listened to his grandmother's tales of black magic in Cuba. She associates the malevolent practices with a people who "didn't speak any Yoruba and their ancestors come from . . . the Congo . . . " (174). Miguel then begins to research Bantu religions for more clues on these malevolent practices.

Santería is not immune to danger. The narrator tells us that the main principle the detective discovered was that *santería* was "bound by ritualistic requirements. Cult practices did not occur haphazardly. It was for that very reason that Gutiérrez knew a murder would take place" (49–50). The implication for Gutiérrez is that *santería's* rituals can include murder.

Curtis's story also alludes to the fear some Latinas/os have of revealing their African ancestry. When he visits the *botánica*, Miguel wonders what Vicki might think about his link to African culture: "He was angry that she made him feel embarrassed that part of him could possibly belong to something so strange, so African" (26). In so doing, Curtis highlights the fact that many Cuban Americans do have ambiguous and complex feelings that link religion, race, and culture in Cuban American communities (De La Torre 1999).

Sex also plays a great role in discussions of the nature of *santería*. Gutiérrez notes, "While lascivious behavior was not unusual in *santería* rituals, it typically was confined to salacious gestures, executed more for their symbolic value than out of real sexual intent." (115). However, the narrator adds that Gutiérrez had also read that "in Africa copulation rituals were common" (115). One of Candy's motives for initiation into *santería* is having sex with Rosa. Again, Curtis's book is predicated on a long history of stereotypes about the sexuality of black Africans (see Hernton 1969; Marriott 2000). On the other hand, Miguel describes himself as a Catholic, but he does not observe associated sexual directives.

But *Shangó* also notes the positive role that *santería* has played in preserving African identity. Krajewski tells Miguel, "You see, rituals like this, where everyone is actively leading chants, singing and dancing, evolved in part out of the slave mentality. For a while, during the ceremony at least, a slave could feel he was somebody, not merely an object, a commodity" (149). And Curtis's book seems to have integrated theories of magic and religion developed by Bronislaw Malinowski (1884–1942). According to Malinowski (1948, 59–60):

> Let us realize once more the type of situation in which we find magic. Man engaged in a series of practical activities comes to a gap; the hunter is disappointed by his quarry, the sailor misses propitious winds . . . forsaken by his knowledge, baffled by his past experience and by his technical skill, he realizes his impotence . . . His nervous system and his organism drive him to some substitute activity. His organism reproduces the acts suggested by the anticipations of hope, dictated by the emotion of passion so strongly felt.

Now compare what Krajewski, the fictional anthropologist, says about the magic rituals of *santería*: "The style of the *orishas*, Miguel, is authoritarian. Much of their public behavior takes the form of psychic aggression, which is one explanation for their almost predictably capricious actions. It's all a way of gaining control. And why? Because the world itself is frightening, and one needs all the help one can muster, including for some, aggressive yet sympathetic deities. It's a question of survival" (150). Curtis also provides an explanatory box that addresses the nature of sympathetic magic, which refers to the idea that imitative acts produce analogous results at a distance (146). Likewise, Malinowski (1948, 60) believed that sympathetic ideas ("like produces like") are a fundamental premise of magic.

Blood forms an important component of Curtis's detective mystery. As in Christianity, blood is an instrument of magical power. Christians believe themselves to be rejuvenated through the blood sacrifice of Christ; the Eucharistic wine turns into blood. However, *Shangó*, unlike Rivera's "First Communion," (discussed below), does not focus on drawing those parallels in order to gain equality for *santería*. Rather, the narrator of *Shangó* sees the use of human blood as illicit, but never mentions how Christianity also uses blood in what might be called magical rituals.

Yet, Curtis uses a rich array of *santería* symbolism in his narrative. Rosa, whose name means "red," has a bedroom lit with a red glow. She dresses in a blood-red robe with white trim. She drives a red Oldsmobile Cutlass with a white top. The first color mentioned in chapter 1 is the red beacon of the patrol car. The next color mentioned is the "pasty white" face of a patrolman. The murder scene is replete with symbols of Shangó, Yemayá, and other deities. The final battle with Rosa is almost choreographed as a partial parallel to ceremonies where Ogun uses a bladed instrument to fight Shangó for the love of Oshun. Shangó's androgynous nature is manifested in his final transmutation that alternates between the female Rosa and the "African male."

In sum, Curtis premises his novel on stereotypes about African religions even as he attempts to provide a sympathetic or didactic portrayal. Of course, we need to be careful about ascribing to Curtis the beliefs of the characters and narrators. Curtis may be striving to represent the very real opinions voiced by *santeros* regarding Mayombe. However, it is also clear that the narrative world he has created mirrors many of the prejudices about African traditions that one might expect in Eurocentric literature.

Comparative summary

The works of Laviera, García, and Curtis exemplify some of the diverse attitudes that Latinas/os have toward African religions. Laviera sees African traditions as an antidote to the hierarchical and patriarchal European traditions. He has a very positive attitude toward *santería*. Cristina García exemplifies a sympathetic but more multivalent view. Curtis is more "utilitarian" in that he will use stereotypes to achieve an entertaining novel. His purpose resembles the use of *santería* for entertainment in a film such as *The Believers* (1987), where accuracy is not necessarily the priority. There is commonality among the texts in the positive acceptance of at least some Afro-Caribbean traditions, as is the case with some current Christian Hispanic theologians (see Cardoza-Orlandi 1995).

Whether it is actually a matter of gender or not, there is a difference in focus between García and the male authors we have featured. For the most part, García's characters resort to *santería* to enhance relationships, personal and cultural. Pilar is interested in *santería* because of links with her grandmother. Grandmother-granddaughter relationships have been noted as important for Chicana authors (Mirandé and Enriquez 1979, 194–198). Felicia is often interested because she wants relationships with men. However, Curtis's characters want just sex and power, as with Candy. Even when there are relationships involving females, they focus on power over the object of love. Laviera focuses on power to counteract the Church.

Other works that might be read for comparison include Roberto Fernandez's *Raining Backwards* (1988), which meditates on memories about Cuba that fade into fantasies. Passing interest in African traditions in Mexican American literature is exemplified in Ana Castillo's *So Far From God* and Anzaldúa's *Borderlands/La Frontera*. The differing degree of attention to African traditions is one way in which sub-groups of Latinas/os reflect their distinct religious heritages.

Notes

1. I follow Murphy (1993) in the transcription of Yoruba names and words used in *santería*. Briefly, he does not treat names of deities as foreign words and no accentuation is usually represented.

2. My translation. Original Spanish: "A los congos . . . se les asignó el papel de brujos, e injustamente."

3. Curtis uses names of friends who are scholars for his characters. Arreola is presumably based on his coauthor (see Arreola and Curtis 1993).

Chapter 3

Catholicism

atholicism is certainly the religious tradition most often represented in U.S. Latina/o literature. Compared to Protestantism and
African traditions, Catholicism was a presence, even if in varying
amounts, in most sections of the Americas for a longer period of time.
Accordingly, this chapter will require a bit more attention than the others. The history of Catholicism among Mexican Americans, Puerto
Ricans, and Cuban Americans has seen a renaissance in recent years (see
Sandoval 1990; Dolan and Deck 1994; Dolan and Hinojosa 1994; Dolan
and Vidal 1994), and it is not our purpose to rehearse five hundred years
of this history. The focus is on some of the basic and overlapping socio-
historical issues relevant to this study of U.S. Latina/o literature.

Socio-historical overview

Catholicism refers here to the branch of Christianity that acknowledges
the pope as the ultimate human authority in matters of religion. The
claim of a virtually unbroken succession of popes since the time of Saint
Peter in the first century is part of the Catholic tradition. Whether one
accepts this claim or not, the Roman Catholic Church is historically the
most powerful and single largest Christian denomination in the world. It
has helped to define "Christianity" for most of Latin America. The
Catholic Church has developed much of its doctrine and practice on the

57

basis of the decisions of periodical ecumenical councils composed of the highest representatives of the Church. Some of the most famous councils include those of Nicea (325 C.E.) and Chalcedon (451 C.E.), which were crucial in the development of Christian conceptions of God and Christ.

The Council of Trent (1545–1563) has been a primary source of Catholic doctrine from its conclusion, to about the middle of the twentieth century. This council is often described as a reaction against the onslaught of Protestantism that was storming western Europe in the sixteenth century. The Catholic Church sought to bring cohesion and strict orthodoxy on issues ranging from the canon of Scripture to the role of the Church in interpreting Scripture (as opposed to Protestant principle that believers can interpret Scripture for themselves). As Orlando Espín (1994) notes, much of Latin American Catholicism can be seen as the survival of pre-Tridentine (pre-Trent) traditions, particularly in the development of folk Catholic practices, which might not have been approved by Tridentine standards.

Vatican II (1962–1965), the most recent of the ecumenical councils, has had a significant impact, but for a relatively shorter amount of time (see Alberigo and Komonchak 1996, 1998, 2000). It was convened by Pope John XXIII, and brought representatives from a much larger portion of the globe than was possible at Trent. Much of U.S. Latina/o literature discussed in our work can be understood as part of a narrow transition from the pre-Vatican II to the post-Vatican II Church. Vatican II, among many changes, allowed the use of vernacular languages in Mass (as opposed to only Latin), declared a more dialogical attitude toward other religions, and restored vocations that helped to empower Latinas/os (e.g., the permanent diaconate).

In any event, Catholicism, in its orthodox form and even after Vatican II, is characterized by the emphasis on seven sacraments (Baptism, Confirmation, Eucharist or Communion, Penance, Anointing of the Sick, Holy Orders, and Matrimony) as crucial elements of the religious life (*Catechism* 1994, 289). These sacraments are efficacious *ex opere operato*, meaning by virtue of their performance (*Catechism* 1994, 292). Of these sacraments, the ones that are the most special subjects of discussion in U.S. Latina/o literature are Baptism, Confirmation, Communion, and Penance.

In order to understand U.S. Latina/o literature, we may also note important aspects of the sacrament of the Eucharist, the celebration of which is commonly known as "Mass." The Eucharist, originally a memorial of Jesus' last supper (1 Cor. 11:26), is called "the source and summit of the Christian life" (*Catechism* 1994, 334). One of the Eucharist's key moments is transubstantiation. As the *Catechism* (1994, 347) expresses it, "By the consecration of the bread and wine there takes place a change of the whole substance of the bread into the substance of the body of Christ our Lord and of the whole substance of the wine into the substance of his blood . . . transubstantiation." The intake of the bread and wine is supposed to take place in a state of spiritual cleanliness. Otherwise, it is considered a grave sacrilege to partake of this celebration.

Another Catholic characteristic often integrated in U.S. Latina/o literature is the emphasis on the cult of the saints and the use of devotional images. Such figures include the Virgin of Guadalupe, as well as an innumerable host of names. The cult of the saints has been largely eliminated in Protestantism, which emphasizes direct communication with God rather than through any intermediaries. Vatican II de-emphasized the cult of the saints, but many Latinas/os continued pre-Vatican II practices in this regard.

Insofar as Latin Americans and U.S. Latinas/os are concerned, it is important to realize that Catholicism did not uniformly reach all the territories claimed by the Spaniards. For example, Lisandro Pérez (1994, 147), author of a respected history of Cuban American Catholicism, remarks, "The Church never had as profound an impact on Cuba as it had on the rest of the Spanish colonies in the New World." There was a chronic shortage of priests in Cuba, and the rise of the sugar industry also meant that many sugar barons were unwilling to let their workers take time off to go to church on Sundays or any other days. Similar shortages of priests and resources affected large areas of Mexico and other countries in the Americas.

The close association between Catholicism and imperialism is important in understanding the anti-clericalism of some authors. Allan Figueroa Deck notes that "Anti-clericalism co-exists in Mexican Culture along with a strong traditional Catholicism" (cited in Burns 1994, 187). In Mexico, anti-clericalism was quite strong in the decades following the Revolution of 1910. A constitution had been approved in 1917 that contained a number of anti-clerical measures. President Plutarco Elias Calles (1924–1928) even suspended the practice of Catholicism on July 31, 1926. Mass, baptism, and religious marriages were banned. Such measures prompted an anti-government revolt, the so-called Cristero War, which exposed the failure of the government's dechristianization efforts (see Bantjes 1997; Meyer 1976). In Cuba, the historical linkage between Catholicism and imperialism led to the complete overthrow of the

Catholic Church in Cuba under Fidel Castro, though separation of Church and state had been moving forward since the United States colonized the island (Pérez 1994, 155–156; see also Betto 1990; Short 1993).

Aside from anti-clericalism, another common socio-historical theme is the negative experiences that Latinas/os encountered as they attempted or were forced to become part of the churches controlled by Euroamericans when former Spanish territories became part of the United States. For example, in the aftermath of the Treaty of Guadalupe Hidalgo in 1848, the control of Catholic churches in the Southwest shifted to an American hierarchy controlled mainly by European priests who were often hostile to Mexicans (Hinojosa 1994, 19). Domination by a non-Latina/o hierarchy persists even today. In fact, the first Mexican American bishop, Patricio Flores, was not ordained until 1970.

In New York, it was the Irish hierarchy who often excluded Puerto Ricans from full participation in the Church. The potato and sugar, if one were to be reductionistic, are partly responsible for the conflict between Irish and Puerto Rican Catholics. In the 1840s, the great potato famines of Ireland prompted the emigration of thousands of poor Irish into New York and other areas of the Northeast (Kinealy 1995). The Catholic population of New York City rocketed from about fifteen thousand in 1815 to about four hundred thousand, or nearly half of the total population (Díaz-Stevens 1993, 65). The large numbers of Irish made them the dominant Catholic ethnic group in New York. In Puerto Rico, the corporatization and mechanization of the sugar industry by the middle of the twentieth century helped to displace small farmers, and this created unemployment that drove many Puerto Ricans to the United States (Sánchez Korrol 1994, 11–50). The relatively cheap airline fares that were available after World War II contributed to the first large-scale immigration by air.

When Puerto Ricans arrived in New York, particularly after World War II, they found a Church controlled largely by the Irish. A language/national parish model had been instituted in the mid-nineteenth century in order to separate English-speaking Catholics from newer immigrant groups (Díaz-Stevens 1993, 72–73). Each ethnic/national group was to have its own churches. This model caused economic and other inequities. The decision by Francis Joseph Cardinal Spellman (1889–1967) to shift away from the national/language parish model often focused on Americanizing or even "re-Catholicizing" Puerto Ricans rather than on allowing them cultural equality (Vidal 2004, 53–55). In fact, the national parish model is often favored by Puerto Ricans themselves. As it was, Catholic churches in Puerto Rico had a long history of ethnocentric American leaders.

Catholicism was viewed as "superstition" by the Protestant elite who governed Puerto Rico after the United States acquired the island (Díaz-Stevens 1993, 53).

Another major problem was the inequality in resources allotted Latina/o parishes. Hinojosa (1994, 21), for example, notes that "in 1890 the Mexicano vicariate of Brownsville and the Anglo-American diocese of Galveston had about the same Catholic population (forty-five thousand and forty-one thousand, respectively), but the Galveston see had more than twice as many priests and six times as many churches." In New York, Irish parishes would often benefit at the expense of Spanish language parishes at the height of the national/language model of Church organization. Similar disparities can be found in most regions.

Liturgical differences between Euroamericans and Latinas/os created a related set of problems (see Francis 2000). Some of these liturgical differences stemmed from the lack of Catholic priests in many areas of Mexico, Cuba, and Puerto Rico. Popular devotions developed that could be performed without a priest (Burns 1994, 176–177). Espín (1994) has argued that the so-called folk Catholicism found in the Americas reflects the pre-Tridentine emphasis on local versions of Catholic rituals; Tridentine orthodoxists wish to promote uniformity throughout the Catholic world.

The emphasis on Tridentine uniformity created conflict in the New World. For example, in New Mexico, the French-born Bishop Jean Baptiste Lamy (1814–1888) ordered the removal of folk religious paintings called *retablos* because they did not reflect approved artistic standards. He acted against the Penitente brotherhoods, groups of people who had created a sort of parachurch organization (Weigle 1976; Hinojosa 1994, 20; Carroll 2002). *Curanderismo*, or folk healing, was discouraged. Some Euroamerican priests thought Latinas/os to be so different in their practices that they were often considered not to be fully Catholic and/or in need of reconversion.

There indeed was truth in the description of the noninstitutional character of a lot of Latina/o worship. Burns (1994, 191) quotes one immigrant woman advising a grandchild as follows, "My son, there are things that pertain to our religion: The Lord, Our Lady of Guadalupe and the Church. You can trust the first two, but not the third." The home remained a focal point of worship as much as the church. Some estimates for San Jose, California in the 1950s, when some of our books are set, note that upwards of 50 percent of homes had "altarcitos" (178).

The alienation from the Church could be felt in the 1960s in the great Chicano movements, which strove for social justice on a broader scale.

César Chávez (1968, 10), the celebrated advocate of farm workers, once complained that Protestants were sometimes more helpful than priests in strikes against growers in Delano, California. The Church's hesitance to help Latina/o activists has been attributed to a variety of factors ranging from lack of sympathy for Latina/o suffering to fear of alienating powerful economic interests (e.g., growers).

The expectation that the Church ought to side with the poor and oppressed grew even more intensely with the rise of what became known as Liberation Theology in the 1960s and 1970s (see Tombs 2002; Avalos 2005). The defining moment of Liberation Theology is usually situated in The Second General Conference of Latin American Bishops at Medellin, Colombia, in 1968. *Peace*, the main document (attributed to Gustavo Gutiérrez) advocates a theology that arises from the social bottom rather than from the hierarchical top. The needs of the poor should determine theology, rather than theology determining the fate of the poor. The core of Liberation Theology can be found in the classic expositions by Gustavo Gutiérrez in his *Teologia de la liberación* (1972) and by Luis Segundo (1925–1996) in his *Liberación de la teología* (1975).

Liberation Theology has been tailored to the needs of Chicanos by, among others, Andrés Guerrero in his *A Chicano Theology* (1987), though it has not garnered widespread support among laypersons. During most of the period that we are studying, Liberation Theology was not fully endorsed by the Church. There were misgivings expressed, particularly in the 1980s at the height of some political conflicts in Central America (Sigmund 1990, 154–175). Among the misgivings was that Liberation Theology was moving toward advocating violent means to overthrow imperialistic structures.

Vatican II sought to address some of the problems discussed previously in this book. One important change was the tolerance for vernacular liturgies, in which Masses could be celebrated entirely in Spanish (Vidal 1994, 140; see *Sacrosanctum Concilium* 36(1) in Flannery 1975, 13). Vatican II also restored the permanent diaconate, which allowed many Latinas/os to ascend to leadership positions without the need for celibacy or educational preparation that was often beyond their means (Vidal 1994, 141). Although these changes are recurrent themes in some works of U.S. Latina/o authors, we cannot even assume that all Latinas/os are aware of some of the profound changes brought by Vatican II. As Vidal (110) notes, even in 1988, about 59.8 percent of Puerto Ricans had not even heard of Vatican II.

But Vatican II also left many issues unresolved and created new ones. For example, Latinas/os are proportionally underrepresented in the

Church hierarchy. About 3 percent of priests are Latino, although perhaps over half of American Catholic laity will soon be Latina/o (see Cadena and Medina 1996, 100). Women still cannot be priests nor ascend to the highest levels of the hierarchy. Moreover, many feminist scholars contend that the Church is patriarchal in many other ways (Daly 1973, 1985; cf. Lorde 1981). Likewise, homosexuality creates many tensions in policy and theology (R. L. Smith 1994) even if there has been some "favorable attitudinal change" toward homosexuality in the nation as a whole after AIDS (see Pratte 1993). Abortion and contraception create large disparities between lay practice and official policy.

A number of large statistical surveys have been completed on Hispanic religiosity by, among others, Gonzáles and La Velle (1985) and R. De La Garza et al. (1992). Some of these studies help us to place U.S. Latina/o authors in the context of the beliefs of the larger community of Latina/o Catholics. For example, when asked if they had felt rejected by the Church, no more than 3.5 percent of Hispanics surveyed thought such rejection best described their experience (González and La Velle 1985, 122). Among Latina/o groups, Puerto Ricans had the highest number of those who felt rejected (7.3 percent), while other groups reported less than that or zero (125). The opposite side of the survey was not so positive. When asked if they "felt welcome," only under a third could affirm that this best described their experience (118).

We can also see that education does make a great difference in the Latina/o participation in Catholic life. For example, of Hispanic Catholics who "never/almost never" attend Mass, Gonzáles and LaVelle point out that the highest percentage (11.1 percent) falls among those with graduate education (1985, 75). Hispanic Catholics with graduate education also have the largest percentage (25.9 percent) of members who do not think abortion is wrong, compared to Hispanic Catholics with only a high school education (12.2 percent). Hispanic Catholics with a graduate education are more likely to disbelieve that contraception is wrong (48.1 percent) when compared to those that only have a high school education (37.7 percent), according to González and La Velle (46). Hispanics with a high school education are more apt to believe in intercession by the saints (72.2 percent) when compared to those with a graduate school education (59.3 percent) (39). Only Hispanics with a graduate school education reported any percentage (7.4 percent) who did not believe in God at all (31).

Given this simplified synopsis of Hispanic Catholicism, we can turn our attention to the attitudes of U.S. Latina/o authors toward Catholicism. It is not a simple matter of U.S. Latina/o authors reflecting their Catholic communities. U.S. Latina/o authors are sociologically an elite, educated group who do not share all of the religious practices and ideas of most Hispanics. In effect, these authors often reflect the typical opinions of the highly educated Hispanics in the surveys cited above. However, many of these authors did grow up in a Catholic milieu apart from which their work cannot be properly understood.

Case Study 1: *The Revolt of the Cockroach People* (1973)

The mysterious Oscar Zeta Acosta certainly bore a hostile attitude toward the Catholic Church, judging from his semi-autobiographical novel, *The Revolt of the Cockroach People* (henceforth *The Revolt*). This novel was a sequel to his *Autobiography of a Brown Buffalo* (1972), which reports his rejection of Christianity and religion altogether. *The Revolt*, however, portrays its main character as wanting to reform rather than overthrow Catholicism. The protagonist still described himself as "a Roman Catholic" on at least one occasion in this book (76). Consequently, the book does represent attitudes toward Catholicism, especially in the 1960s.

Oscar Zeta Acosta was trained primarily as a lawyer. Born in 1935 in El Paso, Texas, Acosta was actually raised in the San Joaquin Valley of California. Acosta served for four years in the Air Force upon his graduation from high school. He converted to Protestantism for a time, but later left Christianity. He attended the University of San Francisco Law School, and was admitted to the bar in 1966.

Between 1968 and 1973, Acosta became a celebrated lawyer, defending Chicano activists such as Rodolfo "Corky" González. He garnered some one hundred thousand votes in a losing bid for the sheriff of Los Angeles County. Interestingly, he once helped teach a course on religion at the University of Southern California. Marco Acosta (Oscar Z. Acosta 1989, 259) reports that his father Oscar disappeared in June 1974 while in Mazatlán, Mexico. Though presumed dead by many, Acosta's whereabouts remain a mystery. The University of California at Santa Barbara now holds a formal collection of Acosta's papers (Stavans 1996).

The opening chapter of *The Revolt* centers on a scene at St. Basil's Roman Catholic Church in Los Angeles on Christmas Eve, 1969. But Buffalo Z. Brown (Acosta's activist alter ego) is not at St. Basil's Church to worship. As Brown expresses it, "It is Christmas Eve in the year of

Huitzilopochtli, 1969. Three hundred Chicanos have gathered in front of St. Basil's Roman Catholic Church. Three hundred brown-eyed children of the sun have come to drive the money changers out of the richest temple in Los Angeles" (11). Brown also complains that the worshipers, many from Beverly Hills, refer to the protesters as "savages" as they enter into the church. Brown says, regarding his fellow protesters, "Most of them have never attacked a church before. One way or another, I've been doing it for years" (12).

Brown describes the physical temple as "[James Francis Cardinal] McIntyre's personal monstrosity. He recently built it for five million bucks: a harsh structure for puritanical worship, a simple solid excess of concrete, white marble, and black steel" (11). A few weeks earlier, Brown had actually spoken with the cardinal, after appearing uninvited at the cardinal's office. Brown asks the cardinal to provide scholarships for Chicano law students, some of whom are also present at this meeting. When the cardinal extends his middle finger, Brown merely offers to shake hands, something that infuriates the cleric. The meeting is concluded with Brown being unceremoniously escorted out. These conflicts lead then to the protest at St. Basil's Church.

The protest outlines some juxtapositions that will figure prominently in the rest of the first chapter, the most important part of Acosta's book for our purposes. First, Brown sees himself as "just like Jesus" (13) in fighting the Catholic establishment. As portrayed by the Gospels, Jesus' foils were the Pharisees, Sadducees, scribes, and other members of the Jewish establishment. Brown sees the Catholic Church as the equivalent enemy today. The racist and Eurocentric nature of the Church is reflected in Brown's comments about the art and liturgy of the Church: "Inside, the fantastic organ pumps out a spooky religious hymn to this Christ Child of Golden Locks and Blue Eyes overlooking the richest drag in town" (12). Such a transformation of Jesus from a probably dark Middle Eastern man into a Nordic figure has long been observed by many historians of art and religion (see Thomas 1979).

As the protest scene develops, a Chicano counter-Mass is enacted before the temple. Instead of the the Eucharist, the Chicanos eat tortillas, considered to be "the buttered body of Huitzilopochtli, on the land-baked pancake of corn, lime, lard and salt" (12). A guitar plays "Las Posadas" in honor of "the White and Blue Hummingbird, the god of our fathers" (12). The singing is followed by prayers for the dead and the living. Brown claims that never before have the sons of the conquered Aztecas worshiped their dead gods on the doorstep of the living Christ.

When the church service is finished, the protestors attempt to enter St. Basil's, but they are stopped and told that there is no more room. At this point, Brown draws a direct comparison to the time when Jesus found no room at the inn. But the Chicanos bang on the thick glass fronting the temple, screaming, "Let the poor people in! Let the poor people in!" (15). This chant invokes a main theme of Liberation Theology, which teaches that the poor and lower strata of the Church must receive priority.

As the Chicanos enter amidst the singing of Christmas carols, an usher strikes Gilbert Rodriguez, one of the protestors. Rodriguez at first hesitates to strike the usher, but then the protestors realize it is not really an usher, but a police officer. So the usher receives an uppercut to the jaw. A full riot now ensues, with candles flying and people running about, shouting slogans such as "Viva la Raza" (Long live the people/race). The narrator notes that the host, "the Body of Christ is on the red carpet" (18). The police finally manage to gain some control, and Brown's forces regroup and plan to return the next day. Brown calls this "the first religious war in America" (21).

The "Basil 21," as these protestors are denominated, return on Christmas Day, as promised. The media is there. Now they describe themselves as a "Jewish underground." The government and the Church are out to exterminate "the Jews of Nazi America" (78). Most of Brown's time thereafter is spent giving interviews, in which he seeks to expose corruption within the church and to enlist the Church's help in gaining reparations for lost Mexican lands (77).

But not all Chicanos are happy with Brown's anti-Catholic rhetoric. His secretary has received distressing calls from her own brother in New Mexico. She adds that "Chicanos in New Mexico take their Catholicism very seriously." Brown explains: "But we aren't against religion, we're not attacking religion . . . It's the power of the church, the administration of funds. We want the Church to become more democratic. We want them to become more involved in social-action programs. The people make up the Church. They should be the ones who control it" (79).

Brown and his fellow protestors camp out at the church for another three days, emphasizing nonviolence. On Sunday morning they take Communion and confess their sins to each other rather than to a priest. As the book continues, Brown reveals more about his religious attitudes. He speaks of his missionary phase in Panama, during which he became a Baptist around 1956. He becomes acquainted with the Bible, but later he reads a book that is just as impressive: Konrad Lorenz's *On Aggression*. Eventually, Brown opts for a secular life and abandons religion altogether.

In any event, the Basil 21 are tried for the riots in which they participated. Two of the defendants are former priests who have married. Duana
Doherty, a former nun, is also on trial. Brown turns their defense into a
trial of the Catholic Church. He begins one of his speeches with the history of Catholicism in the Americas. Some of his historical review is
worth repeating: "[Cortéz] outlaws human sacrifices. He outlaws the religion that has shed the blood of thousands . . . And then he burns the
books so that people will not be tempted to return to their heathen ways
. . . they rape the women . . . If you want to become a Spaniard, be baptized and take a Christian name . . . Church and State are one" (160).

In short, Brown sees Catholicism as an imperialistic enterprise that is
no less violent and cruel than the Aztec religion. He continues to explain
that the protestors rioted at the church because the Church does not treat
them as equal. They sing, "Oh come all ye faithful . . . to jail and court"
(161), thus revealing a discord between their words and their actions. The
trial results in six being found guilty (including Doherty, the former nun),
and fifteen found innocent. However, the trial brings new attention to the
Chicano struggle in Los Angeles. More trials and tribulations follow, but
they do not really reflect as much about Acosta's religious views as the
events connected with the St. Basil riot.

Critical discussion

Buffalo Z. Brown typifies some of the changes in the Catholic Church
that were taking place in the 1960s. In the aftermath of Vatican II, the
Church was trying to answer to the needs of its members. However, many
Chicanos did not think that the Church was going far enough. This was also
the time when Liberation Theology was coming to the foreground, and
many of Acosta's arguments echo those made by Liberation theologians.

The appeal to Aztec gods is not only a reclamation of Latina/o religious
identity but also a reaction to what is perceived to be a religious form of
European imperialism. *Huitzilopochtli*, the war deity, is called "the principle [sic] ancient diety [sic] of the Chicanos" (33). The calendric reference
to "the year of Huitzilopochtli, 1969," implies that a Christian calendar
and Aztec calendar should be shared. The Aztec god is additionally featured in a poster in the office of Gilbert, a fellow protestor. Tortillas substitute for the host of the Eucharist.

Despite his proclamations against racism, Brown may evince some
racism of his own. Acosta's anti-Jewish sentiments seem to surge when he

refers to "shrinks with their Jewishness gone awry" (31) as one of the causes of his anger against the establishment. At the same time, Acosta seeks help from a Jewish leader, who refuses, saying that not all in his congregation are as liberal as he is (83). Acosta portrays his own group of activists as "Jews in Nazi America." On another occasion, Acosta passes a monument commemorating the victory of a battalion of Mormons over the last contingent of Native Americans and Mexicans in 1848. Acosta spits on this monument (59). So, again, Brown judges religions by how they serve the interests of Chicanos.

In sum, Acosta represents someone who believes that the Catholic Church does not represent its original religious roots. Acosta says that he is not against religion, but rather against what he perceives to be a corrupt form of religion. His idea is closely allied with the ideas of Liberation Theology, even if they are not explicitly cited. He believes the Church ought to be an instrument for the poor rather than the refuge of the rich. For Acosta, change must be forced upon the Church from within and without.

Case Study 2: *Family Installments* (1982)

Ana Maria Díaz-Stevens (1993, 149), one of the foremost scholars of Puerto Rican religion, deems *Family Installments* to be an apt commentary on Puerto Rican and Irish American relations in New York. *Family Installments* (1982), which tells the story of a family's transition from Puerto Rico to New York, is the work of Edward Rivera. He was born in Orocovis, Puerto Rico, and grew up in Spanish Harlem. After high school graduation, he held a variety of odd jobs, then spent about six months in Heidelberg, Germany, as part of an army stint. He received a B.A. in English in 1967 from the City College of New York, and later an M.F.A. from Columbia University.

Although there are allusions to religion throughout the book, the most coherent discussion of religion occurs in the chapter titled, "First Communion," which is replete with satire and reflections on the fissiparous tensions between Irish American and Puerto Rican Catholics. The chapter is significant and coherent enough to merit an entry in *Growing Up Latino: Memoirs and Stories*, the anthology edited by Augenbraum and Stavans (1993). Accordingly, the focus is on this chapter rather than on the entire book.

As "First Communion" opens, the main character, Santos Malánguez, is moving to fight with another boy. Santos, a first-grader, has an adopted brother/friend named Chuito who gives him a piece of buttered bread. The bread, purchased from an eight-fingered grocer named Arsenio, was stolen by a boy named Antonio Carretas. When Santos tells Chuito what happened, the latter begins to urge Santos to fight Antonio. Santos loses the fight, which is broken up by Ms. Lugones, his teacher.

Less than a year after he leaves the first grade, Santos lands in a school called Saint Misericordia's Academy for Boys and Girls. Santos comments that Saint Misericordia (Saint Mercy) is actually called "Saint Miseria" (Saint Misery) by the students (73). What is supposed to be an institution teaching mercy, actually teaches violent solutions to problems. At Saint Misericordia's it is common and expected for a teacher to inflict some sort of physical violence on the students from time to time. However, Santos notices that teachers in public schools cannot lay a hand on students. Aside from the corporal punishment, Santos complains about the emotional distress caused by the idea of losing one's soul if one sins.

Otherwise, one of the most significant complaints is how the Irish Catholics treat their fellow Puerto Rican Catholics. Santos notes, "For one thing, they were Irish, all of them, so why should they give a damn for people like me?" (75). And yet, these nuns do care for the Puerto Rican kids at times, something that confuses Santos. He comes to see that the nuns can be both coldhearted and generous. But there are many instances where Puerto Rican culture is excluded. For example, Maestro Padilla, the Puerto Rican organist, struggles to include Puerto Rican music in the liturgy. Santos observes: "Maestro Padilla had been booming his idea of music down on us: a combination of sacred sounds, the strictly prescribed stuff, with intermezzos of all four Puerto Rican national anthems, which I had no doubt was endangering his immortal soul, and possibly the soul of his number one enemy, Pastor Rooney, who was officiating with two other priests up at the altar and probably cursing the choirmaster under his breath in between snatches of Latin" (97).

Pastor Rooney has warned Padilla about playing "unauthorized" music, but Padilla continues to play "La Borinqueña," the Puerto Rican national anthem, at a volume that shakes the church.

The issue of the proper liturgical languages is also raised in the story. Father Rooney prefers Latin over English and is not willing to use Spanish. Moreover, Rooney speaks in a mixture of Latin and English, paralleling the mixture of Spanish and English spoken by the Puerto Rican members. The Irish pastor's selection of an unintelligible Latin instead of English and Spanish seems irrational to Santos.

The theme of the Church's emphasis on rationality and civilization recurs as Santos attempts to unravel contradictions between the acceptance of the Eucharist by the Catholic Church and the views of the nuns about Puerto Rican gastronomy. Such contradictions are foregrounded when a nun named Sister Mary Felicia chastises a girl named Marta for some repulsive personal habits. The nun sees Marta's behavior as a continuation of the behavior of her "ancestors the Caribs, cannibalistic Indians from the jungles of South America" (76). The nun explains how "primitive" these Caribs were, as they had not even discovered friction on their own, "It was the Europeans, the Spaniards, who had brought them friction, the True Faith, and other forms of Christian civilization" (76).

The reference to the cannibalistic Caribs who were civilized by the Spaniards can be seen as the central irony of the story. The First Communion, which was a ritual brought by the Spaniards, also involved the eating of flesh, not to mention the drinking of blood. This is accentuated by Father Rooney's use of Latin mixed with English "*Hoc est* [= this is] my body and blood" (78). The nun's allusion to the friction brought by the Spaniards seems yet another ironic commentary on the Eurocentric nuns.

Later, during First Communion, Santos speaks about transubstantiation, whereby the host and wine of the Eucharist are transformed into the body and blood of Christ. Santos comments, "Our Savior's flesh, fit for human consumption. Some of us cannibals back in the pews couldn't wait to get our teeth into Him" (98). This obviously mordant remark foregrounds the idea that the Catholic Church is practicing a sort of cannibalism which it regards as uncivilized when practiced by other religions.

The host of the Eucharist also serves as a central symbol to expose the fragmentation of the Christian body through prejudice and ethnic tensions. When Santos is finally about to take the host into his mouth, it breaks in half on his own nose. As Padilla, the organist, breaks into "En Mi Viejo San Juan," a favorite Puerto Rican tune, the priests frantically try to recover the broken host. Santos loses bladder control, wetting his shorts. At the same time, Santos recalls the theological distinction between "essence" and "accidents," meaning the properties that are not essential to a particular entity. Thus, the host may be broken, but the essence remains a unified whole. Santos remembers the contrast drawn between the eternally unified essence of the host and the irrecoverable unity of Humpty Dumpty, whose story he has heard in school.

In the end, the priests tell Santos to go back to the pews, as he is not ready to receive the Eucharist. He is now excluded from this ceremony. At the end of the story, Santos's father asks him to avoid another accident at his next attempt at First Communion. But Santos wonders, "But didn't he know it wasn't up to me?" (106). In a subsequent chapter, Santos abandons religion, "Giving up the Holy Ghost and the rest of the religious business was a serious decision, the most serious I'd made to date" (147).

Critical discussion

As have other Latina/o writers we have examined, Rivera uses a central sacrament of the Catholic Church as a lens to discuss broader socio-religious problems. The Caribs's flesh-eating is somehow uncivilized to the nuns, but the intake of Christ's blood and flesh is deemed holy. Thus, the Eucharist exposes the theological inconsistency that, in turn, exposes a broader ethnocentric and irrational viewpoint espoused by the nuns. We must note that comparisons between the Eucharist and Mesoamerican sacrifice have existed since at least the time of Bartolomé de las Casas, who defended Amerindian rights to their ceremonies even as he declared himself against human sacrifice per se (see Goizueta 1996).

"First Communion" undergirds the theme of ethnic dissension in the Church by repeated references to fragmented bodies. Pagán, the grocer, has only eight fingers. There is a reference to Santos, "Without teeth. All gums" (71). In a reference to the artwork of the church, Santos notes: "Not only the painted saints but the statues, too, many of which were missing vital parts. The Christ Child on Saint Christopher's back had lost one of His hands and looked as though He might slip off the saint's back any day now, and another saint, Cecilia, I think, had lost her dulcimer, or harp, or whatever that strange-looking instrument she played was called" (92).

When the host breaks, one of the nuns speaks of "His body broken in pieces" (104). Additionally, there is a discussion of how Humpty Dumpty's demise differs from the fragmentation of the host. The latter retains its essence, while the former does not. The use of Humpty Dumpty as a metaphor is repeated by Díaz-Stevens (1993, 199) as she describes the fragmentation of New York Catholicism, as well.

Indeed, Rivera plays with the word "piece" a few times. In reference to the mistreatment of Padilla, Santos's mother says, "I wish they'd raise his salary, so we can have some peace in that church" (93), where "peace" can be misheard as "piece." Here having "some piece in that church" could mean wanting to be part of this fragmented church. In a more clear example, Santos comments, "I didn't even get the three broken pieces. I had my tongue out again, but all I got was a piece of advice" (104–105).

Rivera seems to reflect well the slightly higher than average dissatisfaction reported with the Church among Puerto Ricans. However, Padilla's advocacy of the Spanish language and Puerto Rican songs is not necessarily reflective of the preferences of all Latinas/os. There are generational and national differences. Hispanics over seventy prefer the Mass in Spanish at a rate of 74.4 percent, as compared to only to 44.3 percent for those under thirty (González and La Velle 1985, 166). Still, a sizable proportion that prefers the Mass in Spanish is still significant. Although the story has a very humorous tone, it is crafted to express the more serious and broader issues of unity.

Another chapter of *Family Installments* addresses the issue of contraception. Chuito, who becomes more religious as a young adult, argues that birth control will some day be regarded as a virtue by the Church. Chuito observes, "The Church evolves" (200). Here Rivera's character does reflect well the sentiments about contraception found among younger Hispanic Catholics. Only 31 percent of Hispanics under 30 believe that "using artificial means to prevent pregnancy is wrong" (González and La Velle 1985, 45–46).

Rivera's characters also evince some Christian misconceptions of the Old Testament. For example, Santos notes that his father did not hit his children. In fact, his father "couldn't stand violence. He couldn't understand, he said, how the Old Testament tolerated it, why it 'glorified' it. An eye for an eye was a disgrace, he used to say" (204). However, as has been pointed out numerous times by various scholars, the New Testament is actually much more violent. Whereas the God of the "Old Testament" punishes sinners within their lifetime, the authors of the New Testament advocate an even harsher punishment that lasts forever (Matt. 10:28).

Case Study 3: *So Far From God* (1993)

The title of *So Far From God* clearly indicates the religious nature of the book. The author is Ana Castillo, who has been a celebrated Chicana writer since the 1980s. According to published biographies and interviews (see Binder 1985, 28–38; *http://anacastillo.com/ac/bio/index.shtml*), Castillo was born in 1953 in Chicago, where she spent most of her young life. She received a B.A. in Art in 1975 from Northwestern Illinois University. Castillo also earned an M.A. in Latin American and Caribbean literature from the University of Chicago. Her Ph.D. in American Studies was earned at the University of Bremen, Germany.

Castillo's first significant work was *The Mixquiahuala Letters* (1986; see Campos Carr 1993). Castillo describes herself as "a great devotee of the Goddess of the Americas, of Our Lady of Guadalupe" (Cinader and Finch 1998). She has voiced her own dissatisfaction with the paradigm of the patriarchal God of the sky, as well as with biblical laws that devalue the biology of women. In an interview, Castillo says, "Although not all Mexican women or all Latinas are Catholic, we are one of the Church's greatest constituencies . . . we're very religious beings" (Cinader and Finch 1998).

So Far From God is set in New Mexico, mostly in the 1970s and 1980s. Castillo introduces readers to a mother with four daughters, all with extraordinary spiritual traits and bearing names with religious connotations. The mother's name is Sofia, which derives from the Greek word for "wisdom." The daughters are Esperanza (hope), Fe (faith), and Caridad (charity). The youngest daughter is known only as "La Loca" (the crazy one), her Christian name having been forgotten by the time of her twenty-first birthday (25). They all live in a home by the ditch at the end of the road. Their father had abandoned the family. Castillo's views on religion are revealed as she details the life experiences of each of these women and other characters.

The book begins with a story of La Loca's resurrection when she was three years old. She suffers some sort of seizure and stops moving.

They have a wake, and Father Jerome, the priest, advises them on "funeral decorum" (22). He admonishes them not to allow death to shake their faith in God, the Father (22). But Sofia wants answers to why God lets such bad things happen, and the priest's sermon is unsatisfactory.

Then Esperanza, the oldest daughter, lets out a shriek. The crowd sees the young girl sitting up inside the coffin as if just awakened from a nap. When the priest attempts to move toward the child, she levitates into the air and lands on the roof, shouting, "Don't touch me, don't touch me" (23). The girl's warning seems to be a gender-reversed version of Jesus' warning to Mary immediately after his Resurrection in John 20:17 to not touch him. La Loca would refuse to be touched by anyone for the rest of her life.

The priest does not know how to categorize this occurrence, and suggests that La Loca may be a demon (23). Sofia objects to the suggestion that there could be anything diabolical about her daughter, then beats the priest with her fists and rebukes him for "backward thinking" (23). Other people are astonished that Sofia is rebuking the priest in such a manner.

Meanwhile, La Loca claims that, while "dead," she went to three places, which are identified as hell, purgatory (mispronounced as pulgatorio / "the place of fleas"), and heaven. She says that God has sent her back to help them all. She enjoins them to have faith. When the priest asks her to come down so that he can pray for her, La Loca corrects him, "No, Padre . . . Remember, it is *I* who am here to pray for *you*" (24).

La Loca eventually is diagnosed as an epileptic, though this did not explain how she is able to levitate. La Loca also develops a phobia of people, being repulsed by their smell and living in fear of their germs. She becomes known briefly as "La Loca Santa" (the holy madwoman), but soon the "holy" part is dropped, and she just becomes La Loca, "the mad girl."

La Loca never goes to Mass, despite protests from Father Jerome. In fact, La Loca tells the priest that she could tell him a thing or two about the wishes of God. In sum, La Loca represents a woman who achieves holiness apart from the sacraments of the Church, and who proclaims her authority over the official patriarchal Church.

Esperanza spends her life trying to find herself and is the only daughter to go to college, receiving a B.A. in Chicano studies (25). Esperanza later earns an M.A. in communications. She is a devout Catholic in high school; in college, she tries Marxism but remains a Catholic. She becomes an atheist in graduate school, but now prays to Grandmother Earth and Grandfather Sky (38). Esperanza lives for a time with a man named Ruben, who renames himself Cuauhtemoc, in honor of his Chicano cosmic consciousness. Ruben leaves Esperanza, then returns to tell her that he is now a member of the Native American Church. Ruben tries to teach Esperanza about the role of women in the universe, and his thoughts are always supported by his other Native American or Chicano male friends.

Since Esperanza has no female Native American friends, she cannot verify any of Ruben's claims about the nature of the cosmos or the role of women in it. Esperanza begins to think of herself as little more than a ritual object in these ceremonies (36). She eventually concludes that a religion based on supposed indigenous traditions can still be patriarchal as long as men are in control of the group.

Esperanza eventually becomes a TV reporter and goes to cover the Middle East Gulf War. She becomes a prisoner of war and is later killed by her captors. The clairaudient La Loca had been informed of Esperanza's demise by La Llorona Loca, a woman who wails for eternity her murder of her children (161). Sofia, basing herself on Catholic theology, doubts the existence of this entity. Esperanza occasionally seems to return "ectoplasmically" as an "earth-bound" ghost (186).

Fe, the most stable of the four daughters, works in a bank (27). She had been engaged to a man named Tom Torres, but he calls off the engagement. The news, relayed by a letter from Tom, causes Fe to generate one continuous shrieking scream for at least ten days. In fact, her scream damages her vocal cords. La Loca prays for Fe, especially because Tom deemed commitment to a woman akin to having a meal with Satan (32). Despite her own experience with pain, Fe can sometimes be uncompassionate toward La Loca. Fe marries her myopic cousin, Casimiro ("I almost see"). He comes from a long line of sheepherders and has the odd habit of bleating like a sheep. Fe dies of cancer after being exposed to dangerous chemicals at a local plant. Unlike her sisters, Fe does not resurrect.

Caridad, the third oldest sister, completes only a year of college. She was in love with Memo, who is not very faithful to her. She has three abortions, all administered by La Loca. The family decides to keep the abortions secret for fear of excommunication and the arrest of La Loca (27). One day, Caridad comes home badly beaten and mutilated after being left at the side of a road by unidentified assailants. She is bedridden for a year before being miraculously made whole again by La Loca's prayers. Caridad never goes to Mass, but instead practices Yoga (65). Caridad also acquires the gift of prophecy. Caridad's favored companion is a horse named Corazón, which is later found dead of a bullet wound as it tries to return to Tome, the town where Caridad has her home (53).

Caridad eventually comes under the tutelage of a local healing woman named Felicia ("happy"), who is originally from Veracruz, Mexico. Felicia has had a tragic life filled with dead husbands and children. Felicia chose Caridad as a student because the latter was incapable of hating anyone (77). The *curandera* teaches Caridad that "nothing you attempt to do with regards to healing will work without first placing your faith completely in God" (59). Yet, according to the narrator (60):

> Felicia was a non-believer of sorts and remained that way, suspicious of the religion that did not help the destitute all around her despite their devotion . . . she did develop faith, based not on an institution but on the bits and pieces of the souls and knowledge of the wise teachers that she met along the way . . . And finally, she came to see her God not only as Lord but as a guiding light, with His retinue of saints, His army, and her as a lowly foot soldier. And she was content to do His work and bidding.

Felicia uses store-bought candles for her Catholic rituals, and when the priest cannot bless them, she does it herself. One of the most important rituals that she performs is "cleansing," which is meant to relieve a person's stress and help find purpose in life (69). The person being cleansed usually stood in the middle of the room, with arms spread in the form of a cross (70). The patient is rubbed with the egg of a black hen to remove the evil of intentional harm. The ritual begins with a prayer expressing the lowliness of human beings before the paternal God (71).

On Ash Wednesday, Felicia usually goes on a pilgrimage to Chimayo, New Mexico. This is the place where, according to legend, a Penitente brother dug at a brightly illuminated spot and found a statue of Our Lord of Esquipulas, which was originally from Guatemala (73). The puzzle of how this Guatemalan statue arrived in New Mexico enhances the holiness of the site (see Weigle 1976, 37). The narrator suggests that Catholics were late in recognizing the miraculous value of the site precisely because they were the newcomers to the land (75).

In another episode, Doña Felicia is said to have had a falling out with the Santo Niño de Atocha, the Spanish saint who is reputed to have saved Christians from Muslims (82).

Felicia recoiled at the thought that salvation was based on nationalism. All of these comments highlight the contempt for institutional Catholicism on the part of Castillo's female characters.

Doña Felicia's grandson Francisco, a seventh son, is a Penitente, a member of a special group of religious laypersons common in the Southwest (Weigle 1976). When Francisco spoke to "Little Chico," a Puerto Rican army buddy, the latter said that his uncle was also a *santero* in Puerto Rico. The narrator tells us that Caribbean *santeros* maintain a kind of secret membership, just as do Francisco's Penitente brothers. However, the narrator adds that *santería* rituals integrated women and distributed divine power much more democratically (96).

Francisco becomes a woodcrafter of santos, and his favorite workplace was beneath a cedar tree. He also tries to improve his Christian life by peforming a myriad of Catholic rituals and litanies all day long (193). Yet, all of these rituals are futile. Francisco cannot even approach the holiness of the saint for whom he was named. According to the narrator, "God was too great and too remote for Francisco" (100), another allusion, reflected also in the title of the book, to an institutional God who does not show himself readily.

Friends think that Francisco, who always dresses completely in black, needs to be married. In one episode, Francisco is told by his friend, Sullivan, to go to the fair to see if he could find a girl. Francisco warns Sullivan that God punishes adultery with death (196). Sullivan, however, has another belief system in which death means that he would become a "Cloud Spirit, sacred and nurturing to this Earth and to my people" (196). Death, in this supposed Native American religion, does not have the potentially torturous connotations of the Christian system. Francisco becomes a stalker of Caridad, whom he one day abducts with the power of words. He eventually is found hanging from a tall piñon tree. God is indeed far from Francisco.

In any event, Felicia suggests that Caridad, who is suffering from a series of bad dreams, go up to Ojo Caliente, site of healing mineral waters. Caridad is not seen until a year later, when people find her living in a cave in the Sangre de Cristo mountains. Then, she becomes the object of pilgrimages by people in search of healing, among other things. Caridad does return home after about a year and becomes known as a channeler. However, her "cynical sister Fe" thinks that Caridad's year-long absence really had more to do with some failed love affair (119). One day, Caridad and a friend named Esmeralda fling themselves from a cliff, and their bodies are never found. It is said that "Tsichtinako was calling" (211). Tsichtinako is a female deity of the Acoma Indians, who live on top of a cliff-lined mesa, the site of perhaps the oldest continually inhabited community in America.

In the penultimate chapter, the author tells of a procession on Holy Friday. It is one of the rare occasions that La Loca goes out into the world, and by now she has become a cult figure. A company even begins to manufacture votive candles with her picture on them. In describing the procession, the narrator intersperses some commentary along with a re-enactment of the stations of the cross. A few comments bear repeating, "When Jesus was condemned to death, the spokesperson for the commit-tee working to protest dumping radioactive waste in the sewer addressed the crowd . . . Jesus bore His cross and a man declared that most of the Native and hispano families throughout the land were living below poverty level, one out of six families collected food stamps . . . Jesus fell, and people all over the land were dying from toxic exposure in factories" (242).

In short, the author identifies the sufferings of oppressed Latina/o and indigenous people with the sufferings of Christ.

After each sister dies, La Loca becomes even more eccentric, watching TV mindlessly. She was particularly fascinated by the famous Marian apparitions at Medjugorje. La Loca contracts AIDS even though she shuns human contact. She eventually does die. She is buried in the churchyard of the Church of Our Lady of Guadalupe. According to the narrator, the sainthood of "La Loca" did not depend on official proofs, such as stigmata or thorn marks (248).

77

In the final chapter, Sofia becomes the leader of M.O.M.A.S. (Mothers of Martyrs and Saints). One has to be the mother of at least one daughter to be considered for membership. The narrator informs us that "eventually, Masses were held by women clergy, not just men, including some who were married" (250–251). Their international meetings became a reunion of the dead, "some transparent, some looking incarnated" (251). The criterion for membership is that the mother had to have borne a "santo or martyr from your own womb" (252). The narrator adds a criticism against Saint Augustine (354–430), the supremely influential Christian theologian who described the womb as "being between feces and urine" (252).

The narrator also attempts to dispel the rumor that the mothers would sit on chairs similar to the ones that the Church used to prove that a pope was not a woman. This legendary chair policy reaches back to the story of a pope named Joan, who was supposedly stoned to death for masquerading as a male Pope in the ninth century. From then on popes have to prove that they are indeed men by submitting to an examination of their sex organs on a special chair. The narrator ends with a very incisive criticism of the Church's approach to women (252): "After all, just because there had been a time way back when, when some fregados all full of themselves went out of their way to prove that none among them had the potential of being a mother, did it mean that there *had* to come a time when someone would be made to *prove* that she did?"

Critical discussion

As the last sentence of the book (quoted above) indicates, this story is a sustained critique of patriarchal religious structures. The critique manifests itself not only in the comments of the narrator and life experiences of the characters, but also in the very selection of characters and overall structure of the novel. First, the names of the women are derived, in part, from the seven virtues outlined by Catholic doctrine. According to the Catholic Catechism (1994, 444), the foremost of the "cardinal" virtues is "prudence" (= wisdom), which "guides other virtues by setting rule and measure." Sofia, of course, is the one who guides the daughters, the three eldest of which have names that parallel the three "theological virtues" outlined by the Catholic Catechism (446–447), namely, Faith, Hope and Charity.

At the same time, we see that the women's virtues don't always correspond with the meaning of their name. Fe (faith) is described as cynical.

Caridad (charity) is not always charitable. Esperanza (hope) loses hope. Sofia, however, does eventually triumph. La Loca is odd and probably represents the utmost in nonconformity to Catholic orthodoxy. In any event, the author seems to imply that the Catholic virtues are not always what they seem to be.

Nevertheless, Sofia and her daughters illustrate that authentic religious experiences can be found by women outside of the official hierarchical structure of the Catholic Church. La Loca has gone to and come back from the world beyond with a newfound assertiveness that confounds the priest, who lacks spiritual discernment when confronted with La Loca's resurrection. In fact, La Loca says that she can teach the priest about religion rather than the reverse. She achieves sainthood without the benefit of the bureaucracy. The cases of Caridad, who returns "ectoplasmically," and La Loca seem to indicate that incorporeality poses no hindrance to a woman's "spiritual" life. Sofia also is not afraid to challenge the priest when he insults her daughter. The Church, in fact, is an impediment to the spiritual development of women.

All religious traditions are evaluated according to their view of women. Thus, we find that the Native American Church, at least in the form followed by Ruben, comes under criticism because it is also exploitative and meant for the benefit of men. The evaluation of *santería* includes the fact that they are more gender-inclusive than Catholicism. Religion itself must be evaluated on whether it serves the welfare of women.

The story of Francisco also shows that the sacramental institutions of the Catholic Church are powerless to effect personal transformations, particularly on men. Men generally are not viewed positively. Ruben, for instance, cares little but for sexual satisfaction at the expense of women. The father of the girls abandons them. Francisco is a hypocrite. The priest is not very spiritually aware nor caring, and Saint Augustine is a misogynist.

Although Castillo seems quite informed on religion in comparison to other Hispanic writers, she also works with a number of assumptions that have questionable historical validity. The story of Pope Joan, for example, may have little or no historical validity. Although charges that this story is a Protestant invention seem to be without merit, the historicity of Pope Joan cannot be firmly established. While Stanford (1999) believes that there is some historical validity, the first written accounts are not found until hundreds of years after her supposed existence. As mentioned in the discussion of *Borderlands*, the idea of a universally beneficent set of matriarchal religions would probably be criticized by other feminist authors (Eller 2000; Frymer-Kensky 1992). Whether or not one agrees with her view of history and religion, Castillo has attempted a very extensive and multifaceted critique of patriarchal structures, religious or otherwise.

Case Study 4: *Happy Birthday Jesús* (1994)

Ronald L. Ruiz's *Happy Birthday Jesús* is one of the most severe portrayals of Catholicism found in recent U.S. Latina/o literature. In fact, the message of the book seems to be that Catholicism does not help society, but rather helps to create a sociopath. *Happy Birthday Jesús* was Ruiz's first book, and it reflects much about his long experience with the American justice system. Ruiz, a lawyer, served as district attorney for Santa Cruz County, California. According to his autobiography (Ruiz 2000), he was born and raised in Fresno in a family of Mexican immigrants.

After becoming the first in his family to graduate from high school, Ruiz received a degree in English from St. Mary's College in Moraga and received his law degree in 1964 from the University of San Francisco Law School. He worked in the offices of the district attorney, as well as a private defense attorney, handling a variety of offenses ranging from drunken driving to death penalty cases. *Giuseppe Rocco* (1998), Ruiz's second novel, garnered the national Premio Atzlán award for the best novel written by a Hispanic in 1998. Ruiz said that he no longer practices "Catholicism or any kind of religion" (per. comm. March 30, 2002).

The title of the book is filled with irony because there is nothing happy about the birthday of Jesús Olivas, the title character. A defense attorney for Olivas believes his very name is part of the problem (68): "People in this country don't go around naming their kids Jesus. That's almost like asking for it, like putting a curse on someone. Look what it's done to you. You don't go around naming your kid after the Son of God." The parallels between Jesús Olivas and the biblical Jesus become a pivotal theme in the story.

The book begins as Olivas, the main narrator of the story, is being released from prison for the attempted murder of his priest, Father Galván. The narrator eventually makes clear that Olivas's actions against his priest result from a lifetime of torment from an oppressive Catholicism. A woman lawyer, who oversees Olivas after his release, briefs her colleagues as follows, "She told them about my family, about my life in Fresno, about my education and religion" (9). After his release from jail, Olivas revisits his church, which "Aside from our house, I had probably spent more time in that building than any other in Fresno" (19). He enters the darkened tabernacle, and begins to curse at the Church, "You Motherf***er. You Motherf***er" (19).

In his early life, Olivas's skepticism of the Church revolved around the catechism classes to which he was subjected. The portion he recalls is as follows (41): "Why was I born? I was born to know, love, and serve God in this world and to be happy with Him in the next. Who made me? God made me. Why did God make me? God made me to know, love, and serve Him in this world and to be happy with Him in the next. Who is God? God is the All-knowing, All-Powerful, All-Present, Eternal Good."

In some ways, the book is about how Olivas' life aims to expose the falsehood of all of these teachings.

First, Olivas wonders why he was born, since birth only leads to death. Worst of all, death might lead to an eternal torture in a fiery hell. Besides, Olivas's image of God was not that of a happy being, but of one who was always angry with him. All of his catechism classes led eventually to confession and Holy Communion, but he is reluctant to confess a sin that was haunting him—he hated his grandmother, which violated the commandment to honor your parents from Exodus 20:12.

Olivas, who never knew his father or mother, was raised by a zealously religious grandmother named Soledad ("solitude"). She always dresses in layer upon layer of black. Once, when he was late from church, his grandmother forced him to wear a diaper. Later his grandmother testified against him at his trial. For this and other humiliations, Olivas hates his grandmother.

Communion and confession also are a source of terror for Olivas. At about age eight, he steals a hammer. He is reluctant to go to confession for fear that he would be found out. And he is reluctant to participate in Communion, thinking it a sacrilege to take in God's body and blood in a state of sin. He finally decides to undergo Communion without confessing his sin, and the worry about God's punishment so overwhelms him that he vomits after intaking the host. He finally goes to another priest to confess and does not vomit his food this time. Olivas reports his grandmother's thoughts regarding the episode, "She said it was the work of God, and together we prayed our thanks" (52).

As he enters adolescence, sex becomes a principal source of agony for Olivas. He begins masturbating at the age of five or six. By the time he is in middle school, a priest has come to scare youths away from such activity (125). The priests describe it as "self-abuse," and they stress the idea that it will consume both body and soul. One priest suggests a link between masturbation and leprosy, and warns that this disease will literally eat its

way through the flesh down to the bone (126). Olivas's psyche is so affected by these sermons that for a short period he even believes that he has
contracted leprosy. Olivas simply cannot understand why a few moments
of pleasure deserve an eternal torture in hell.

In any event, Olivas's grandmother eventually discovers that he sometimes does not go to Communion because of this. She warns him that if
he misses Communion, he will be punished (129). Nonetheless, Olivas
learns to justify his masturbation: "I had so many mortal sins on my soul
that one or two more wouldn't matter" (129). He also reasons that most
people did not die at thirteen years of age. Later he even masturbates in
the middle of a work site, no longer caring whether he is caught.

Olivas's story additionally focuses on the theme of sexual sin among the
clergy. One example is the story of Father Martinez, who had come to
town for about three years as a substitute for the regular priest. Olivas's
grandmother volunteers Jesús for the job of altar boy, so he goes to the
church to help this temporary priest. The priest is secretly having sex with
the local prostitute, Chole Carabello. Yet, the priest seems very judgmental of the congregation, berating them even for talking loudly. At one
service, he becomes enraged by the din of the people and proclaims that
because he is God's "instrument," the congregation must be respectful
toward him. When he tells the congregation how he has endured years of
discipline for God, a man in the crowd decides to challenge him, "Self-
discipline! Don't talk to us about self-discipline when you have none
yourself" (137).

Indeed, some of the townspeople know about the priest's sexual secret
and are disgusted with his despotic behavior during services. On a subsequent evening, they taunt the priest as he hides in the church with his
altar boy. Despite a crowd of people who want to get into the church,
Father Martinez begins to relate to Olivas the story of how he became
involved with Chole. At the end of the episode, Olivas says, "Finally I
asked him to hear my confession. He forgave my sins" (155). Olivas's confession of his sins to the errant priest offers yet another irony in the story.

A parallel story addresses clerical pedophilia. While in jail, Olivas
meets a man named Tommy Lee Smith, who has killed his priest. Smith
is a Irish Catholic boy who is the center of his household; meals and
other activities revolve around his schedule. As he matures into youth, a
priest named Father Joe takes interest in him, calling special public
attention to Tommy whenever he takes Communion. Father Joe takes
Tommy on a special retreat, and Tommy awakes to find the priest sexually abusing him.

According to Tommy, despite all of the sermons on sin voiced in the church, the priest represents "true evil, because he cloaked himself in good" (64). In one of these sexual episodes, Tommy stabs the priest to death. Other priests try to make it appear that Tommy had gone into the priest's room instead of the reverse. Tommy pleads guilty, only to regret it later. The lesson, as Tommy voices it, is, "And maybe some day, if nothing else, they'll understand that men aren't born monsters . . ." (65).

The juxtaposition of sex and religion is also threaded into Olivas's uneasy friendship with Chole, the prostitute. She looks at him as her lover, friend, and son. She lives right across from the church, reflecting a spatial juxtaposition of religion and prostitution. Chole, described throughout as literally a stinking and filthy specimen of humanity, has an unconditional love for Olivas. Her nemesis is Olivas's grandmother. One day a drunken Chole grabs Soledad by her shawl and tells her (91): "I know who you are. You might be fooling everybody in this whole f***ing town, but you're not fooling me. You're no better than me, Soledad Olivas. You're just a f***ing whore, too. And your daughter was a whore, like you. And his father was a pimp who turned her out just like he turned me out."

Thus, Chole exposes the hypocrisy of Olivas's grandmother, something he also sees as characteristic of most religious figures in his life.

Despite Chole's undying love for Olivas, the latter is quite angry and abusive toward her. On his eighteenth birthday, Chole makes a cake for Olivas. Her sycophantic attention to him is so overbearing to Olivas that he beats and rapes Chole. He pushes her face into the cake. He leaves her bloodied before he continues on to the church, where he commits the attack that sends him to jail. The time he has served in jail, however, has not diminshed his hatred for his priest or the Church.

After his release from jail, he looks for Chole, who has always shown him nothing but love. Just before finding Chole, Olivas has set in motion his plan to kill Father Galván. He goes into the church, and acts out a mock Communion. He takes out the chalice and the host, saying (308):

> But I didn't pray to It, I talked to It, whispered to It, real close. I said, "All right, ****sucker. On the third day You rose again from the dead. But on this third day You and everything here is gonna die. And it's going to be a slow, ugly death. I want you to think about that, a slow, ugly death. Because three hours wasn't enough. You only hung on that cross for three measly hours, and I've seen three million hours of pain and hurt and suffering. I've seen three million hours of hanging. So You're gonna get more than three hours this time. Let's see if You can stop me, Big Guy."

He then leaves the church, looks for Chole, and gathers materials for his final assault on Father Galván.

But Olivas learns that his intended target, Father Galván, is no longer at the church. He has gone to Rome to see if he can convince the Vatican to canonize Soledad Olivas, who died while Olivas was in jail. Jesús finds Soledad's tomb and sees that his grandmother is already regarded as a saint, and people visit her gravesite. His wicked grandmother has been canonized in effect, if not officially. It takes him four trips to haul the kerosene that he will use to burn the temple down.

Olivas has set his sights on a young white priest who has taken Galván's place. When the priest turns on the lights, Olivas pounces on him and begins stabbing him in a frenzy. Olivas rips out the heart of the priest and lights the church on fire. The church has become a sort of burning hell. He then goes and finds Chole, who is living in a chicken coop. She looks old and barely recognizable. In the final paragraph Olivas says, "I got them for us, Chole. I got them." His final sentence comes as an apparently dead Chole is being cradled in his arms, "Chole, I love you" (313–314).

Critical discussion

Except perhaps for the young priest killed in the final chapter, *Happy Birthday Jesús* has no positive portrayals of Catholic characters. The Catholic grandmother is a tyrant. Priests are hypocrites and pedophiles. The congregation can be just as abusive and vengeful as the clergy. The sacraments are instruments of terror. The institution as a whole seems to create sociopaths. From Olivas's viewpoint, Catholicism is a religion that glorifies the short-lived suffering of its God-man, Jesus, and ignores the endless sufferings of millions of human beings. God himself seems to be without excuse for the misery he inflicts on or allows in the world. In sum, the Catholic version of religion is not a positive phenomenon. It is not even comforting. Religion does not help people become better. Religion is the cause, not the solution, of our social ills.

In a study of anti-Catholic attitudes in American literature, Marie Ann Pagliarini (1999, 116) says, "Central to anti-Catholic literature was the representation of Catholicism as a menace to the pure American woman and the Protestant family." Ruiz, however, sees Catholicism as a menace to the Hispanic Catholic boy and family. Of course, Ruiz mainly portrays one individual in one community. But Ruiz's personal rejection of religion and Catholicism seems to be consistent with the book's criticism of the power of religion to wreak personal and social destruction. The only character who exhibits unconditional love is not really religious, but rather a prostitute. If the author does have a positive view of some alternative form of religion, it is not to be found here. So it might be said that this book is not balanced in its critique of religion or Catholicism.

As do other U.S. Latina/o authors, Ruiz uses counterliturgies to drive his narrative. We have seen this in the case of Tato Laviera, who creates a sort of counter-Mass focusing on African deities in *La Carreta*. In *Happy Birthday Jesús*, the sacraments are instruments of terror. Confession and the Eucharist are a means of social control. Other symbolic reversals may be seen in the burning of the church in order to create a sort of burning hell, which was yet another idea used to terrify and control church members.

Jesús Olivas is the match and antithesis of the biblical Jesus. They both, of course, share the same name. Like the biblical Jesus, Olivas has been subjected to suffering and is seen as an outcast, though Olivas believes that his sufferings are infinitely worse than those of the biblical Jesus. Olivas's friend Chole is a prostitute, and Jesus is often associated with Mary Magdalene, often portrayed as a prostitute in post-biblical traditions.

Ruiz also is keen on pointing out the logical flaws of Catholic theology. In particular, hamartiology, the doctrine pertaining to sin, comes under some severe scrutiny. The idea that divine punishment is not proportional to the quality or quantity of sins becomes an incentive to exaggerated sinning. If one receives the same punishment for killing one human being as for killing thousands, then why not kill thousands? If confession and repentance erase sins, then these practices are a license for more sinning as well. In short, what appear to be Olivas's "crazed" crimes are actually a logical consequence of an orthodox hamartiology.

Case Study 5: *Mr. Ives' Christmas* (1995)

The attitudes toward the Catholic Church found in *Mr. Ives' Christmas* is almost at the other end of the attitudinal spectrum, compared to *Happy Birthday Jesús* and *The Revolt of the Cockroach People*. *Mr. Ives' Christmas* was authored by Oscar Hijuelos, who was the first U.S. Latina/o author to have garnered a Pulitzer Prize (1990) for literature. In terms of prominence, therefore, Hijuelos certainly belongs in a Latina/o literature canon. Although Hijuelos is of Cuban parentage, he is not really part of the more influential anti-Castro community that dominates the ethnic identity of most Cuban Americans. Nonetheless, as a Cuban American, his voice deserves to be heard.

Oscar Hijuelos was born in New York City in 1951. He earned a master's degree in creative writing from the City College. His first novel, *Our House in the Last World*, was published in 1983. His most famous story is the Pulitzer Prize-winning *The Mambo Kings Play Songs of Love* (1989), which is about two brothers who become celebrated musicians in New York. A more recent novel, *A Simple Habana Melody* (2002), has received positive reviews.

Mr. Ives' Christmas is imbued with the soul of Charles Dickens's *A Christmas Carol* (1843). Like the famous English author, Hijuelos tells a story centering on redemption within the context of the Christmas season. Unlike the nineteenth century work, the novel by Hijuelos is much more explicit about religion. More specifically, *Mr. Ives' Christmas* centers around the comfort and peace that can be found in a Catholic Church. The Church is found in the first and final scenes of the book, as well as in crucial episodes throughout.

In the very first paragraph of the book, the narrator tells us that Mr. Edward Ives, a young man living in the 1950s, often finds his way to Saint Patrick's Cathedral in New York. He reminisces about attending Mass as a child with his adoptive parents, and the memories are so strong that he is moved to the verge of tears. Ives also visits another church in Brooklyn, which has a diverse congregation. There are many other churches in his neighborhood in which he shows some interest (56).

At Christmastime, Ives loves to think about his own origins as he contemplates the baby Jesus. Ives was an unwanted child whose biological parents gave him to a foundling home (4). He speculates that his father might have been a fisherman. His mother might have been very young and poor, perhaps even a prostitute. Sometimes he sees aspects of his own appearance in Hasidic Jews he meets. He thinks of himself as white, though others consider him a bit swarthy. One day around Christmastime, a man came to choose a baby to adopt and ended up adopting Ives. Although Ives is outwardly courteous, he "had lived with a notion that he was worthless" (15).

Otherwise, Ives is a generous man, giving his own inheritance to his sister so she can start a business. He finds himself preaching about the misfortunes of others. For Ives, God's most common form was the "goodness and piety of others" (93). Even in the religion of others, he saw a benign God, not a vengeful one. Indeed, his possible multiethnic heritage seems to make Ives open to ethnic and religious diversity. Ives likes to help

Hispanic families. Ives speaks Spanish; his best friend is a Cuban named Luis Ramirez. Ives's own daughter, Caroline, marries Ramirez's son Pablo.

Ives's future wife, Annie McGuire, is an art teacher at a Catholic girls' school on the Upper East Side. She wears a thin, nearly imperceptible, crucifix. Her family does not much like Ives and thinks that artists are undesirables. Annie is the first in her family to attend college. Despite her sexual promiscuity, she loves the idea of living as a Catholic (48). She apparently has been molested by her own father. Ives and Annie marry around Christmastime and attend Mass on Sundays. But Ives anguishes after having sex with Annie, who studied the *Kamasutra*, the Hindu sex manual. Sometimes Ives finds it hard to reconcile his passions with his piety.

Annie and Ives have a son named Robert, whose life and murder becomes the focus of the story. Ives has endeavored to teach his son about religion since Robert was very young. Robert feels as if he had two homes, their apartment and the church (73). Despite having a girlfriend named Celeste ("heaven"), Robert planned to enter the Franciscan order. After Robert returns from Italy to receive the pope's blessing, he has a dream. He sees Jesus standing waist high in the water and as a boy his own age. Jesus beckons him, and Robert interprets that as meaning that he should become a priest.

Ives does initially have some misgivings about Robert's decision, but later seems proud. Mr. Ives's dream, in fact, is to see Robert officiate at Mass, and he keeps a picture of Robert shaking hands with Pope John XXIII. Robert "had memorized his Baltimore catechism, memorized all the altar-boy Latin for the Mass in the good old days before it was changed by the reforms of the Ecumenical Council [Vatican II]" (88). Robert still has youthful temptations, and Ives helps him overcome them—e.g., when a Hispanic neighbor undresses with her window open, Ives sends her a note asking her to close the window (90).

Robert's attraction to the priesthood can be seen as an extension of Ives's own deeply contemplative and spiritual disposition. Not long before the murder of his son, Ives has a defining spiritual experience as he is walking amidst the New York crowds. As he is waiting for a traffic light to change on Madison Avenue, Ives (100):

> began to feel *euphoric*, all the world's goodness, as it were, spinning around him. At the same time, he began to feel certain physical sensations: the sidewalk under him lifting ever so slightly, and the avenue, dense with holiday traffic, fluttering like an immense carpet, and growing wider and

stretching onward as if it would continue to do so forever, an ever-expanding river of life. And the skyscrapers that lined Madison Avenue . . . began to waver . . . bending as if the physical world were a grand joke. And in those moments he could feel the very life in the concrete below him . . . it was as if he could hear molecules grinding, light shifting here and there, the vibrancy of things and spirit everywhere. In one slip of a second anything seemed possible.

Soon, the sun appears many times its normal size. Four swirling winds fill the sky, each with its own color: cardinal red, saffron, gray, and brilliant violet. The winds come from four directions, "spinning like a great pinwheel over Madison Avenue and Forty-first Street" (101). The vision ends almost as soon as it begins, and Ives returns to normal after the traffic light changes.

Ives wonders why his vision did not seem Christian (101). That night Ives has a dramatic increase in libido (104), and yet he thinks a lot about death (105). He has a vision of the Garden of Eden as a place of perpetual childhood lived in peace and love, where even orphans and foundlings are welcome (105). Yet, he tells no one, not even his wife, of his visionary experience for six months.

The experience moves Ives to explore religions more carefully. He contacts his Jesuit friend, who tells him to read the words of Meister Eckhart, Saint John of the Cross, and Søren Kierkegaard. He also begins reading books on reincarnation and psychic phenomena. One lecture, given by an Indian writer named A. I. Explixa, particularly impresses him. He uses a pencil to mark the most important paragraph, which reads, in part (108): "To commune with the divine, with the unseen, which is only an extension of what all people call reality, is to experience the world ashimmer . . . One feels like a pebble at the bottom of a stream of rushing water, awaiting not just the warmth of the sun, but the very hand of God to seek it out through the current."

Explixa, whose real name is Ranjit Gunanand, was once so despondent that he sought to kill himself with a gun. As he is about to shoot himself, he notices a dove crying. He also sees the Hindu god Krishna, and decides to give his life over to understanding the Un-understandable. What Explixa says later sticks with Ives forever: "Some men seek enlightenment, others not, but find it in any case . . . Buddha, the Christ, the prophet Mohammed—in other words, the great mystics—are but receptacles for the grace and wisdom of the Eternal Principle: 'God flows through all of us, to some degree'" (110).

Annie, for her part, has some experiences that make her cogitate on the nature of the world. Once, while acting as a substitute teacher in high school, she reads a Dickens novel and highlights the moral that there is no greater reward than goodness to your fellow man. Yet, some of the kids ridiculed this idea. Another time, Piri Thomas, the famous Nuyorican author, comes to speak about how hanging out on the street was not really cool. He is met with jeers and boos, and Annie's defense of Thomas is met with equal disdain. She finally decides that ignorance will persist in the world regardless of how many people preached for goodness (121).

All the experience with religion by both Annie and Ives is merely a prologue to the murder of their son. On that pivotal day, Ives and Annie are walking toward their building when they came on a crime scene in front of the Church of the Holy Ascension. They soon find out that the victim is their son. The apparently senseless motive involved Robert looking at another youth in a way perceived to be wrong. The killer is Daniel Goméz, a mulatto Puerto Rican, who is even arrogant about his crime. The boy has been in trouble before, and he is attracted to anti-Jewish conspiracy theories. Robert is buried on Christmas Eve morning of 1967. His grave marker is a simple Celtic cross.

Ives is inconsolable for a long time after Robert's death. He spends time in Robert's room, reminiscing about his son and thinking about the afterlife. Among Robert's personal effects is a book with a row of three religious symbols: an ankh, a Chrismon, and a crucifix (141). Ives also keeps a white leather-bound New Testament, a fat German Bible, and a baptismal card, among other objects related to his son (8).

Ives's exploration of various religions assumes new significance in light of Robert's death. Ives collects pamphlets from many religions: Eastern, Islamic, and Judaic and about Transcendental Meditation, among others. He becomes open-minded enough to attend other churches, including a largely African American church. Despite his religious nature, he even attracts sympathies from an atheist named Maria, an office worker who attends his son's funeral, though she previously vowed never to set foot in a church. However, Ives's love of Latina/o culture diminishes somewhat because of the Puerto Rican teen who killed Robert.

The theme of forgiveness becomes a central part of Ives's life. Through a priest named Father Jimenez, Ives arranges a meeting with the family of his son's murderer. It is not a pleasant meeting. The mother of Daniel Goméz, feeling the meeting as a bit forced, explodes into a harangue in Spanish. She breaks away from a prayer of forgiveness suggested by the priest, and she denies that her son committed the murder. Nonetheless, the meeting produces a photograph of the murderer's grandmother hugging Mr. Ives. The photograph bears the inscription, "Forgiveness?" (145).

Ives's pursuit of forgiveness eventually expands into an obsession with saving the soul of Daniel Goméz. Ives sends him magazines and books in prison. But Ives's hopes that the penal system will reform Goméz are shattered when he kills two more people eighteen months after his release. Yet, Ives persists in trying to convert Goméz, sending him a letter, along with a Bible and pamphlets. Ives feels some satisfaction when Goméz publishes a short composition titled, "Raising Pigeons in the City" (176). The story, though seemingly mundane, is a testament to Ives's encouragement of education.

Others are not so forgiving, especially after Ives takes up drinking to drown his grief. The owner of one bar, Mr. Malloy, even suggests killing the murderer. Malloy premises his argument on the idea that God does not care enough to execute justice, and so Ives must do it himself (147). Malloy, therefore, is a believer in the *Deus absconditus*, who absents himself from the administration of justice. Instead, Malloy argues, it is human beings who must administer justice. Ives eventually rejects all talk of revenge.

Forgiveness is also not on the mind of Ives's best friend, Luis Ramirez, who thinks that Ives should be either canonized or put away for his saintly behavior toward his son's killer. Ramirez's unforgiving reaction is linked to his disbelief in God. While grieving after the death of his own wife, Carmen, Ramirez exclaims that he does not believe in God, even as he himself wears a crucifix (229). Ramirez comes to believe that one ought not fear death, but rather the afterlife. He thinks that the afterlife must be painful because his wife comes back from the dead to visit him with a pained look on her face (232).

Annie wants no part of any program to save Danny Goméz's soul. She thinks that Ives's attempted friendship with Goméz is an unfortunate consequence of his grief (178). Annie wants to put Robert's death behind her, but Ives sees it as as the crucial moment of his life (180). Toward the end, the two drift into separate lives.

Caroline goes in an entirely different direction after her brother's death. She joins the Peace Corps and discovers "the mystical" (215). Indeed, she sends crates filled with Hindu and Buddhist paraphernalia back to Ives's home in anticipation of her return. When she returns home, she finds the act of saying grace at the table a bit anachronistic. She had come to see Jesus as a sort of swami rather than the One Supreme God. She has come to believe that just breathing can seemingly unite her with a universal serenity.

Caroline also speaks of a mystical experience that parallels that of Ives, except that it takes place in "an avenue of incredible temples, and crowds and crowds of Hindus" (217). As she sits enjoying an evening with a friend, Caroline sees Sanskrit or hieroglyphic scripts rising out of the sacred Ganges and floating in mid-air. These scripts flatten out like banners and then suddenly coil into a cylinder that comes hurtling toward her and her friend, who sees the same thing. The people to whom they report this story think that the beatific visions means they have good Karma, but she does not take herself so seriously. While she does relate this experience to her family, it is only after she marries Pablo that she reveals that Robert was somehow part of that apparition.

When Goméz is released from prison again in 1992, he asks to speak with Ives (193). But Ives no longer feels the same level of compassion after receiving a letter from a woman who eventually marries Danny Goméz. Her casual tone about her love for a killer strikes him as odd, and he begins to see that it was unjust for Danny Goméz to enjoy a loving future while his son lies dead. The key questions for Ives become, "Who inherited the earth . . . who deserved to prosper, who deserved to suffer?" (196). He has not corresponded with Goméz for five years, though he writes letters on behalf of Goméz to the parole board. Ives begins to feel dishonest in saying anything redeeming about his son's killer.

Goméz continues to make a plea to meet with Ives, and the latter finally agrees near another Christmas day. Annie refuses to go along, but Ramirez drives Ives to Goméz's house. The latter is working in a restaurant he owns. Goméz, who now weighs 300 pounds, is physically sick in anticipation of the meeting. He wears a penitent expression when he greets Ives. Contrary to expectations, Ives is not demonstrating a tormented countenance. Instead, Ives moves forward, with a restrained smile and gentlemanly disposition, to embrace Goméz. The latter cries, as he awkwardly attempts to return the gesture. Goméz thanks Ives for coming to see him. Ives comes to believe that his dead son is present in the room and approving of Ives's actions (242). The priest who helps to set up the meeting with Goméz, thanks Ives, "Only God knows how much good you have done . . . Feliz Navidad" (243). Ives leaves an envelope for Danny Goméz, which is to be opened after they part. The envelope contains a picture of Robert at age seventeen. On the trip back home Ives tells Ramirez that he is glad he met with Goméz, who had turned out all right in Ives's estimation.

In the final episodes, we find Ives reminiscing about Christmases past. Robert is there in those memories, and so are his adoptive parents and friends. He remembers his own mystical experience on Madison Avenue. The narrator reveals Ives's thoughts about Christ's final resurrection (248): "With painted but transcendent eyes, bearded and regal, He would come down the central aisle toward Ives, and placing His wounded hands upon Ives' brow, give His blessing before taking him away, and all others who were good in this world, off into His heaven, with its four mysterious winds, where they would be joined unto Him and all that is good forever and ever, without end."

Clearly, the ghosts of Christmas past now bring a forgiving peace and joy to Ives's future thoughts.

Critical discussion

The central theme of this book is forgiveness as one of the greatest gifts of God. The theme is enveloped within a Christmas story, which can be seen as the starting point of God's own plan of forgiveness for humanity. Ives is the human counterpart of God in heaven. Like God, the Father, Ives forgives the killer of his son. Despite his struggles with the loss of his son, Ives's act of forgiveness, along with other religious ideas, also has the practical consequence of bringing peace to his life.

It is also clear that Ives has a very positive attitude toward the Church. He bears no real criticisms of the priesthood or any sacramental institutions. His church is a place of refuge, where good memories flow. Most of the central events of Ives's life, including the death of his son, happen in or near a church. There is nothing ostensibly bad that ever happens because of the Catholic Church. If Ives reflects Hijuelos's own views of the Church, then it is no accident that the story begins and ends in a church.

But this positive view of the Church may also be cause for criticism from other Latina/o authors. Hijuelos does not seem interested in the very real problems of ethnic divisions within the Church in New York City. Acosta might complain that Hijuelos bears no criticism of the sometimes imperialistic history of the Church. All the problems seem to happen outside of the Church. Thus, some might argue that Hijuelos overlooks the fact that Catholicism can bring distress as well as relief to individuals. Just as Ruiz might be accused of having a completely jaundiced view of religion, Hijuelos might be accused of having too much of an uncritical approach to Catholicism.

However, Mr. Ives's view of Catholicism is not quite orthodox. At some points his faith does waver, as in the following statement, "And, in those days when he believed strongly in God . . ." (70). Otherwise, Mr. Ives seems quite open to pluralistic paths to God. He gravitates toward a mystical strain of Catholicism that often has many parallels to other religions around the world. Thus, Hijuelos is consonant with liberal Christian scholars who also see parallels between Jesus and other religious figures (see Borg 1999). The idea of joining up with God and partaking of a living universe is consistent with many Eastern conceptions of religion. Mr. Ives is not judgmental toward his daughter when she experiments with Hinduism and Buddhism. Even Ives's report on an apparently Protestant fiery preacher seems to be nonjudgmental; for him, the search for God and goodness is what counts. Therefore, Ives would be in the minority (21 percent) of Catholics who have a favorable view of alternative religious groups, according to González and La Velle (1985, 152).

Hijuelos's use of biblical symbolism is quite interesting. The mystical experiences of Ives bear some similarities to some in Ezekiel 1. For example, that biblical prophet has a vision of a north wind, which soon beckons the appearance of four creatures and a great wheel. The vision of Caroline, which involves scripts floating in the air, has faint similarities to a vision in Zechariah 1:5, where one finds a flying scroll. In Hijuelos's story, there is a pregnant model named Mary, which Ives connects to the biblical Mary, especially because it was near Christmastime (35).

Christological symbolism is present, as well. We find that Ives often meditates on the baby Jesus as a parallel to his life. Jesus was born at an inn according to Luke 2:7 (contra Matt. 2:11), and Ives sees that as a parallel to his experience as a foundling. Ives's son Robert is pierced by a bullet without cause, and Jesus was also killed despite his innocence, according to the Bible. Ives expects the resurrection of his son, just as he expects the resurrection of Jesus.

All in all, Hijuelos (or Mr. Ives) does not reflect the experience of Hispanic Catholics insofar as feeling "welcome" in the Church. As mentioned above, only under a third of Hispanics could affirm that this best describes their experience (González and La Velle 1985, 125). Thus, Ives is describing the experience of more assimilated or Anglophonic members. Of course, Hijuelos is not obligated to furnish a story about downtrodden Latinas/os in New York churches. Hijuelos also is not obligated to represent anything other than Ives's experiences. On a purely statistical level, however, Hijuelos is in the minority in representing a very positive picture of the Catholic Church.

Comparative summary

Most of the authors have negative or ambivalent attitudes toward Catholicism, and they illustrate a number of perspectives and periods.

Acosta represents well the 1960s, with its activist criticism of institutional religion and the growing interest in Liberation Theology. Castillo offers a feminist perspective that criticizes patriarchal institutions to an extent not found in any of the male authors we have considered. Rivera sheds light on ethnic conflict between Catholic groups in New York City in pre-Vatican II days. For Ruiz, Catholic theology leads to sociopathy seemingly everywhere. His discussion of clerical pedophilia seems prophetic in light of recent revelations. Ruiz continues a theme that began at least as far back as Maria Monk's *The Awful Disclosures of Maria Monk* (1836), which also spoke of the terrors inflicted upon a young girl by pedophilic and murderous priests and nuns. Hijuelos seems representative of the more conservative 1980s and early 1990s, when traditional institutions were in vogue again.

For the purposes of comparison, one might profit from reading John Rechy's *The Miraculous Day of Amalia Gómez* (1991), which provides a viewpoint of women and Catholicism by an openly gay male author (see León 1999). In the Pulitzer Prize-winning *Angela's Ashes*, Frank McCourt (1996, 127–131) reminisces about his experience with First Communion, furnishing an Irish boy's parallel to the Puerto Rican boy's experience in Rivera's "First Communion." Maria Escandón's *Esperanza's Box of Saints* (1999) also tells of the struggles of a woman to fit Catholicism with the realities of the world. Victor Villaseñor's *Rain of Gold* (1991), which tells the story of two branches of a family, bears a large spectrum of views. Yet, it is very difficult to find wholly positive visions of Catholicism among U.S. Latina/o authors, especially after Vatican II.

Chapter 4

Protestantism

O ne of the most significant developments in the entire history of Christianity is occurring at this very moment. Latin Americans and U.S. Latinas/os are shifting from Catholicism to Protestantism at a rate perhaps unseen since the sixteenth century in Europe (see Stoll 1990; Davis 1994; Greeley 1997; Maldonado 1999). Protestantization is already changing Latina/o culture as we have known it, and is now strong enough to be reflected in U.S. Latina/o literature, though still not to the same level as Catholicism.

Socio-historical overview

Protestantism is defined here as a major form of Christianity that derives from groups that separated themselves from the Roman Catholic Church beginning in the sixteenth century, particularly in Central and Northern Europe and in England. The principal initial Protestant figure was an Augustinian monk named Martin Luther (1483–1546), who became incensed at abuses that were wreaking economic ruin upon Germany (Ozment 1980, 195–198). Eventually, Protestants came to encompass most groups that no longer acknowledged the pope as the supreme authority in religious affairs. Today, Anglicans, Baptists, Lutherans, Methodists, and Presbyterians are classified as Protestant. Protestants can hold a wide variety of beliefs, but common ones include viewing the Bible as the ultimate source of authority, salvation through faith (and not through sacraments), the priesthood of all believers, and, in most cases, the elimination of the cult of the saints and the Virgin Mary.

The fact that Catholicism was the official religion of Spain and its empire in Latin America explains the relative insignificance of Protestantism among Latin Americans for most of the last five hundred years. Even at the beginning of the twentieth century there were only a few Protestant churches (especially Episcopalian, Presbyterian, and Methodist) in Latin America. Mexicans living in what is now the American Southwest were among the first Latin Americans to interact at a significant level with Protestants, and particularly with Anglo Protestant settlers in Texas. The end of the Mexican War in 1848 provided a new impetus for the work of Protestant missionaries, who sometimes saw Mexican Americans as an initial step to the conversion of Mexico to Protestantism. According to the Hispanic Churches in American Public Life survey, some 23 percent of U.S. Latinos are Protestants (Espinosa et al. 2003, 14).

Protestantism made its first significant inroads into Puerto Rico after the U.S. gained control of the island in the aftermath of the Spanish-American War of 1898. By around 1910, Protestants had some 15 missionary societies, 120 churches and 326 missions in Puerto Rico (Nelson 1989, 879; Silva Gotay 1998, 105–148). These developments have influenced the rise of Protestantism among Puerto Ricans who have moved to the U.S. mainland, particularly since 1950. Some scholars estimate that over 10 percent of Puerto Ricans in New York were Protestant already by the 1970s, with Pentecostal varieties being dominant (Garrison 1974, 301–302). About 20.7 percent of Puerto Ricans born in the U.S. mainland are Protestant (De La Garza 1992, 37).

Although Episcopalians were active in Cuba in the middle of the nineteenth century, Protestantism in Cuba became significant only after the Spanish-American War (M. Ramos 1986). Many Cubans who moved to the United States, converted to Protestantism and returned as missionaries to Cuba. Some scholars estimate that 5 percent of the Cuban population was Protestant by the beginning of the Fidel Castro regime in 1959 (Nelson 1989, 315). The Castro revolution had a negative impact on Protestants, but it did not eliminate them completely. Many exiles established Protestant churches in the United States, and especially in Miami. About 10.2 percent of Cuban Americans born in the United States are Protestant (De La Garza et al. 1992, 37).

While some studies cite a strong continuity in Catholic affiliation among Latinas/os in some local areas (for example, Austin, Texas),

Andrew Greeley (1997, 12) estimates that some 600,000 persons per year leave Catholicism mostly for Protestantism, though Davis (1994) sees this shift as more continuity than conversion (see also Pantoja 2001, 169). The rate of conversion to Protestantism is highest among Puerto Ricans and lower among Mexican Americans. The Southern Baptist Convention alone has an estimated 1,500 Hispanic congregations, and adds about 150 per year, according to Greeley (1997, 12).

Within Protestantism, evangelicals and Pentecostals are gaining a lion's share of conversions from Catholicism. "Evangelical" is a term with a complex history and meaning. Etymologically, "evangelical" derives from the Greek, pronounced approximately "evangelion" (εὐαγγέλιον) and refers to the good news associated with the Gospels. Today, most evangelicals speak of being "born again," and believe in the virgin birth, deity, and imminent return of Jesus Christ. Most evangelicals also believe that society ought to be ruled by biblical principles.

Evangelicals usually distinguish themselves from groups such as the Jehovah's Witnesses, Mormons, and Seventh Day Adventists that are perceived to be unorthodox in some central teachings. Conservative strains of evangelicalism (for example, fundamentalism) may be strongly anti-Catholic. Among the foremost popular representatives of American evangelicals are Charles Colson, Jerry Falwell, Billy Graham, Carl F. Henry, and Pat Robertson (see further, Noll 1986; Wuthnow 1989).

Gallup and Castelli (1989, 94), who use the "born-again" experience to identify evangelicals, estimate that 6 percent of American evangelicals are Hispanics, and that evangelicals constitute the vast majority of Hispanics who are Protestants. De La Garza and others (1992, 28) report that 20.2 percent of Cuban Americans consider themselves "born-again," along with 29.2 percent of Puerto Ricans (U.S. born), and 30.1 percent of Mexican Americans, even though the proportion of self-professed Hispanic Protestants could be much less. This disparity indicates that the "born-again" criterion must be used with great caution in identifying Hispanic evangelicals

One of the major strains of evangelicalism among Hispanics is Pentecostalism, which stresses that miracles and other supernatural phenomena (for example, speaking in tongues, faith healing, and Holy Spirit baptism) depicted in early Christianity are still achievable and should be actively cultivated (see Hollenweger 1997; Dayton 1987). In New York City, Pentecostal Puerto Ricans reportedly outnumber all other Protestant Puerto Ricans combined. HCAPL reports that some 64 percent of all Latino Protestants are "members of Pentecostal or Charismatic denominations or claim to be Pentecostal, Charistmatic, or spirit-filled" (Espinosa 2003, 16).

There is no single reason to explain the shift to Protestantism. Many Mexican immigrants sometimes brought anti-clerical sentiments acquired in Mexico. Hispanics in the United States often felt alienated from an American brand of Catholicism that was not willing to adjust to their cultural distinctions. Protestant churches were often willing to train and provide Hispanic ministers for Hispanic congregations, even while trying to "Americanize" them. While becoming a Catholic priest can be a lengthy process, Protestant ministry and leadership can be achieved relatively quickly. Protestantism often filled niches where Catholicism was weak or absent, as was the case in northern Mexico as late as the mid-twentieth century (see Rubio Goldsmith 1987; Avalos 2001). Switching to Protestantism also may be part of assimilation to American culture, which is perceived to be predominantly Protestant. Moreover, Protestants may use aggressive methods of proselytizing that cater to social needs.

Although Protestantism among Latinas/os in the U.S. is not monolithic, many scholars see the movement toward more independence from Anglo-dominated hierarchies as a major trend. The Assemblies of God and other Protestant denominations now have large Spanish divisions managed almost entirely by Hispanic ministers. Many Latina/o Pentecostal churches, and particularly the Puerto Rican Assembly of Christian Churches, are independent of any larger Anglo denomination (Garrison 1974, 304). The increasing participation of women is expected in most denominations. Central and South American immigrants, particularly from Honduras and Guatemala, may add significantly to the proportion of Hispanic Protestants in the United States.

Latina/o Protestants are also impacting Catholic policy, and two principal paradoxical responses have resulted (see Ruiz 1996). One is a counteroffensive to stop the shift to Protestantism, as reflected in the National Pastoral Plan for Hispanic Ministry approved by the U.S. Bishops in 1987. The other response is a type of ecumenism that acknowledges the future vitality of Hispanic Protestantism and stresses common interests among Latinos of various religious traditions. The latter response seeks a Catholic modus vivendi with Protestantism that is relatively free of strife.

Case Study 1: *Savior, Savior, Hold My Hand* (1972)

Savior, Savior, Hold My Hand begins after the author, Piri Thomas, has been released from prison (see chapter 6 for more biographical information). As reported in *Down These Mean Streets* (1967, see chapter 6), Thomas had earlier converted to Islam. Piri Thomas was born John Thomas Jr. in Spanish Harlem in 1928. According to an interview with Thomas, the name Peter was added later by his father who thought an Anglo-sounding name would give him a better opportunity to succeed (Hernández 1997, 172). The name "Piri" (Pee-ree) reflects the Puerto Rican Spanish pronunciation of "Petey," a hypocoristic form of the more formal "Peter." His family consists of two brothers and one sister, in addition to other children who died in childbirth. Thomas has lived in Puerto Rico on a number of occasions, but he has spent most of his life in New York City. As of the late 1990s he was living in the San Francisco area.

Thomas describes his religious background in the following excerpt from an interview (Hernández 1997, 175):

> My beautiful mother, Dolores Montañez, was a Seventh Day Adventist which is the closest you could get to Jews. We didn't cook when the sun went down on Friday until the sun went down on Saturday. We didn't eat pork, and we ate very healthy food. My father was a deathbed Catholic; the only time he went to see the priest was when he was ready to kick the bucket. But I liked my Tía Angelita's Pentecostal church the best, because I could jump and dance in the spirit, shout *Aleluya y gloria a Dios*! In Mami and Papi's churches I had to sit very quietly, with my ass getting cold.

As is the case with many Latina/o families, there are representatives of both Catholicism and Protestantism among the Thomas family members.

Savior reflects one of the strongest trends in Protestantization, namely conversion to Pentecostal strains of Protestantism. Thomas first encounters Pentecostalism through his aunt, who is a member of the Spanish Mission Pentecostal Church. Although he has attended meetings numerous times with his aunt, it is his release from prison that moves him decisively toward Pentecostalism. Thomas explains his attraction to Pentecostalism in *Savior* (19–20):

> The most beautiful thing about the Pentecostals was their ability to pour themselves into the power of the Holy Spirit . . . It was a miracle how they could shut out the hot and cold running cockroaches and king size rats and all the added horrors of decaying rotten tenement houses and garbage-littered streets, with drugs running through the veins of our ghetto kids . . . Those who looked for God to come closer were blessed with El Bautismo del Espiritu Santo, and they spoke a language that I could not understand.

99

Thomas centers here on many of the key components of Pentecostalism. As mentioned, Pentecostalism stresses the empowerment of the believer in the act called "Holy Spirit baptism," which endues the believer with various powers to carry out the Christian mission. This tradition reaches back to the biblical book of Acts (chapter 2), where the disciples, after the ascension of Jesus, are waiting to be empowered for their mission. A wind comes upon them and fire is seen upon their heads.

"A language that I could not understand" refers to what is commonly called glossolalia. Pentecostals believe that they are speaking in either tongues of angels or some human language that they otherwise don't know or never have spoken before. In fact, glossolalia is the principal sign of Holy Spirit baptism in Acts 2. The scientific community usually does not believe that glossolalia is anything other than involuntary muscle movements of the tongue during emotional experiences (Samarin 1972). Pentecostal services are typically much more spontaneous, participatory, and vivacious compared to mainstream Protestant services. Aside from the music, Thomas also likes the fact that "Everybody smiled at each other and called each other Hermano o Hermana" (69).

One evening, he dresses up to go to church. He hears conversion testimonies, which are a common part of Pentecostal services. These testimonies usually relate how a person led a miserable life and how the person's life turned around when he or she was "saved" by Jesus. Often these testimonies are followed by an altar call, in which a pastor or evangelist invites people who are not Christians to convert. Thomas hears the call and interrogates himself about whether he can do it. One obstacle is his fear of what street toughs will think of him.

Nonetheless, he gathers up his courage, and walks down the aisle toward the altar. The pastor asks unbelievers in the audience to accept Jesus as their savior (75). Then Thomas narrates his own conversion (75): "I nodded yes. Then I cried aloud, 'I do.' . . . I waited to feel Christ's most sweet hand of salvation break the stones in my heart and light up the darkness of my soul. But it didn't happen. I felt good, but not like Brother Rivera had. Maybe I was a harder rock than he had been . . ."

When he arrives at home, Thomas tells his aunt his doubts about whether Jesus has actually saved him. His aunt, however, tries to reassure him that God works differently with each person (76).

Thomas soon finds himself immersed in the Bible. Within months, he becomes a member of the Young People's Society in his church. He begins to direct services. He even composes songs, one of which also becomes the title of his book, *Savior, Savior, Hold My Hand*. In short, Thomas is illustrating another important characteristic of Pentecostalism, which is the democratization of power. The belief in Holy Spirit baptism means that even new converts are considered to have the power and ability to serve in leadership positions without the lengthy seminary training required for the priesthood in Catholicism.

A former street thug, Thomas now preaches on the streets. One of his first testimonies is worth repeating in part (81): "I was lost, born, bred, and grew in sin. But Jesus took my hand and led me to where I now stand." Despite his wish to be saved, however, Thomas does not always feel that he is experiencing what other Christians do. He also experiences constant temptation to return to the street life. In one instance, he meets up with an old friend named Oscoot, who tries to convince Thomas to help distribute drugs. Thomas refuses, telling Oscoot that he is a Christian.

It is at this Pentecostal Church that Thomas meets a girl he wants to date. Her name is Anita Luz Rivera, and she lives with her sister. Thomas fears that his criminal record will be a problem. He had a past relationship with a girl named Trina, but she moved on with her life while he was in prison. Nonetheless, on Valentine's Day he decides to give Anita some candy and a note expressing his feelings toward her. After many courtesies, they do enter into a courtship.

Just before his marriage, Hermana Díaz, a member of Thomas's church, tells him that the Lord had directed her to speak to him. She warns him diplomatically not to be brutal on their marriage night (128–129). Thomas is hurt by the implication that he might still be an animal, incapable of making love without physically hurting his bride.

Nita and Piri marry and establish a household in a white neighborhood that also hosts a brand of Christian racism. Thomas overhears people asking about who sold a house to a "n****r," meaning Piri. He overhears the answer, "Don Baldwin did, and that man is not a ni****r. He's a Porto [*sic*] Rican." (217). Piri, who calls this "cruel racist Christian talk," lets the conversants know that he has overheard their hypocritical remarks. Thomas decides to sell his house and only encounters more prejudice when a real estate agent suggests that he not sell to blacks. Piri scolds the agent and decides that he will sell the house himself to whomever he pleases.

His next serious encounter with white Christian racism occurs as he works for a youth program that is run by a man named John Clause. Thomas and Clause introduce their youths to services at the "Great Church," which is predominantly white and wealthy. The pastor begins with a message welcoming his listeners and encouraging them to bring their friends (255). But soon Piri notices the disdain of the membership for the nonwhite youths who come to the church with him.

Thomas grows disillusioned with that "brand of Christianity" that wants Christ's love to be expressed "on their own terms" (257). Piri mentions his discomfort to Clause, but the latter makes it seem to be only Thomas's problem.

In a subsequent episode, a fourteen-year old boy named Chiquito is scolded by a man for cursing. Chiquito also writes letters threatening the life of the people in the youth club, and Clause wants to have him arrested. Thomas tries to understand Chiquito's anger, and he eventually blames it on "these ivory-tower Christians" (315). When confronted by Piri, Clause denies that racism is a problem and tells Thomas that he is "young in the Lord" (315).

Thomas tells Clause that Chiquito is practically homeless, sleeping on roofs, cellars, and parked cars. He married at thirteen because he was so lonely. Thomas thinks that Clause should be more forgiving. For his part, Chiquito complains that God does not hear his prayers when he has nowhere to sleep. God isn't "worth a damn" according to Chiquito (317). In any event, Thomas comes to see the interrogation of Chiquito as a sort of crucifixion, which is followed by a resurrection of sorts when the Children's Court releases him.

Yet another confrontation results when a man named Lenny Roberts comes to work at the youth club. Roberts treats the young white youths much better than the Hispanic youths. When Thomas hears of this differential treatment, he nearly stops inviting Roberts to make the rounds with him. A verbal confrontation ensues, and Thomas sarcastically suggests that wealthy Christians come into minority communities with lots of Bible knowledge, but without any understanding of the culture (326).

Eventually, Thomas asks, "Are you prejudiced against non-white people?" Roberts admits he has prejudices but that he is working as a Christian to overcome them. This is not good enough for Thomas, who calls him "nothing but a hypocrite" (327). When Roberts retorts that Thomas is the one who is "not a Christian," Thomas responds, "You could be right, man. You could be right" (327). The two avoid each other after that, and Thomas eventually quits the club.

Thomas's attitude toward the Bible also becomes more cynical as he discovers its contents. He recalls an episode (354) at a Christian summer camp when some of the kids were discussing 1 Timothy 6:1-2, which he quotes as follows: "Let all who are under the yoke of slavery regard the master as worthy of all honor so that the name of God and the teachings may not be defamed. Those who have believing masters must not be dis-respected on the ground that they are brethren. Rather, they must serve all the better since those who benefit by their service are believers and beloved."

The youngsters cannot believe that Paul is advocating slavery. Upon seeing the passage, Thomas says to himself (355): "Diggit, Paul you dug slavery. Instead of a real Christian putting slavery down, you're telling people to dig their slavery and like it all the better because their masters are Christians. Paulie baby, you should have stayed under the name of Saul instead of taking a Christian alias."

Thomas believes that some of the Scriptures need an overhaul. He urges the youths not to take the whole Bible as God's Word for today.

In the final chapter, Thomas' disillusionment with Christianity becomes more evident. His wife notices that he is not going to church as often as before. He responds that he is still a believer in God, but is disil-lusioned by the hypocrisy he sees (358). He affirms that no amount of church attendance or prayer will bring about social change. He has come to see prayer as good for the soul, but not a way to cure social ills. When his wife tells him that "God is with us," he remarks that this idea is part of their social problems, "We cover our eyes with God and become con-tent to live in these damn conditions" (360). He protests that he cannot carry a cross while he is nailed to one as an oppressed person in this soci-ety. His final sentence is, "Hey, Jesus Christ, I betcha' there must be a mil-lion ghetto crosses out there" (361).

Critical discussion

Pentecostalism, one of the most vibrant forms of Protestantism among Latinas/os, endures a frank critique in *Savior, Savior, Hold My Hand*. Thomas's experimentation with Pentecostalism is not wholly satisfactory. He enjoys the social aspects of the church, such as friendliness and singing. But he does not believe that the supernatural will overturn social ills. In fact, it may be part of the problem as far as he is concerned. Thomas does not consider the Bible as completely God's Word either, but rather the words of men like Paul whose morality is no longer valid, if it ever was. Thomas has been influenced by the many religions he has studied in prison and beyond. He seeks to unify religions rather than just practice one. Thomas describes himself as a spiritual man who is not really tied to a single denomination or religion.

Thomas's experience with Pentecostalism is probably similar to that of many Pentecostals, except that he is honest about it or has thought about it critically. For Thomas, the idea that Holy Spirit baptism somehow will transform a person often comes up against reality. Pentecostalism, like other forms of religion, can be used to mask and endure rather than transform societal problems.

From a Pentecostal perspective, Thomas was probably not "saved" or did not persevere sufficiently to attain the regeneration and joy he sought. Thomas also seems to be as dogmatic as the white Christians he criticizes. From a secular critical perspective, Thomas's own view seems to overlook that "real Christians" may indeed have been supporters of slavery (see Garnsey 1996). The anti-slavery he views as Christianity, therefore, may represent a modern abandonment of New Testament Christian views of slavery.

Thomas also wants whites to understand his culture, but he may not understand theirs. If Thomas can excuse Chiquito's behavior as a product of his experience, why can't he excuse white people's behavior as a product of their experience? Accordingly, conservative Anglo-Americans might object that individual responsibility, which may need to be at the heart of social reform, is undermined by Thomas's selective excuses. Thomas sees Chiquito as a victim even when he threatens the life of others, but Thomas cannot see Jerry Roberts as a victim of his own culture. Consequently, Thomas does not believe Clause or Roberts are to be forgiven just as much as Chiquito.

Case Study 2: *Run, Baby, Run* (1968)

Whereas Piri Thomas provides ultimately an ambiguous or even cynical attitude toward Pentecostalism, Nicky Cruz provides an uncompromisingly positive attitude. Not as well known as Piri Thomas among academics, Nicky Cruz may be much more popular in the Latina/o world. He claims to have sold over eight million copies of his book, which has been translated into forty languages worldwide. Born in Puerto Rico, by some accounts in 1938, Nicky Cruz is a minister in the Assemblies of God Church, the largest Pentecostal denomination in the world. As he tells it, his single experience with Catholicism was unsatisfactory (138; all citations are from the 1992 revised edition): "When I was a child my parents had taken me to church. It was full of people. The priest mumbled and the people chanted back at him. It was a miserable hour. Nothing seemed to apply to me. I never went back."

Here Cruz exemplifies what was often deemed wrong with the pre-Vatican II Church. Its use of Latin, instead of the vernacular language, made Catholicism distant and irrelevant for many people. Cruz, therefore, was never really Catholic, and this opened the way for Protestantization.

His book begins as he is about to be sent to New York from Puerto Rico at the age of fifteen. His opinion of Puerto Rico involves religion from the very start: "Puerto Rico . . . is also a land of witchcraft and voodoo, of religious superstition, and great ignorance" (15). His parents are spiritualists who make their living casting out demons, and "supposedly contacting dead spirits" (15). He recalls that his house is a sort of headquarters for "all sorts of voodoo, seances, and sorcery" (15). His father appears to be very well read in these occult practices, and he retains a respectable library. Cruz recalls a childhood full of fear and resentment, in part because his large family meant little attention for each individual child. His father metes out harsh punishments, locking Nicky in a pigeon cage once for stealing from his mother's purse and also beating him on that occasion.

But Nicky reserves most of the hatred for his mother. One evening, as Nicky tires of playing with his brother, he enters the house where his mother is in a spiritist trance. When one of her clients comments on how cute Nicky is, his mother, seemingly possessed, replies that Nicky is not actually her son, but rather the son of Satan himself (18). She then orders him out of her presence, "Get out, DEVIL!" (18). Nicky vows that he would make her pay and repeats over and over how much he hates her. Other signs of sociopathic behavior include his obsession with killing and mutilating animals and developing an "unusual craving for blood" (21). Nicky's behavior eventually prompts his parents to send him to live with his brother Frank in New York City. His father sobs once, calling him a little bird that is now flying away.

The arrival in New York is difficult. Cruz sleeps in the subway, where people hurl epithets like "sp*c" at him. Within weeks after enrolling in the tenth grade, he is involved in fights with gangs. Frank pleads with him to avoid gangs, but it is no use. Nicky fights so fiercely that he develops a reputation in his neighborhood. Eventually, he becomes the leader of the Mau Maus, one of the most feared gangs in New York.

Nicky's gang not only fights other gangs, but the group also preys on innocent people. As Cruz describes it, "Each day was full of frenzied criminal activity" (71), including the gang rape of a woman on her way home. He reports that five of his gang members "went with her twice," which is typical of the nonvulgar language Cruz uses. At the same time, Cruz suffers innumerable wounds and injuries from his fights.

Cruz's family begins to worry about him. His brother Louis, who lives in the Bronx, encourages Nicky to come live with him. Nicky insists that the gang is his family and all he needs (80). Yet, Cruz is often tormented by dreams of his family. He dreams that his father is a wolf and his brother Louis a bird. He wishes his father would "come to New York and cast the demons out of me. I was possessed with guilt and fear . . ." (81). Cruz's mother and father do come to New York, and his father diagnoses Nicky's problem as an actual demonic possession (93).

Specifically, his father thinks that Nicky has five demons. Frank and his father hold Nicky down as his father begins to perform a sort of exorcism ritual. He commands each demon to leave Nicky, as he slaps both sides of Nicky's head. His father shouts, "There's a demon in his tongue. Out, demon, out . . . There it is. I see it coming out" (93). When the ritual is over, Nicky storms out of the house cursing.

A judge eventually diagnoses Nicky as an emotionally disabled human being who cannot love anyone (111). So the judge recommends that he see a psychologist named Dr. John Goodman. In return, Nicky will stay out of jail unless he gets in trouble again. But Nicky tries to kill Goodman, and the latter exclaims, "Unless you change, you're on a one-way street to jail, the electric chair, and hell" (114).

One hot Friday in July, Nicky Cruz hears about a big circus down by a local school in Brooklyn. When he arrives, he sees a man playing "Onward Christian Soldiers" on a trumpet. A skinny, short man begins to preach when the music stops. Cruz says he feels an eerie sort of silence sweeping over him and his surroundings, as if his father's witchcraft is active again. The preacher opens his Bible and reads John 3:16, "For God so loved the world that He gave His only begotten son, that whosoever believes in Him, should not perish, but have everlasting life" (120).

Then the preacher challenges the gang leaders around him to talk with him. Some do, and Nicky mocks them. Now, some of the young people ask Nicky if he was afraid to go up to confront the skinny preacher. The preacher identifies himself as David Wilkerson and walks up to Nicky with a hand outstretched. Nicky tells him to "Go to hell, Preacher." But Wilkerson says, "You don't like me, Nicky . . . but I feel different about you. I love you. And not only that, I've come to tell you about Jesus who loves you, too" (122).

Cruz attempts to discredit Wilkerson, calling him a communist. But Nicky realized that he is unequipped to fight Wilkerson's approach. Cruz said, "If he had come at me with a knife, I would have laughed at him and kicked him in the teeth. But he came saying, 'I love you'" (123). So he rushes away from the whole scene, as if being pursued by the devil himself.

Wilkerson later shows up at the door of Nicky's basement room, again extending his hands to Nicky, only to receive a slap on the face.

Wilkerson remains undeterred and tells Nicky that Jesus also suffered much torment, and yet was able to ask God to forgive his tormentors (124). But it is too late. Even after Cruz has forced Wilkerson out of his room, he could hear the words "Jesus loves you" over and over in his head (125).

The next morning Wilkerson is back in front of Nicky's apartment. This time Wilkerson gives Nicky a diagnosis, "You talk tough but inside you're just like all the rest of us. You're afraid. You're sick of your sin. You're lonely. But Jesus loves you" (126). Cruz said, "Something clicked. How did he know that I was lonely?" (126).

A few weeks later, Cruz and many other gang members attend a service by Wilkerson at a larger arena. Despite much commotion and hatred among rival gang members, Wilkerson seems serene. He calls people up to the altar to "receive Jesus," and Nicky goes up this time. Wilkerson asks him to kneel along with his friend Israel. Wilkerson touches Nicky's head and asks him to call upon God. Nicky's conversion statement comes next, "O God, if You love me, come into my life. I'm tired of running. Come into my life and change me. Please change me" (141). An overwhelming sense of joy comes over Nicky as he cries and hugs his friend Israel.

Cruz joins a local church named Iglesia de Dios Juan 3:16, which becomes his base of operations, especially after he receives his Holy Spirit baptism. He goes to preach in Puerto Rico, where his mother makes a dramatic profession of faith at one of his services. Although his father apparently never did convert, he seemed to have become more calm about life (189).

Nicky goes to Bible school and meets a girl named Gloria, whom he later marries. They return to New York to work with Teen Challenge, a youth group developed by Wilkerson. Cruz goes back into gang territory, as well, in order to gain more converts. His first convert, Pedro, moves in with Nicky, but Gloria eventually thinks this arrangement is unworkable. The couple also manages to have a daughter named Alicia Ann.

But Cruz is not as successful as he had hoped to be in New York. When he sees that his erstwhile best friend Israel has gone back into the gangs, Cruz becomes depressed. He resigns from Teen Challenge and goes to California to start a new life. The depression, however, does not lift so easily, and he notes that he has even lost his religious fervor (248). He does come out of his depression, and Israel eventually does return to Christianity. The book, as originally published in 1968, ends with Nicky Cruz dreaming of a ministry dedicated to the inner city.

In the 1992 edition of the book, Cruz looks back over the last thirty years since the first publication of the book. He speaks about his efforts to evangelize Europe, especially in light of the fall of communism. He says, "You may not consider it [England] a mission field; however, according to a recent census, Sunday services at English churches have lost one thousand people every week over the last ten years. That adds up to a half-million people in a single decade" (266). He also speaks out against pornography, homosexuality, and *santería*.

Critical discussion

Cruz represents a U.S. Latina/o writer with a zealously positive attitude toward Pentecostalism. He believes that this is the best approach to life. He accepts without question the ideas of miracles, speaking in tongues, and Holy Spirit baptism. He accepts the idea that God can change people from the worst criminals into new creatures. For him, the Bible is unquestionably God's Word. Unlike Piri Thomas, who is open to non-Christian religions, Cruz is uncompromisingly against anything other than Christianity. He sees Afro-Caribbean religions as devil worship. Indeed, Cruz has retained a very real Pentecostal belief in demons and demon possession. He sees disaffiliation with organized churches as a sign of falling away from Christianity. He cannot conceive of God-belief without church attendance, as his comments about England show.

Cruz's story is otherwise very similar to that of Piri Thomas. They both were angry young men who were in gangs. They both experienced racism. They both converted to Pentecostalism. Nicky Cruz has probably sold more books and been translated into more languages than Piri Thomas. Cruz is also much more famous among Latinas/os than Thomas. Cruz can still fill a stadium, whereas Thomas may not. However, Cruz is not as highly regarded as Piri Thomas among Latina/o academics and literati. For example, Nicky Cruz appears nowhere in the literature section of Kanellos' *Reference Library of Hispanic America* or in similar reference works.

Cruz's treatment among academics and literati cannot easily be attributed to literary form. *Run, Baby, Run* is very similar to *Down These Mean Streets*, which was published only the year before. Both Cruz and Thomas write with a gritty realism that is meant to show street life at is worst. True enough, Cruz has often toned down the dialogue, omitting some of the expletives that Thomas would use. But otherwise, Cruz's book is no less and no more "literary" on purely formal grounds.

Latina/o academics simply may not see as "literature" works by zealous Pentecostals or highly committed Christians. Indeed, it is very difficult to find any writer who is a highly committed Pentecostal, Protestant, or Catholic in the canons of U.S. Latina/o literature. Academia probably finds intolerable anyone who believes that non-Christian religions are all evil or demon worship. The argument here is not so much that Cruz should be admitted to the canon; rather it can be argued that his exclusion exemplifies again how U.S. Latina/o authors resemble Anglo-American academics, who do not prefer any form of zealous and organized Christianity.

Indeed, The Chronicle of Higher Education (http://chronicle.com/weekly/almanac/2001/nation/0102901.htm) reports that in 1998–99 some 45.9 percent of full-time faculty members regarded themselves as "liberal" and 6.7 percent as "far left." Only 12.9 percent regarded themselves as "conservative," and only .4 percent as "far right." Therefore, most U.S. Latina/o authors probably do not represent the growing population of Protestant and Pentecostal Latinas/os who are shifting Latina/o culture toward more conservative bents.

Case Study 3: *Klail City* (1987)

Klail City comes from the fertile mind of Rolando Hinojosa, one of the most respected Latina/o writers in the canon. Born in 1929, Hinojosa belongs to a family who can trace their presence in the Rio Grande Valley of Texas to the days before the United States conquered that piece of Mexican land. The son of a Mexican American father and an Anglo-American mother, Rolando Hinojosa was immersed in a bicultural world. He joined the army in 1946 after graduating from Mercedes High School. After serving in the military, he completed an undergraduate degree at the University of Texas at Austin in 1954 and began a career in teaching at Brownsville High School.

In 1960, after several occupations, Hinojosa enrolled in graduate studies in New Mexico. He later entered the Spanish doctoral program at the University of Illinois, Urbana, completing a dissertation on Benito Pérez Galdós. Since 1969, he has been teaching at universities in San Antonio,

Kingsville, and Minneapolis. He is now professor of English at the University of Texas at Austin. Recognition as a writer has come relatively easy for Hinojosa. He received the Premio de las Casas de las Americas (Havana) for his first novel *Estampas del Valle* (1972).

His development of the fictional world of Belken County has occupied several of his works, which are denominated the "Klail City Death Trip series." These chronicle over sixty years of Anglo-Mexican relations in the Rio Grande area of Texas. His work is part of a larger set of "border narratives" receiving special attention in Chicano literary criticism (see Saldivar 1991). Hinojosa also writes bilingually, as exemplified in his first novel, *Estampas de Valle*, which was written in Spanish before it was translated into English.

Klail City is perhaps the crucial novel in the Klail City Death Trip series. Its Spanish version won the Casa de las Américas prize. The prologue tells us that Hinojosa makes use of hundreds of cast members and three narrators: Rafe Buenrostro, Jehu Malacara, and P. Galindo. Most of the cast goes around "asking why they were put on this earth" (7). We also see a sort of commentary on Protestantism in the prologue (7):

> Now, this writer doesn't live in a cave, by the by. And so, he has also heard of people who claim to have been born again. This writer finds that hard to take, let alone swallow. The writer attributes this attitude to his upbringing and to his father, a man of long intellect but of very short fuses. This writer also notes that those people don't talk about resurrection after three days; at least not yet, anyway.

The phrase "born again" probably refers to evangelical Christians. Indeed, Gallup and Castelli (1989, 93) regard the self-description of "born again" as a primary mark of evangelicals in their surveys.

In any event, the best comments on Protestantism occur in the chapter titled "Brother Imás," which details the interaction of a traveling evangelist named Tomás Imás with Jehu Malacara ("bad face"), who shares narrative duties with Rafe Buenrostro ("good face"). Jehu Malacara lives in Flora ("flowery"), a name laden with irony. There is indeed nothing florescent about Flora as we enter into the crucial episodes concerning Malacara.

The chapter opens with the funeral for Bruno Cano, a citizen of the town of Flora. The funeral is being conducted by Father Pedro Zamudio with whom Bruno had a spat the night before. Cano had fallen into a hole in his search for gold bullion thought to be buried in the backyard of a *curandera* named Panchita Zuárez. Father Pedro comes upon the scene and refuses to extricate Bruno, presumably because the latter is trespassing on private property. In any case, Bruno becomes so incensed that he curses the priest's mother. The priest does not want to bury Bruno on sacred ground, but he is persuaded by the Carmona Brothers, Lisandro and Sabás.

At that time, Jehu Malacara, a fifteen-year-old youth, is working as an acolyte for the priest. After the seven-hour funeral on a very hot day, Jehu sees the priest working on the fiery, vengeful sermon that he will deliver the following Sunday against the Carmona brothers, in particular. Malacara, who regards himself as a prisoner in Flora, describes the sermon, "The parishioners were among the first casualties, then the town of Flora came under fire, after that the Valley went up in flames" (81). Hinojosa thus gives us an ironic portrayal of a town, which, though named for flowers, has actually been turned into a fiery hell by the Catholic priest. A sarcastic parenthesis adds (80), "Oh, if Rome knew what went on in the outside world away from the view and sight of L'Osservatore . . . " (The abbreviated name of the Vatican's official periodical is L'Osservatore Romano, which means "The Roman Observer.")

When Sunday arrives, however, Malacara decides to leave Flora with a Protestant named Brother Tomás Imás. The irony of the surname, which means "and more," is evident in the description that follows the introduction of the name, "Some parents have gone nose first and straight to Hell for less" (81–82). The Protestant preacher, who is frequently fond of alliteration, describes his work as the "Lord's Path, Preaching Precious Parables to Philistenes [sic] and other livestock that had wandered, raced, or strayed from the Lord's Lovely Light" (82).

Malacara describes Imás's mission as saving people from fiery pits, and Flora certainly seems like one of those pits. The portrayal of Imás continues with the comment that he also insists on eating one hot meal a day, which he expected his audience to provide to him. His specialty was the "mexicano branch of Christianity, the pickings [of which] were far from lean" (82). The narrator tells us that Valley Mexicans had already been rendered somewhat incredulous by the events of 1836 and 1848, when Anglos seized control of Texas with many broken promises as consequences.

Malacara recounts how he met Imás. On the Thursday after the funeral, Malacara is on his way to fill the hole in which Cano Bruno has died. He spotted a man named Edelmiro Pompa talking to a "fuereño" (an outsider) who speaks a very unique variety of Spanish. As Malacara tries to insert himself between Pompa and Imás, the latter stretches out his hand and introduces himself, "One of God's Good Guests, Tomás Imás. I Sing and Say Psalms for Salvation" (83).

The Protestant asks Malacara where he is going, and the latter replies that he is going to cover a dead hole for a dead person. However, Malacara explains that the dead body is not in the hole (83). Imás replies, "There must be a logical explanation, youngster. A basis of historical reasoning for covering an empty hole?" (83). This latter comment also might be construed as the narrator's own criticism of the credulity of Christians concerning Jesus' empty tomb story. Malacara, who tells Imás that he is an acolyte, also wonders if this outsider is a priest. Imás answers that he is a Lutheran priest. Edelmiro then asks if he is a "holy roller," which brings an immediate rebuke from Malacara (84).

Imás tells Malacara that he is spending Friday in Flora but leaves for Klail City the following day. Imás asks Malacara to join him, then goes on his way. Pompa warns Malacara not to allow the priest to see him chummy with the evangelical preacher (85). The two old friends then go to fill the empty hole, but they do not finish the job, as swimming is deemed more important. The unfinished job claims another victim in Anacleta Lobos, a forty-year-old bachelorette.

Malacara is frightened and runs to the Klail City-Flora bridge to wait for Brother Imás. The youth is hungry, having missed at least three meals by now, but Imás does show up around midday on Saturday. When Imás approaches, Malacara tells him he is ready to leave, but Imás does not say a word. Instead he reaches into his knapsack and pulls out two oranges, the larger of which he hands to Malacara. The last dialogue of this chapter bears repeating: "'Jehu?' 'Yes, brother.' 'In the Name of the Lord.' 'Amen.'" (88).

In the next chapter, Malacara sees what his job as assistant will entail. He will help Brother Imás to sell books, the Bible among them. We learn that Imás is about thirty years old. He was born in Albion, Michigan, and his grandparents were from Mexico. His father started out as a field worker, but later acquired an indoor job as an electrician's assistant, and eventually became the owner of his own electrical shop. Imás had never seen a church, even at the age of sixteen. Then he joins the army, and while there, encounters two Mormons. Imás experiments with Mormonism, and afterwards joins some Pentecostals, whose numbers were growing in Dearborn during that time (92). He leaves a good job at the Ford Motor Company and becomes a pillar in a local Pentecostal church.

After that he goes off to the South to sell Bibles "to them who sorely needed them" (92), which seems to be a commentary on Imás's innocence or on the lack of Bible literacy in the Bible belt. He goes back up to Albion to tell his family that he is ready to "begin his life as a victim and lover of God." (92). He joins a Bible school in Wisconsin, but the institution teaches him little he did not already know, such as "helping the fallen, loving one's neighbor as one's self . . ." (93). The irony here, of course, is that helping the fallen is literally what the Catholic priest did not do in Flora.

Imás meets up with the Edmunsons, an Anglo-Swedish couple who teach him his peculiar brand of Spanish. The Edmunsons learned it in the Belken County area. They also apparently convince Imás to join their own Lutheran denomination, which has a flock of Mexicans in the Valley. Malacara discovers that some of the sacred music played by Imás was actually taken, via the Edmunsons, from Mexican songs composed by Maestro Olivas, a local Valley musician. Imás protests that the Edmunsons, being honest Christians, would not take a song. Instead, Imás suggests that they characterize the act as "borrowing" rather than "taking" (95).

Soon Malacara is trying to sell Bibles himself. He inexplicably opens one of his sales pitches with Deuteronomy 23:1, which speaks of excluding those with mutilated genitals from the Israelite priesthood (97). Malacara tells his audience that the Bible does not lie. He adds that the audience need not even understand English because salvation does not depend on understanding what one reads (97).

Malacara also discovers that Imás does not use a dramatic alliterative speech when speaking privately; Imás has a different persona in public. But Imás's alliteration also begins to infect Malacara's rhetoric. He tells the audience that the translations "Perpetual Providence Provides" are not as important as "the act" (98). He thereupon butchers a passage from Job (24:15-16), which is never specifically cited, as follows (98): "Let me read what Job says to Eliphaz: 'No eye shall see me; And he puts a veil over his face. He digs through houses in the darkness.' Here, here, here allow me to translate: 'El ojo (eye) que mire (that sees) pondrá (will put) buena cara (a good face) a las casas (to the houses) que tengan este texto (of darkness).'"

Of course, Job is speaking about adulterers and not himself. And Malacara mistranslates though an inverted reference to his own name is found ("a good face"). Likewise, the audience might see as irrelevant his final and thrice-repeated quote (98), "Is this Naomi?" (from Ruth 1:19).

In any event, Malacara sells Bibles all over Belken County. He charges three dollars, and the profit is barely enough for one hot meal. As he says, "Who could want more?" (99). He adds that he still serves Father Zamudio and credits the latter with showing Malacara the right path. Malacara extols his own knowledge of both the Old and New Testaments

(98). He poetically calls Imás, "a Lutheran believer/of sainted breast; / Strong deliverer, / though humbly dressed" (99). Imás's days as a traveling evangelist end when he suffers a rattlesnake bite while trying to preach to field workers. Protestantism does not take permanent root with Malacara, who returns to a normal life as a Klail City high school student.

Critical discussion

Although only a couple of chapters in length, the story of Brother Imás reveals much about the narrator's view of Protestants. First, Imás is viewed as an outsider. The other Protestants, the Edmunsons, are also outsiders. Mexican culture is still seen as predominantly Catholic, and Protestantism is seen as an Anglo influence. Imás is from the North and the Edmunsons are as non-Mexican as can be (Anglo-Swedish).

Second, Protestants are viewed as either self-deluded or somewhat disingenuous. Imás's public persona is not the same as his private one. His dramatic alliterative rhetoric is artificial, much like what is said of many Protestant evangelical preachers. There is an element of salesmanship and hucksterism in Protestant approaches to religion. They are selling the Word of God that should presumably be free. At the same time Brother Imás can be generous, as when giving the larger of two oranges to Malacara. In some ways, Imás resembles Don Quijote in trying to save the incredulous people of the Valley.

Hinojosa also broaches some of the reasons why people convert to Protestantism. In the case of Malacara, he is young and perhaps tired of his Catholic upbringing. The harsh rhetoric of the priest actually helps push Malacara toward Protestantism, though Malacara later credits the priest with showing him the light. Imás has never really been a Catholic and is exposed to proselytization by non-Catholic groups ranging from Mormons to Pentecostals in the army and in the workplace.

In many ways, Hinojosa's allusions to reasons for conversion correspond to what we find in reality. The attitude toward Protestantism is mixed here, just as is the case with Catholicism. The episodes concerning Malacara's experimentation with Protestantism come full circle when one recalls what the author said in his prologue concerning the claim of being born again, "This writer finds that hard to take, let alone swallow." In any case, neither branch of Christianity has heroic figures in Belken County.

Comparative summary

Protestantism is still an evolving theme within U.S. Latina/o literature. It does not have the long history and cultural dominance of Catholicism, at least thematically, in U.S. Latina/o literature. Portrayals range from the somewhat comical and disingenuous Tomás Imás to the gritty realism of a Piri Thomas or a Nicky Cruz. Yet, there are not many other works with which to compare the ones featured in this book. It may be that Protestants do not seem to be writing novels of the types featured here. On the other hand, the literary elite of Latina/o literature do not recognize a Nicky Cruz as part of the canon, even if his writing style and general life story is very near that of Piri Thomas, who has enjoyed wide acclaim. Zealous pro-Protestant authors do not seem to be rewarded by Latina/o intellectuals. As such, this differential treatment shows that U.S. Latina/o authors and scholars reflect values that are typical of college-educated Anglo-Americans.

Chapter 5

Judaism

The turbulent history of Judaism and Christianity is replete with irony and tragedy. The irony is that Christianity began as a Jewish sect. The tragedy is that Christianity has often behaved savagely toward its religious parent. The study of U.S. Latina/o works relating to Judaism are not very numerous or extensive, one of the few examples being Maya Socolovsky's study (2003) of Achy Obejas, a Cuban American of Jewish ancestry who wrote *Days of Awe* (2001). We will show that U.S. Latina/o authors express attitudes, ranging from sympathetic to unsympathetic portrayals of Jews. As such, our work complements Sol Liptzin's *The Jew in American Literature* (1966) and Louis Harap's *The Image of the Jew in American Literature* (2003) insofar as we now include Latina/o literature under "American literature."

Socio-historical overview

In simplest terms, Judaism refers to a religion that traces its historical roots to the people at the center of the Hebrew Bible, which Christians commonly call the "Old Testament." The entire Hebrew Bible is called the Tanak, an acronym for the Torah, Nebi'im ("prophets") and Kethubim ("writings"), which form the principal parts. Judaism emerged out of groups that worshiped a deity called, by most modern scholars, Yahweh— the national God of ancient Israel. Membership in Judaism is usually conferred through birth, with the maternal side conferring membership in stricter traditions. The Torah (often translated as "law" or "teaching"), believed to be part of a covenant between Yahweh and the people of Israel, contains the main tenets of Judaism. These teachings, attributed to a man named Moses (traditionally dated to about 1400 B.C.E.), are found mostly in the biblical books of Exodus, Leviticus, Numbers, and Deuteronomy.

The Talmud (ca. 500 C.E.), which is often seen as the oral Torah, has also been authoritative for many traditional Jews (see Mielziner 1968; Neusner 1970, 1982–89). The Talmud is the main repository of legal rulings, or *halakah*, that extend and bring more precision to the Torah. If the Torah speaks about not working on the Sabbath, it is in the Talmud in which one finds disquisitions about what "work" means. The Talmud also contains a wealth of other traditions that help to formulate Jewish life and identity. Two main editions of the Talmud are recognized: the Babylonian and the Palestinian (or Jerusalem). The Babylonian edition is usually the most authoritative among Jews who still hold it as a primary rule of life in America.

The main practices usually associated with traditional Judaism include circumcision and the observance of the Sabbath and various feasts, including Passover, Yom Kippur (Day of Atonement), and Rosh Hashanah (the fall new year). Judaism is also often associated with Zionism, which refers to the movement advocating the restoration and maintenance of Israel, the ancestral Jewish homeland. Since the final destruction of the second Jewish temple in 70 C.E. by the Romans, the synagogue has served as the main place where Jews gather to transmit and practice their religion.

Judaism has been quite diverse in its historical manifestations. There were numerous sects that existed from the earliest written records. Today three main movements, which relate to the understanding of the role of the law in modern life, are identified: Orthodox, Conservative, and Reformed. Orthodox Jews see themselves as the most observant followers of the law of Moses, which is considered to be immutable and of divine origin. Reformed Judaism does not regard the Torah as of divine origin and sees Jewish practice as more a matter of culture than of obedience to divine commands. Conservative Judaism observes the law but also is open to changes. More extreme forms of Orthodox Judaism might not even regard Reformed Jews as Jews.

The United States is now home to some five million Jews, the first of whom arrived as early as 1621 (Dimont 2001, 1). By 1730 the first official synagogue, Shearith Israel, was built in the Wall Street area of New York City. By the late nineteenth century, the Reformed, Conservative, and Orthodox movements had taken shape in America, especially at the hands of immigrant rabbis such as Isaac Wise and Solomon Schechter. The story of Judaism in America can be summarized as one in which Jews struggled to adapt a very hierarchical religion to a democratic America. Previous waves of Jewish immigrants also looked at successive ones as needing either Americanization or modernization. One of the largest challenges today is the preservation of Judaism in the face of assimilation and intermarriage. Max Dimont (2001, 207), a popular historian of American Judaism, sees America as the home of the most influential Jewish community in the world.

Interaction between Jews and Spanish-speaking cultures reaches back centuries before the Spanish arrived in the Americas. Spain enjoyed an era during which many famous Jewish figures, like Maimonides (1135–1204), would leave an imprint on Jewish life for centuries to come. In 1350, Spain began a vigorous effort to convert Jews to Christianity (3), and in 1492, Spain expelled Jews who did not convert to Christianity. These Jews migrated to other countries around the Mediterranean, and they are widely known as Sephardim (to distinguish them from the Ashkenazim, Jews of predominantly Eastern European origin).

In Latin America, Jews settled as early as 1503, especially in Brazil. As Dimont notes, Surinam, Barbados, Martinique, and Jamaica, among other places in the Americas, became the home of a growing Jewish population (8). The Inquisition, however, was transplanted into the Americas as early as 1503, and this made Jewish life uneasy some of the time. The portrayal of Jews in post-independence Latin American literature can be traced at least as far back as Justo Sierra O'Reilly's *La Hija del Judío* (*The Daughter of the Jew* [1848–49]), which relates the courtship of a Catholic boy and a Jewish girl against the backdrop of the inquisition in Yucatán, Mexico.

Vatican II aimed to move the Catholic Church toward reconciliation with modern Jewry. In "Guidelines on Religious Relations with the Jews" (1974), the Catholic Church declared that in regard to communication with Jews, "from now on, real dialogue must be established" (Flannery 1975, 744). The document specifically repudiates the idea that the Jews killed Christ and reaffirms the Jewish origins of Jesus and Christianity. More recently, Pope John Paul has apologized for the Church's past treatment of the Jews.

The apology came in the form of a historic document titled *Memory and Reconciliation: The Church and the Faults of the Past* (1999) and a sermon on the first Sunday in Lent on March 12, 2002.

Protestantism has had a wide variety of views concerning Jews, ranging from the virulent anti-Judaism of Martin Luther's "On the Jews and their Lies" (1543), to more pro-Zionist versions seen in among many fundamentalist Americans, who nonetheless do not see Jews as being saved outside of Jesus (see Malachy 1978; Halsell 1989; Merkley 1998).

Interaction between Jews and U.S. Latinas/os usually occurs in large cities, such as Los Angeles, Miami, and New York, which have large populations of both Jews and Latinas/os. Fortunately, we now have some data concerning these relations, thanks to the first national survey of Latina/o-Jewish relations released in March of 2001 (for all results, see http://www.ffeu.org/ Latina/o-jewish_project.htm). Less than 2 percent of either group thought that relations between Jews and Hispanics were "excellent." According to a more recent survey by the Anti-Defamation League 2002, 24), 44 percent of Hispanics born outside the United States have "Anti-Semitic propensities" compared with 35 percent of those born in the United States. For example, 54 percent of Hispanics born outside the United States believe that "Jews were responsible for the death of Christ," compared with 26 percent of U.S.-born Hispanics (Anti-Defamation League 2002, 24). Some 22 percent of U.S.-born Hispanics believe Jews are "more willing than others to use shady practices to get what they want."

Of course, there are a few Jews (about 1.8 percent, according to the Latina/o-Jewish survey) who also identify themselves as Latinas/os. As Ruth Behar notes in her foreword to Caroline Bettinger-Lopez's *Cuban-Jewish Journeys* (2000, xiii), "No longer is it unusual to find Jews from Venezuela, Chile, Argentina, Mexico, Puerto Rico and Cuba living in this country who are committed to maintaining both their Latinness and their Jewishness in equal parts." Jewish-Latina/o figures include Ilan Stavans, the noted Mexican-born scholar of U.S. Latina/o literature, and Aurora Levins-Morales, the Puerto Rican writer.

Case Study 1: *The Autobiography of a Brown Buffalo* (1972)

Oscar Zeta Acosta, discussed in chapter 3, has an ambivalent and even hostile attitude toward Jews. This is best exemplified in his *Autobiography of a Brown Buffalo*, which was written before his *The Revolt of the Cockroach People*. Acosta's remarks are not systematic, but they are sufficiently numerous to warrant at least a brief examination. The *Autobiography* begins as Acosta (Brown) is already advanced in his legal career in the 1960s. Generally, he is living a fast life, full of sex, drugs, and social activism. We first meet him as he is staring in a mirror, conducting an imaginary conversation with himself and other figures in his life. One of those figures is Dr. William Serbin, a Jewish doctor, who has been treating Brown since the late 1950s.

At one point in this imaginary dialogue, Acosta in the character of Brown broaches the subject of his constipation, he says; "Dr. Serbin, my Jewish shrink butts in. 'Don't tell me you believe that stuff about the Chinese putting the leftovers back in?'" (13). Brown adds, "Lately Dr. Serbin has taken to following me wherever I go" (13). Brown argues that he has a physical ailment, namely constipation, rather than some mental illness. Dr. Serbin suggests that his constipated feeling is a symptom of holding something back, but Brown responds, "Everything's bulls**t! You and your accusations. All of them . . . they're just Jewish fairy tales" (13).

As the imaginary dialogue begins to tax him, he refuses to continue his conversation with "that Ivy League black-haired bastard" (13). Dr. Serbin had begun to treat Brown in the late fifties. Prior to that Brown had another psychiatrist, named Dr. Rubenstein. Eventually, Brown decides to leave Serbin. His parting words bear repeating, "After ten years I turn my back on that Jew with his ancient history hangups" (42). Not much positive is said about Jews in the rest of the book.

Critical discussion

Although not a systematic or even extensive expression of Latina/o anti-Judaism, Acosta exemplifies what may be more common. Many Latinas/os have assimilated stereotypes of Jews from their own Catholic heritage or from a Protestant-American background. Acosta's anti-Jewish slurs can be seen as another instance of his vulgar racism and bigotry, as he also refers to Chinese as "Chinks" and homosexuals as "fags" (43). Some may argue that Acosta is parroting a sort of formulaic racism rather than expressing a philosophical anti-Judaism. He also may be identifying madness with anti-Judaism. There are similar comments on Jews from Lourdes in Cristina García's *Dreaming in Cuban*.

Case Study 2: *El Bronx Remembered* (1986)

New York City, not surprisingly, is the setting for two stories about Latinas/os and Jews in Nicholasa Mohr's *El Bronx Remembered* (1986), which contains a series of stories about Puerto Rican children growing up in the Bronx. Born in 1935, Mohr is a native New Yorker whose parents immigrated from Puerto Rico. At the age of eight, Mohr suffered the death of her father, who left a family of seven children. The artistic talents she demonstrated early in her life helped her gain confidence later. She attended the Art Student's League of New York after graduating from high school in 1953. She traveled in Mexico, especially as an admirer of Diego Rivera with his powerful message about social change.

In 1959, she went to Brooklyn Museum of Art School, but eventually shifted from painting with brushes to painting with words. Her first book, *Nilda* (1973) was named "Outstanding Book of the Year" by the *New York Times*. She has now written over thirteen books, including, *Felita* (1979), a collection of stories titled *Rituals of Survival: A Woman's Portfolio* (1985), and *The Magic Shell* (1994). She has produced illustrated children's books, including *The Song of El Coqui and Other Tales of Puerto Rico* (1995) and *Old Letivia and the Mountain of Sorrows* (1996). Her reputation has resulted in her presence in numerous anthologies of Latina/o authors.

The two stories of *El Bronx Remembered* that address Jewish-Puerto Rican relationships are "Mr. Mendelsohn" and "The Wrong Lunch Line." In "Mr. Mendelsohn," the title character is an Orthodox Jew who lives next door to the Suárez family in a Bronx apartment building. As the story opens, we find Mr. Louis Mendelsohn asleep late Friday night in the living room of the Suárez family. It is almost midnight, and Mrs. Suárez awakens him so that he can go back to his apartment, which is only three feet away down the hall. Mrs. Suárez holds her door ajar as she watches to see that Mr. Mendelsohn safely enters his own apartment, the door of which has seven locks.

The next morning, on the Sabbath, Mr. Mendelsohn comes back to the Suárez apartment. Mrs. Suárez, who is constantly worrying that he does not eat enough, fixes breakfast for him. One of the Suárez boys, Julio, asks Mendelsohn why he prefers to eat in the crowded Suárez kitchen instead of in his own apartment, which has six rooms. Mr. Mendelsohn replies, "First of all, today is Saturday, and I thought I could bring in my food and your mama could turn on the stove for me. You know, in my religion you can't light a fire on Saturday" (50). When Julio persists in his questions, Mrs. Suárez interjects that Mr. Mendelsohn is no bother, and tells the boys to get ready for a doctor's appointment.

As the conversation continues with Mrs. Suárez, Mendelsohn tells her how he raised six sisters, all of whom are now married. He visits them only on the holidays. He has been living in the Bronx for forty-five years, whereas the Suárez family has been there for only six months. Mr. Mendelsohn also tells the Suárez family of the changes he has seen: "The Bronx has changed. Then, it was the country. That's right! Why, look out the window. You see the elevated trains on Westchester Avenue? Well, there were no trains then. That was once a dirt road. They used to bring cows through there" (54).

Georgie, one of the younger Suárez boys, adds that his father was lucky to have been riding a horse while living in Puerto Rico. But Mendelsohn reminds Georgie that they are the lucky ones today, as they have good clothes and a good school. Yvonne, Georgie's sister, adds that the family would like to buy a house, instead of renting.

Tato, the youngest boy, is a special favorite of the old man. Mendelsohn plays with him and reads to him. Some days, Tato and Mr. Mendelsohn nap together. Although he sees the family every day, Mr. Mendelsohn especially enjoys spending Sundays with them. The narrator says; "Only the High Holy Days and an occasional invitation to a family event . . . would prevent the old man from spending Sunday next door" (59).

The first Sunday that Mr. Mendelsohn spends with the Suárez family, he is circumspect about the food. Mrs. Suárez keeps insisting that he eat. He remarks, "You know, I'm not allowed to eat certain things. In my religion we have dietary laws. This is not—pork or something like it, is it?" (60). Mrs. Suárez assures him that it is only chicken and adds that she prepares everything cleanly. From that Sunday on, Mr. Mendelsohn never questions the food served by the Puerto Rican family.

The next episode finds Mr. Mendelsohn speaking with his sister Jennie in his new quarters. The Suárez family has moved to a better house in Yonkers, where "It was more like the country there" (60). His sister has helped him to move to a safer neighborhood, but all Mr. Mendelsohn can think about is visiting the Suárez family. He also wishes to go to his old *shul* (synagogue). Jennie assures him that his new neighborhood has a *shul* and that no one he knows lives in his former habitat.

One day, the Suárez family goes to visit Mr. Mendelsohn. He sees the family walk into the lobby of his new retirement community. The nurse at the front desk, however, tells the family that "Deliveries are made in the rear of the building" (63). Mr. Mendelsohn tells the nurse that they are his friends and are there to take him out to their place. Even though the family has gone through some changes, he still is very much at home with them.

In the next episode, Mr. Mendelsohn dies of a heart attack. His sisters, Sara and Jennie, are collecting his personal effects, and they come upon a picture of Tato. They conclude that the boy "must be one of the people in that family that lived next door in the old apartment on Prospect Avenue. You know—remember that Spanish family?" (67). Sara wonders whether they should return the picture, but Jennie thinks that might seem rude and suggests just putting it away. The sisters then deliberate about whether to tell the Suárez family that their brother has died. The story ends with Jennie's question to Sara, "What do you say?" (67).

In "The Wrong Lunchline," set in 1946, Mohr explores Puerto Rican-Jewish friendships in school. Like "Mr. Mendelsohn," this story involves food. As this story opens, we find Yvette (no surname given), a Puerto Rican girl, and Mildred Fox, a Jewish girl, waiting for the school lunch bell to ring. The school had announced that Passover lunches would be provided to Jewish children during that week. The girls' close relationship is signaled by their hand-holding as they go up to the counter where the Jewish children are picking up their lunch trays.

The narrator tells us at this point that the girls lived only a few houses away from each other. Yvette lives in tenement at the top floor of a four-room apartment shared with "parents, grandmother, three older sisters, two younger brothers, and baby sister" (70). Mildred, an only child, lives at the back of her parents' candy store. Almost every evening, after supper, the girls play in front of the candy store. Yvette also visits Mildred's apartment frequently, enjoying the Hershey's chocolate bar that Mildred's father often gives her.

As the two girls stand in the Jewish lunch line, a Latina girl named Elba Cruz calls out questions to Yvette, "Why are they getting a different lunch from us?" (70). Yvette responds, "It's their special holiday and they gotta eat that special food, that's all" (71). Elba persists in asking why, and Yvette can only explain that "Else it's a sin, that's why" (71). The interrogation continues, with Elba asking why it is a sin. Mildred tells her that it is Passover, and Elba asks what that means. Mildred explains, "It's a Jewish holiday. Like you got Easter, so we have Passover. We can't eat no bread" (71).

Yvette dismisses Elba's contention that she is in the wrong line. Elba tells Yvette that the teacher is coming, and will kick her out of the line. At the same time, Yvette poses her own question, "Why can't you eat bread, Mildred?" (71). Mildred tells Yvette that she can only eat *matzo*, unleavened bread. She adds that she cannot mix meat and milk together either.

Before long a teacher comes and interrogates Yvette, "You! You there!! . . . What are you doing over there?" (72). Yvette sheepishly retorts that

she is going to get some lunch. The teacher asks whether Yvette is entitled to a free lunch, and Yvette affirms that she is. The teacher then asks,
"Well . . . are you Jewish?" (73). Yvette remains silent, and the room suddenly became quiet in order to hear her answer. Another teacher comes
to investigate, and the first teacher explains that Yvette "is eating lunch
here with the Jewish children, and I don't think she's Jewish. She does-
n't—I've seen her before; she gets free lunch, all right. But she looks like
one of the . . . She looks Spanish" (73).

After Yvette's affirmative answer to a more direct question ("Are you
Spanish?"), the teacher orders Yvette to follow her to the office of Mrs.
Rachel Ralston, the vice principal, who scolds Yvette and threatens to
notify her parents the next time she goes to the Jewish line again. Ralston
adds, "Don't go where you don't belong . . ." (74).

After school, Yvette goes to visit Mildred. They listen to a radio program, but a moment of awkward silence ensues after the program ends.
They do not want to broach a sore subject. Soon the silence is broken
when Mildred offers Yvette some *matzo*. Yvette eats it and comments that
it does not taste like much. Mildred concurs, adding that it tastes better if
you put something good on it. Finally, Yvette blurts out what's on her mind;
"Boy, that Mrs. Ralston sure is dumb" (75). They both laugh, and Mildred
adds, "She's scre . . . screwy!" Then Yvette utters her final conclusion, "Dop
. . . dopey . . . M . . . Mi . . . Mrs. Ra . . . Ral . . . ston . . ."(75).

Critical discussion

Mohr has created stories with very hopeful and positive attitudes about
Jewish and Latina/o relations, which are also a subset of Jewish-Christian
relations. In "Mr. Mendelsohn," the apartment building in which the two
parties meet functions as a microcosm of New York and America. Here the
relative newcomers are symbolized by a Puerto Rican family who arrives
just six months before as the story begins. Judaism, which has a longer history in New York, is typified by Mr. Mendelsohn who has been there for
forty-five years. The generational contrast is in the juxtaposition of Tato,
the youngest Puerto Rican child, napping with Mr. Mendelsohn, a Jewish
old-timer. We also see movement from the inner city to the suburbs as the
Puerto Rican family prospers.

In general, Mohr paints a picture of the harmonious existence that is
possible between Jews and Latina/o Christians. Dietary and Sabbath laws
are cause for compromise and mutual support between the families, rather

than conflict. The Suárez family assures Mr. Mendelsohn that the food is prepared properly. The Suárez family helps Mr. Mendelsohn fulfill his Sabbath laws by lighting the stove for him. Saturday, the Jewish day of rest, and Sunday, the Christian day of rest, co-exist harmoniously.

At the same time, we see that not all Jews and Latinas/os interact in the same intimate way. Mendelsohn's sisters are not always attuned to Mr. Mendelsohn's love for the Suárez family. But the story ends ambiguously hopeful. The question, "What do you say?" can be interpreted as Jennie addressing her sister, or as the narrator addressing the reader. If a sign of hope, the narrator may be inviting the reader to ponder on whether Latina/o-Jewish relations can be as good as indicated in the book.

In "The Wrong Lunch Line," one also sees very positive relations between Hispanic and Jewish children. Adults inject divisions where children do not. The educational system creates divisions that children can overcome. One might speculate that the girls think that the teacher is stupid because the biblical injunctions concerning the Passover meals allow both Jews and non-Jews to partake of them under certain conditions. Note Exodus 12:48-49: "If an alien who resides with you wants to celebrate the passover to the LORD, all his males shall be circumcised; then he may draw near to celebrate it; he shall be regarded as a native of the land. But no uncircumcised person shall eat of it; there shall be one law for the native and for the alien who resides among you."

The simpler explanation, of course, might be that the girls believe the teacher is stupid because she focuses on differences that need not be problems. Once again, Mohr's stories tells us that differences between Jews and Hispanics/ Christians are more artificial than real.

Given the results of the Latina/o-Jewish relations survey we have cited, some could argue that Mohr's stories are not very realistic. Most Jews and Latinas/os don't really know much about each other. There are many major differences in politics and attitudes toward bilingual education, American support for Israel, and the role of the Catholic Church in the Holocaust. Mohr's stories, therefore, might best be seen as expressions of hope rather than a highly representative view of Latina/o-Jewish relations. Mohr's stories may reduce Judaism to dietary restrictions and overlook the real sources of conflict that have existed between Christians and Jews (see Ruether 1974; Klein 1978; Sandmel 1978; Cohen 1999. For the ideology of comparison between Christianity and other ancient religions, see J. Z. Smith 1990).

Case Study 3: "Xerox Man" (2000)

Ilan Stavans is considered one of the most influential scholars of Latina/o studies by the Anglo-American academic establishment. Stavans is also a Jewish Latino. Born in Mexico in 1961, Stavans (2000, 75) describes himself as a descendant of Russian Jews who settled in Mexico. He tells of a childhood lived in isolation from most of Mexican culture, which he encounters more fully when he enrolls in college. He later migrated to the United States and now teaches at Amherst College. In general he describes a life lived in relationship to many identities: Mexican, Mexican Jew, U.S. Latina/o, U.S. Latina/o Jew, and Jew. Other U.S. Latina/o authors and scholars don't always accept him as more than an opportunistic upstart (on this controversy, see Letters to the Editor under the heading "Ilan Stavans and Chicano Writers," in *Chronicle of Higher Education*, February 13, 1998; and the report by Scott Heller, "Living in the Hyphen-Between Latin and American," *Chronicle of Higher Education* January 9, 1998).

The repertoire of Ilan Stavans is quite diverse, including critical essays, as well as creative fiction. But he describes his work thus, "My themes always dealt with God as manipulator of human conscience, and my existential journey could be reduced to a verse by the Nicaraguan modernist poet Ruben Dario, 'To be and not to know . . .'" (2000, 86). It is in this vein that we can examine briefly "Xerox Man," a work that he has identified, in a personal communication in 2001, as illustrative of his interest in religion.

"Xerox Man" was originally published in 2000, though it aired on the BBC in 1999 (Stavans 2000, 301). Stavans says he wrote the story in virtually one night. The narrator, presumed to be Stavans, speaks of his encounter with Reuben Staflovitch at Foxy Copies in New York City. Stavans visits the shop regularly and has a great relationship with the owner, whose name is only given as Morris. One day he asks Morris if he ever feels curious about his customers. At first, Morris denies any curiosity, but then asks Stavans to follow him to a back room. In the closet of this room Stavans sees a huge stack of disorganized papers. The whole scene reminds him immediately of a *genizah*, a repository for unusable Jewish sacred literature.

Morris thinks most of the pile to be trash, but Stavans notices that one of the smaller piles bears papers with Semitic scripts. The pile belongs to Reuben Staflovitch. In response to Stavans's curiosity, Morris says that Staflovitch comes "in with a black doctor's bag about once every two to

three weeks" at around closing time (302). He reserves the Xerox machine
to himself and copies meticulously. He takes out an antique book from his
bag, copies it, and then returns it to the bag. He remains absolutely silent
through all transactions at the shop, and always leaves one page out of his
otherwise fastidiously copied set. Stavans takes out the top page of the pile
and asks Morris if he can take it home. That night, he discovers that the
page is from a Latin translation of Maimonides' *Guide for the Perplexed*,
one of the most famous works in Jewish religious literature.

The narrator happens upon Staflovitch one day as he is walking on
Broadway, then follows him up to the Jewish Theological Seminary and
eventually into an apartment building. Stavans tells Morris of his pursuit,
but the latter retorts, "You might be after a man with no soul" (303).
About a month later, the Stavans enters the subway after a busy day of
teaching at Columbia. He spots Staflovitch, and engages him in a brief
conversation (303–304). Stavans does not have much luck, but asks, "Are
you from Argentina?" He is rebuffed with "Why do you care?" Stavans
recovers with "Well, I am a Mexican Jew myself."

Suddenly, Staflovitch opens up with his theological views. His mission, he says, is "To serve as a conduit in the production of a masterpiece
that shall truly reflect the inextricable ways of God's mind" (304).
When Stavans reveals that he has seen him at the Jewish Theological
Seminary, Staflovitch abruptly ends the conversation, "I don't want to
talk to you . . . Leave me alone. Nothing to say, I've nothing to say"
(304).

Staflovitch is arrested a week later and dubbed the "Xerox Man."
According to the news reports, Staflovitch collects rare Judaica, only to
destroy it in dramatic ways, such as burning. However, he always photocopies the items in full before destroying them. The narrator says,
"Replicas are his sole objects of adoration" (305). As Stavans suspected,
Staflovitch was raised in Argentina, in the home of an orthodox Jewish
rabbi. However, father and son clashed over issues of the role of Jews in
the secular world, among other things.

Staflovitch decides that "ownership of antique Jewish books by
nonorthodox institutions was a wrong in desperate need of correction"
(305).

He also develops a theory that God does not rule the universe, but
rather lets it run chaotically. Staflovitch mimics this chaos by assembling
a book made up of individual and random pages of other books. As the
task of creating a masterpiece by this method seems doomed, Staflovitch
abandons sets of pages in various shops. He sees New York as the closest

city to God because that city practically runs on photocopies. New York is original by the very fact that it mimics itself. In any case, Stavans runs to the shop to rescue the rest of the pages, only to find that a recycling company has already been there. The narrator observes, "Paralipomena: This is the legacy the Xerox man left me with" (307).

Critical discussion

Stavans integrates many themes that he has cited as central to his work as a creative writer. The notion of God as a manipulator finds expression in Staflovitch's vision of God as a promoter of chaos. The Latin American connection is made, and the narrator identifies himself as a Mexican Jew.

The struggle between secularism and Jewish religiosity is mentioned. The allusion to the long tradition of transmitting tradition reaches back at least to the Talmud (*Pirke Aboth* 1:1). Even as Staflovitch reacts against orthodoxy, he retains the Jewish links with the sacredness of books and writing. Muslims, of course, refer to Jews as the people of the book (e.g., Quran, Sura 5:6).

The "Xerox Man" may be read in light of recent debates about whether there even is such a thing as Jewish philosophy anymore. In a recent article, Norbert Samuelson (2002) notes that "Jewish philosophy" today does not mean what it meant for thinkers like Maimonides. In fact, Samuelson almost seems to surrender to the idea that Jewish philosophy now ought to be situated within the study of religion and science. Maimonides has lost its relevance, it seems, for modern Jewish intellectuals. In any event, even in this short story, Stavans has woven a number of Jewish philosophical and religious issues into a compact series of events in New York City.

Comparative summary

Despite the work of a small but active group of Jewish Latinas/os, systematic treatments of Judaism in Latina/o literature from a Jewish point of view are still difficult to find. To what extent Stavans is not regarded by some as having a "Chicano experience" precisely because he is Jewish is also difficult to assess. Indeed, what we sometimes find are Latinas/os speaking of Judaism as a religion of the "other." These treatments range from the vulgar anti-Jewish descriptions by Acosta to a more sympathetic even if oversimplified view we find in the work of Nicholasa Mohr. Insofar as literature is concerned, Latinas/os, for the most part, encounter Judaism in large cities, rather than in small towns of South Texas or other similar areas with Latina/o populations. This is particularly ironic, given that Jews in America have often confronted many of the same problems of ambiguous and conflictive ethnic identities, and Jewish literature is also full of meditations on the role of religion in modern life. The future might bring more stories about the complexity of Jewish Latina/o identities and Jewish-Latina/o encounters.

Chapter 6

Islam and Eastern Religions

ompared to Christianity, Islam and Eastern religions are not as well represented in U.S. Latina/o literature, and so they are best treated together in one chapter. Doing so obviously oversimplifies the great complexity of these religions. However, we can justify this by the fact that this simplification and lack of attention precisely mirrors the simplification found in U.S. Latina/o literature. Accordingly, we treat only selected elements that are relevant to an understanding of U.S. Latina/o literature.

Socio-historical overview

According to the standard Muslim biography of Ibn Hisham (d. 218 A.H./833 C.E.), Islam, a term which refers to "submission" (to God), was born in the Arabian desert in dates which correspond to around 610–622 in the Gregorian calendar.[1] Ibn Hisham narrates that Muhammad, the founder of Islam, claimed to have received revelations which are now embodied in the Quran (the principal written authority of Islam) as well as in a body of tradition (hadith).

However, standard historiographical accounts, as represented by modern writers such as Marshall Hodgson and M. A. Draz, who generally follow Ibn Hisham and other early Muslim sources, are increasingly being questioned by some modern scholars. Everything from the historicity of the life of Muhammad to the reliability of the Quran and the traditions concerning the prophet known as the Hadith, has come under renewed scrutiny (see Crone and Cook 1977; Wansbrough 1977, 1978). The diverse nature of what is called "Islam" is beyond the scope of our treatment. However, according to the authoritative collection of Islamic traditions (Hadith) by al-Bukhari (ca. 810–870 C.E.), there are five basic principles of Islam, which we summarize as follows:[2]

1. Shahada, which is the proclamation that there is only one God, Allah, and Muhammad is his prophet.

2. Salat, or ritual prayer five times a day while facing Mecca.

3. Zakat, or giving of alms.

4. Sawm, which refers to fasting from dawn to sunset during the month of Ramadan.

5. The Hajj, or pilgrimage to Mecca, at least once in the believer's lifetime.

Within the larger Muslim community, or ummah, there are two large branches. The largest branch, Sunni Muslims, holds the belief that the successor of Muhammad should be chosen by consensus, not genealogical ties to Muhammad. The Shiite Muslims believe that the proper successor of Muhammad should have been chosen from the house or family of Muhammad. Despite these and other differences, both branches do agree on major points.

For the purpose of U.S. Latina/o literature, the most important and powerful Muslim movement is the so-called "Black Muslim" movement, which ironically is often not seen as "Muslim" by the larger Muslim communities of the Middle East and Asia. The term "Black Muslim," which is generally disavowed by its adherents, was coined in 1956 by C. Eric Lincoln (1994, xvii), one of the first academics to study the movement. In general, African Americans who have adopted Islam tell of the struggle to assert their Muslim identity not only vis à vis a larger white American world, but also vis à vis a larger Islamic ummah, or community of Muslims (McCloud 1995, 5).

Despite the presence of Muslims in the Americas as far back as the Spanish conquest (Turner 1997, 11), it is in the early twentieth century that any significant Islamic movement emerged among African Americans. The rise in interest was part of a response to the alienation and disillusionment experienced by a mass migration of African Americans into northern cities in the early twentieth century (Turner 1997, 73). Disillusionment with the NAACP, which was often perceived as an upper-class organization, also helped to draw many African Americans to these neo-Islamic movements (Lincoln 1994, 140–141).

The Noble Drew Ali (born Timothy Drew in North Carolina in 1886) was one of the first twentieth-century figures to integrate Islam into a new religious tradition in America. Ali's movement, which began in Newark, New Jersey, actually combined Islam, Freemasonry, and theosophy with creative assertions of black identity. In 1913, Ali founded the Moorish Science Temple of America (Turner 1997, 72–108). His group had grown to some thirty thousand members by the time he was assassinated in 1929 in the wake of a struggle for control of his organization.

During the 1920s, the so-called Ahmadiyya movement also attracted many African Americans. The movement can be traced back to Ghulam Ahmad (1835?–1908), who was born in the Punjab of India. In 1889 he announced that he was the mahdi, a Messianic figure some Muslims have been awaiting (Smith 1999, 74). The Ahamadiyya movement provided "the first multi-racial model for American Islam" (Turner 1997, 110).

Yet, perhaps the most vital and significant of all African American Islamic movements is known as the Nation of Islam. The founder came to Detroit in 1930 as mysteriously as he disappeared without a trace in 1934. His name has been variously recorded as W. D. Fard, Mr. Farrad Mohammad, and Wali Farrad (Lincoln 1994, 12). Fard, whose exact ethnic/racial identity is still a mystery, "announced himself to Detroit Police as 'the Supreme ruler of the Universe'" (Lincoln 1994, 13). He combined Islam with a thorough antipathy for the white race, which he branded as deceptive by nature. A basic tenet is that "Islam is the original religion of all black mankind" (Muhammad 1957, 31). By the time he disappeared, Fard had established a Nation of Islam temple in Chicago, along with an educational system for his organization.

His most fervent pupil, Elijah Muhammad (1897–1975), assumed the leadership of the Nation of Islam after Fard's disappearance. Known originally as Elijah Poole, Elijah Muhammad was born in Georgia. He arrived in Detroit in the 1920s. Before he converted to Fard's message, Poole was captivated by the message of Marcus Garvey and other African American leaders of the time. After Fard's disappearance, Elijah Muhammad moved the headquarters to Chicago, and the main history of the Nation of Islam has been most heavily influenced by him.

Elijah Muhammad's brand of Islam was not deemed orthodox by the majority of Muslims around the world. Elijah Muhammad (1957, 19), for example, believed that Allah "came in the person of Master Fard Muhammad." This belief would violate part of the main profession of Muslim faith (the shahada), "There is only one God, Allah, and

Muhammad is his prophet." Elijah Muhammad's claim to be a prophet is also at odds with most of Islam, which holds Muhammad of the seventh century to be the last prophet.

Elijah Muhammad's attitudes toward Christianity were also quite strident. He describes Christianity as a "religion organized and backed by the devils for the purpose of making slaves of black mankind" (1957, 13).

Elijah Muhammad thought that "the characteristics of the white man is [sic] evil" (13). He believed that the Nation of Islam formed a society that was not really part of America. America would soon fall, and his group would be ready to emerge as the new leaders from the ruins. Nation of Islam members were to avoid pork, alcohol, gambling, and drug abuse. The emphasis on black pride additionally functioned as an antidote to the rampant racism that was part of American society, particularly during segregation.

Aside from Elijah Muhammad, Malcolm X (1925–1965) also became a recognized leader of the Nation of Islam. Originally surnamed Little, Malcolm X (1966, 188) had converted to the Nation of Islam while in prison in 1947–1948. Malcolm X had risen to be the right-hand man of Elijah Muhammad, but eventually fell out with his mentor because of the latter's resistance to a more radical political agenda. Malcolm X may have been assassinated because of his growing differences with Elijah Muhammad.

When Elijah Muhammad died in 1975, there was an intense struggle for succession that pitted Muhammad's son, Wallace Muhammad (aka Warith Deen Mohammed), against other contenders. Warith Deen Mohammed virtually disbanded the Nation of Islam and moved toward more orthodox forms of Islam under a succession of organizational names. Additionally, Warith Deen became, in 1990, the first Muslim to open the Senate with a prayer, signaling a new level of acceptance in mainstream America (Smith 1999, 93). The separatist and more original philosophy of Elijah Muhammad continued under Louis Farrakhan (1933–), the current leader of the revived Nation of Islam.

Outside of Christianity, Islam is perhaps the one major religion that has been most coherently embraced by Latinas/os. According to Jane I. Smith (1999, 66), Hispanics first began seeing Islam in the barrios in the 1970s. La Alianza Islámica, one of the oldest Latina/o Muslim organizations, was founded around 1975 in east Harlem as an offshoot of the Darul Islam movement, which was founded in Brooklyn primarily among African Americans in 1962. The Darul Islam movement has since splintered, and segments have moved toward Islamic mystical (Sufi) traditions. In 1987, PIEDAD (Propagación Islamica para la Educación y Devoción de Ala' el

Divino) was founded in New York, and focuses on Muslim Latinas (67). While definite numbers are not available, one estimate in 1997 placed the number of Latina/o Muslims at around fifteen thousand (http://www .latinmuslims.com/history/spanish_ummah.html). The total number of Muslims in America is still difficult to determine. The World Almanac 2002 (681) places the number at 5.78 million. Ihsan Bagby and his colleagues conducted a systematic survey of mosques, which estimated that a total of six to seven million American Muslims is a "reasonable" estimate, of which an estimated 1,572 Hispanics are participants in mosques (Bagby 2001, 6, 19; http://www.cairnet.org/mosquereport/Masjid_Study_Project_ 2000_Report.pdf).

Compared to Islam, we have only meager information regarding Latina/o practitioners of Eastern religions. By Eastern religions we refer here to any major religions originating from India to Japan. Such religions include Hinduism, Buddhism, Shinto, and Taoism. Most of these religions can be traced back long before Christianity (e.g. Hinduism and Buddhism). Each of these religions have evolved to entail as much or more complexity than Christianity. The scriptural and exegetical traditions associated with some of these religions are as voluminous as anything found in Christianity. Obviously, we cannot justify much socio-historical attention to these traditions when they have so little representation in U.S. Latina/o literature.

Nonetheless, we may note that a few Latina/o authors do show some interest in these religions. We have already mentioned examples in Hijuelos's *Mr. Ives' Christmas*. Piri Thomas reports reading books on Hinduism and Buddhism. For our purposes, we focus "Case Study 2" on one U.S. Latina/o work that contains a relatively coherent integration of Far Eastern religious traditions. This work is Rudolfo Anaya's *Jalamanta*, which could also easily illustrate the use of indigenous traditions, but we already have examples of those.

Case Study 1: *Down These Mean Streets* (1967)

Piri Thomas's autobiographical book, *Down These Mean Streets*, was written during the turbulent sixties, at a time when the Nation of Islam was also in turmoil. *Down These Mean Streets* is still probably Thomas's best known work. In 1995, The New York Times placed the book among "the top ten best books that represented life in New York" (Hernández 1997, 172). Although Islam does not form a central concern of the book, one crucial chapter does illustrate how Latinas/os dissatisfied with race relations find African American Islam attractive. In fact, Thomas's conversion experience has been compared to *The Autobiography of Malcolm X* (Hernández 1997, 171).

Throughout most of his youth and criminal career, Thomas really does not look to religion at all. Even at a point where he was near death after being shot, he described himself to a priest as follows, "'I'm not Catholic, *padre*,' I said. 'I am nothing.'" (237). He wishes to be married in a church, but again that is clearly more to fulfill some middle-class American ideal than because of any sincere belief in the sanctity of marriage. At best, he sees himself as Protestant for the sake of his mother.

Down These Mean Streets tells the story of a very angry young man whose anger comes from the racism he encounters in his neighborhoods. For example, after his family moves to an Italian neighborhood, Thomas encounters the issue of ethnicity. On his way home from school he hears someone call out, "Hey, you dirty f***in' spic" (24). An Italian kid named Rocky was the source, and the remark is followed by a question, "What nationality are ya?" Before he can answer, one of the friends of Rocky says, "Ah, Rocky, he's black enuff to be a n****r. Ain't that what you is, kid?" (24). Thomas protests that he is a Puerto Rican born in a New York City hospital. His life is a repetition of such incidents that only awaken his own race identity.

But the most grievous racism is the one he finds within his own family. From early on, he is aware of the color differences among family members who also deny their African roots. In one instance, his brother José claims that the family has no African blood. José notes that their mother is white, and their father's dark features can be attributed to Indian blood. Thomas responds "Boy, you, Poppa and James sure are sold on that white kick. Poppa thinks that marrying a white woman made him white. He's wrong. It's just another n****r marrying a white woman and making her as black as him. That's the way the paddy looks at it. The Negro just stays black. Period. Dig it?" (145).

After this argument, Thomas heads to the American South, and then to France, England, South America, and other places. The lesson he learns is the same, "Any language you talk, if you're black, you're black" (191).

Thomas returns home after being notified of his mother's death, but the relationship with his family does not improve. In fact, Thomas becomes embroiled in a pivotal physical confrontation concerning his father's relationship with a white woman. An argument erupts, and Thomas lapses into black speech to mock his father, and the father asks why he is speaking as though he "came from some . . . cotton field" (199). Thomas responds, "Is that where you came from, Pops? . . . Ain't that what bugs the hell out

135

of you. Mistuh Blanco in a natural black-face? Let me go, Pops, or I'll put my knee on your phony white balls" (199). Thomas leaves the house again.

Thomas's life away from his family only gets worse. With a group of white men, Thomas embarks on a life of petty robbery and drug abuse. After being convicted for shooting a police officer, Thomas goes to prison, where he begins to explore religions more seriously. The interest begins, in part, as an effort to educate himself and pass the time, "I had already got my high school diploma and three or four certificates on some free courses on anything that ate up time . . . More and more I had been digging into philosophy and different religions" (288).

At about this time, Thomas begins to delve into the meaning of some words that he had been hearing every night, "Allahu Akbar, Allahu Akbar" (288). Initially, he does not know that he is listening to a Muslim prayer in Arabic, "Allah is great, Allah is Great." The words come from a cell below and belong to man named Muhammad, who previously had a Christian name. Muhammad belongs to the Nation of Islam. As might be expected, Muhammad has negative views of Christianity: "Christianity is the white devil's religion. God or Jehovah is the white man's God and he's used his Christianity as a main weapon against the dark-skinned inhabitants of this world. What his blood-letting or slaughter did not destroy, his Christianity ably conquered. Even though Abraham is called the father of the faith, there's where it ends as far as we Black Muslims are concerned" (291).

Thomas says that he and Muhammad became friends and then became brothers. Thomas now thinks of himself as a Black Muslim with the new name of Hussein Afmit Ben Hassen (296).

Thomas's experiment with Islam did not survive his release from jail. In fact, Thomas experimented with Pentecostalism, as detailed in *Savior, Savior, Hold My Hand*. Commenting on why he reverted to calling on Christ instead of on Allah, Thomas says, "Guess I've been a Christian too long" (301). However, Thomas says that one aspect of Islam persisted in his new ideology, "I never forgot one thing that Muhammad said, for I believed it too: 'No matter a man's color or race, he has a need for dignity and he'll go anywhere, become anything, or do anything to get it—anything'" (297).

Critical discussion

Piri Thomas was on the leading edge of Latina/o Muslims, even if his experiment was short-lived. The reason for the rapid exit seems to be that his Christian heritage, weak as it was, still overrode his Muslim identity.

Yet, nothing he does and none of his decisions as a young man are tied to a particular religious concept or to a god. Thomas's religious experience is entwined with his search for a community that addresses racism in a manner that satisfies him at least temporarily. But in general, Thomas has no place for a god in his early life.

Second, Thomas's Latina/o identity was not conducive to the type of Islam that he encountered. The Nation of Islam was then even more sep-aratist than it is now. Latinas/os, whose family members can encompass a spectrum of color, were probably not attracted to an organization which sees black as superior to other colors. The Latina/o experience of racial mixture in itself is a great obstacle to gaining numerous converts to the Nation of Islam. Thomas, while cognizant of racism, was no separatist. However, other forms of Islam that are more racially inclusive may gain more Latina/o converts.

Case Study 2: *Jalamanta* (1996)

As mentioned earlier, Rudolfo Anaya's *Jalamanta* is one U.S. Latina/o work that bears anything approaching a coherent integration of "Eastern" religions. The recognition of these traditions is explicit, as in the follow-ing statement by the title character, "The philosophers of the East have taught of the transmigration of the soul" (132). Sometimes we find dis-tinctive Hindu concepts such as "Suffering is the karmic retribution for our past lives" (61). So already, we have sufficient clues that Jalamanta is interested in discussing Eastern religions.

However, it is best to see Jalamanta as expounding a blend of Eastern and indigenous religions in order to create a religion tailored to suit Anaya, who summarized his own intentions as follows (Dick and Sirias 1998, 182): "I think if you look at all my novels, most of the philosophy of *Jalamanta* has been expressed in them in one way or another. *Jalamanta* was a way of putting it together perhaps in a more concrete form . . . If I don't use the answers that other philosophies or world religions might give me, how do I take from those world religions and world philosophies and compose my own answer to suit me?" *Jalamanta* is the alias for Amado (= "beloved"), a man who had lived in exile in the desert for thirty years. Amado was exiled by the authorities, who are headquartered in "The Citadel" for preaching a heretical doctrine whose nature is revealed later in the book. *"Jalamanta"* itself means "the remover of the veil," the "veil" referring to the ideas that blind us from the truth.

As the story begins, Jalamanta arrives from exile to live with his first love, Fatimah, a healer and nature lover who seems to personify the female principle of nature. Jalamanta spends much of his time in simple subsistence activities and in preaching to groups of people who are grow-ing larger and hungrier for his wisdom. He insists "I am no prophet . . . I only speak of the Path of the Sun" (7). This declaration recalls the words of Amos 7:14, the biblical prophet of the eighth century B.C.E., "I am no prophet, nor a prophet's son; but I am a herdsman, and a dresser of sycamore trees." Jalamanta carried a shepherd's staff made from the twisted roots of a desert tree and bearing a carving of the heads of two interlaced serpents (6–7). He also carries a crystal that shimmers with green light that he places on Fatimah's neck.

As for his basic religious tradition, Amado explicitly says "Pantheism is our inheritance" (161). Pantheism teaches that the universe itself is God. Since human beings are part of the universe, they are a part of God. This doctrine is clear in Jalamanta's assertion that "in seeking unity with the Universal Spirit, the soul was becoming God" (90). The inability to per-ceive the divine is also a major theme of the book. Jalamanta's principal metaphor for this inability is that of a veil, which he describes (26):

> A veil is an illusion that blinds the soul . . . Anger, hate, bigotry, greed, excessive pleasures and gratification, and many other selfish desires take possession of the mind and body. When one gives in to those desires, the care of the soul is neglected and forgotten. Those veils block the nourish-ment of the soul. I teach a way of knowledge, a way to remove the veils that blind the soul . . . The veils that blind the soul have their origin in the dis-trust we have for each other.

Jalamanta also teaches about the value of meditation. As he defines it: "To meditate is simply to take the time to be still for a moment. This moment of silence allows you to participate in the same imagination that created the universe" (38).

The narrator adds later, "How could he explain that their souls were the stuff of the universe, the essence of the Universal Spirit?" (40).

Otherwise, the religion centers on the Sun, a visible representation of the Universal Spirit that is ineffable. The Sun represents the divine com-ing into being of the Universe. The Sun is responsible for all life on earth and for dispelling the night. Jalamanta says, "A prayer to the Sun is a prayer to the Universal Spirit" (44). Jalamanta explains that man has cre-ated gods throughout their evolution, but none has stood the test of time better than the Sun. Harking back to Aztec legends, he declares that a

Sixth Sun is dawning as we leave the era of the Fifth Sun behind (21). Figures he calls the Lords and Ladies of the Light are the light of the Sun.

Jalamanta emphasizes that his religion is derived from oral, not written, traditions of the "elders of the southern desert" (109). In fact, he chides Benago, a sort of Pilate-figure, for believing in a religion that claims to capture the thoughts of God in books (112). Jalamanta's own crisis of faith comes when he realizes that what was "written in the old laws" was nothing but the dogma of the authorities. He sees the ruling religion as guided by "esoteric secrets of a jealous priesthood" (176).

Memory is another important aspect of Jalamanta's system. During his exile, when he had gone to the depths of despair, a healer named Memoria ("memory") came and healed him. Jalamanta teaches that everyone bears, in their soul, a memory of the light emanating from the First Creation (74). The nature of suffering and evil is not omitted. In one conversation, Iago, his childhood friend, affirms that we sin because of our original sin (61). Santos, a friend of Jalamanta, however, believes in karma and reincarnation, and people will reap what they sowed in previous lives (61). Indeed, suffering is real, not an illusion. Jalamanta also teaches that we, not God, bear responsibility for the pain and suffering caused by human beings (58).

Near the middle of the book, we find the "Central Authorities" bringing him to headquarters for an interrogation. One of the representatives of the authorities is Vende ("sell"), who dresses in a brown uniform, brown boots, and a cap with the insignia of three skulls (94). Jalamanta realizes that Iago has betrayed him to the authorities. Soon Jalamanta finds himself before Benago, the inquisitor. Benago admits to Jalamanta that the central authorities also use religion, but to appease the masses. This again illustrates the idea that religion can be used for good or for evil.

When he returns to his community, Jalamanta is queried about his meeting. Some of his listeners wonder if Jalamanta will obey Benago, and these questions spark a discussion about the nature of death and the afterlife. Jalamanta says that death is part of the natural cycle, and even the sun dies and is reborn in its daily and yearly cycle. The soul survives after the death of the body, and joins their common cosmic source (129).

An old man listening to Jalamanta's discourse gently protests that it is not fair that he should die after accumulating so much knowledge and with so much left for him to do. But Jalamanta assures him that it is for the best, as the old man's soul will become part of the cosmic All (131). This response brings a sense of peace to the old man. Earlier we were also told that Jalamanta and Fatimah have a son born while Jalamanta was in exile. The son had died in battle at age eighteen. Jalamanta, however, suppresses his grief with the knowledge that his son's spirit is still with him and Fatimah.

The discussion then turns to the appropriate rituals for a human death. Jalamanta says that grief is natural, but should not veil the souls of the living. He prescribes a four-day ceremony, and each day one must pray in one of the sacred directions of the universe. The soul lingers near a loved on those four days, and then it returns to the eternal light of the universe. Jalamanta explicitly rejects concern with transmigration of the souls, as taught by "the philosophers of the East," because we should concentrate on seeking full enlightenment in our present life (132). Once this enlightenment happens, it will remain a permanent part of the universal spiritual consciousness.

The discourse on death reveals Jalamanta's doctrine about the composition of human beings, or what is called "Anthropology" in systematic theologies. A human being is composed of a "trinity of mind, body, and soul" (133). Jalamanta defines the mind as "the conscious ego of the soul for its time on Earth." It has great power, but it is not immortal. It is born with the body, which also must be nurtured as the temple of the soul. He believes the modern world has privileged the power of the mind at the expense of the soul. Jalamanta also believes that the modern materialistic world has become arrogant in its scientific and technological accomplishments. Of all of the human components, the soul is the most important.

After the discourse on death and anthropology, Jalamanta's attention turns to proper conduct. In general, Jalamanta believes that "Our evolution is always toward a higher consciousness" (139). The person walking in the path of the Sun will not be pessimistic or cynical. A central part of right conduct is love. By practicing love, the community of souls can actually usher in the era of the Sixth Sun. Such an era can be an era of peace and love, and human beings can create it.

The attention of the crowd now turned to the nature of sex. Jalamanta, focusing his attention on a young pair of lovers, opines that the best sexual relationship is one that joins the passions of the body with the passion of the soul. Otherwise, he sees few restrictions. Iago thinks this is a license for promiscuity, especially for the young couple. However, Jalamanta responds that young lovers can learn responsibility to each other if the veils of spiritual ignorance are removed (149). Iago's question is captious because he desires Fatimah, Jalamanta's wife.

Ecology is also tied to religion. Jalamanta's orations on ecology are prompted by a group of "natives whose ancestors had originally inhabited the land" (155). They report that what they call the Great Spirit, Jalamanta calls the Universal Spirit. Jalamanta avers that he believes in the Great Spirit, but he insists that this Spirit, which exists in everyone as the enlightened soul, is the same everywhere. However, Jalamanta adds that the different names and descriptons given to this Spirit by different cultures have resulted in conflicts and war (155). Jalamanta explains that the root of our humanity is the earth. The native group joins in a joyful ritual and nods in approval of his teachings.

Kindra, a witch representing folk healing traditions, forms the subject of another chapter in the book. She believes that the most salient type of sickness is one that affects the soul that has deviated from the enlightened path (158–159). Jalamanta's health care system regards the act of touching as therapeutic (68). Kindra, along with Jalamanta, also believes that human beings have a spiritual kinship with animals. Kindra complains that the majority religions "call such notions pantheism" and accuse her of devil worship (159). She particularly objects to the biblical idea, found in Genesis 3, that the serpent caused the fall of humankind. Instead, she believes that the serpent represents a benign figure who enlightens, not imprisons, humanity with an intuitive knowledge drawn directly from the Earth itself (160). Jalamanta adds that "Pantheism is our inheritance" (161).

In one of the final chapters, Jalamanta confronts the idea of atheism. A woman asks a question predicated on the idea that God is dead. Jalamanta replies that envisioning God acting as a man is responsible for any notion that God is dead (178). Earlier in the book, he had argued with a doctor of philosophy, who clearly represents the scientific physicalist position that there was nothing beyond physico-chemical entities. Jalamanta's reply is that "Science cannot find the soul because its light is the light of love" (84).

The final two chapters emphasize that Jalamanta's teachings have removed the veil of spiritual ignorance. Followers acclaim Jalamanta as "truly a man of the Earth and of the spirit"(189). In the final chapter, the authorities come and arrest him, based on information supplied by Iago. Santos, a disciple of Jalamanta, attempts to defend Jalamanta, but the latter urges restraint. The authorities then announce their crucial charge: "You have preached false doctrines, telling the populace that the soul can become God" (193). The book ends with Jalamanta being hauled into the Citadel, as Fatimah and Santos watch helplessly. The narrator does not tell us what happens to Jalamanta after that, but the lesson, from Jalamanta's viewpoint, seems to be, "Wherever you are, I'll be there" (194).

Critical discussion

Rudolfo Anaya, according to his own words, has attempted the most complete exposition of his religious system in Jalamanta. What we find is a mixture that we had seen before but with more explicit allusions to Eastern religious traditions. The main element that Anaya seems to accept from Eastern religions is pantheism, which is not unique to Eastern religions. There have been plenty of Christian mystics, such as Pseudo-Dionysus, Meister Eckhart (ca. 1260–ca. 1327), Jean Gerson (1363–1429) and Saint John of the Cross (1542–1591), whose ideas have been described as pantheistic. Indeed, Jalamanta seems to favor Christian saints and prophets who followed a mystical path (94).

But many of Anaya's pantheistic ideas are couched in language (e.g., Karma) distinctive to various traditions of Hinduism and Buddhism. The form of Hindu pantheism we perhaps know best is found in the corpus of Hindu writings called the Upanishads (ca. 800 B.C.E.). Here we find the idea that Brahman, the Supreme all-pervading God, is identical with atman, the soul or self (Sen 1984, 19). The doctrine of advaita (non-duality), whose development is usually attributed to the famous philosopher Shankara (ca. eighth century), teaches that the universe and God are identical (Sen 1984, 83).

Ludwig (2001, 92) claims that "the very heart of the human problem, according to Hindus, is ignorance." The theme of ignorance is another important parallel between Jalamanta's religion and Hinduism. In particular, the idea of a veiled perception is certainly a theme reflected in some English translations of the Bhagavad Gita, one of the sacred scriptures of Hinduism. The Bhagavad Gita details the teachings of the Krishna, the Hindu god, to Arjuna, a noble warrior who is pondering the mysteries of life and the universe in light of an impending battle with his own family. In the translation of Bhagavad Gita 7:15 by Juan Mascaró, Krishna says, "But men who do evil seek me not; their soul is darkened by delusion. Their vision is veiled by the cloud of appearance (māyāyapahṛtajñānā). Their heart has chosen the path of evil." In Mascaró's translation, Krishna says, "I am hidden by my veil (yogamāyasamāvṛtaḥ) of mystery" (Bhagavad Gita 7:25). The translation of Barbara Stoler Miller (1998, 74) has "veiled in the magic of my discipline" in Bhagavad Gita 7:25. If we consult the Sanskrit edition of the Bhagavad Gita (Sargeant 1979), we learn that "veiled" or "veil" are probably not the best translations of the Sanskrit terms.[3] Yet Anaya and other readers may be inspired by the translation more than by the original.

The life and character of Jalamanta himself seems to blend those of gods and leaders of various religions. Jalamanta's nature seems to parallel that of Krishna. For example, in one episode where Fatimah spies Jalamanta bathing, the narrator says that he "was the water, he was the light" (122). In the Bhagavad Gita 7:8, Krishna says, "I am the liquidity of the water [apsu] and the light [prabha] of the sun and the moon." Jalamanta teaches that desire is the enemy of the soul, and Krishna says (BG 3:37, 40; Mascaró 1962, 59), "It is greedy desires and wrath, born of passion, the great evil, the sum of destruction; this is the enemy of the soul . . . Desire has found a place in man's senses and mind and reason. Through these it blinds the soul."

There are also parallels to Muhammad, the founder of Islam. Fatimah is the name of Muhammad's daughter. Muhammad's daughter also married a martyr, her husband being Ali, who died in a struggle for succession to Muhammad's leadership. Muhammad spends time in the desert and on a mountain—as does Jalamanta—though one could also find parallels to the biblical Moses and Jesus here.

But the life of Jalamanta bears perhaps the most parallels to the life of Jesus. Like Jesus, Jalamanta abandoned the parent religion and was persecuted for it. Just as Jesus preaches against the "law," so Jalamanta gives up on the "old laws." In John 14:20, Jesus declares that he is "in my Father" and believers are "in me." Similarly, Jalamanta declares that we are all part of God. Jesus wanders and is tempted in the desert, and Jalamanta wanders and is tempted in the desert. Both preach to crowds. There is an episode (76) in which Jalamanta defends a prostitute that parallels the defense of the prostitute by Jesus in John 7:53–8:11.

Jalamanta argues with doctors of philosophy just as Jesus argued with doctors of the law (84). Eventually, the establishment comes to arrest Jalamanta, just as they come to arrest Jesus. Jesus has Judas, and Jalamanta has Iago, who shares his name with a deceitful character in Shakespeare's *Othello*. Santos (= "saints") tries to defend Jalamanta at his arrest, an action reminiscent of Peter's when the Romans came to arrest Jesus (John 18:10). Of course, there are differences, as well. Jalamanta is paired with a woman, and they have a frank sexual relationship. Unlike Jesus, Jalamanta has a son.

In *Bless Me, Ultima*, Tony, the main character, fights a struggle between the solar side and the lunar side of himself. Jalamanta mentions little of this struggle. However, Jalamanta is almost thoroughly heliocentric. The sun is the origin of all light and the main deity of the new system. The albedo of the moon is hardly worth a mention. In short, Jalamanta seems to reflect a synthesis within Anaya that has gone beyond the struggles seen in Antonio of *BMU*.

As in *BMU*, Anaya again juxtaposes a favorable view of those Eastern and indigenous folk religions with an unfavorable view of Christianity, and Catholicism in particular. Organized religion is thought to be the means by which knowledge is kept from people —"the esoteric secrets of a jealous priesthood" (176). His rejection of the Christ's Incarnation is implicit in his denial that "I do not clothe the Universal Spirit in the body of a man or a woman" (46). Jalamanta denies that he is establishing a new church (141), as "church" has negative connotations for Anaya. Anaya's emphasis on the divinity of the soul may be compared to Gloria Anzaldúa's emphasis on the divinity of the body.

Additionally, Anaya portrays Jalamanta's idea of the soul becoming God as antithetical to the religion of "the authorities," which are partial metaphors for Catholicism. However, the idea of human beings becoming God or having God within can also be found among some of the seemingly more traditional Catholics in history. For example, Athanasius, the fourth-century Church father who helped to formulate the orthodox doctrine of the Trinity, gave the following explanation for Jesus' Incarnation: "For he was made man that we might be made God" (Athanasius, *De incarnatione verbi dei* 54:3).[4] Don Quijote proclaims that poetry proves that "God is in us" (*est Deus in nobis*; Cervantes 1997, 2, 163). So perhaps Anaya, like other American writers, has gone to the East to find concepts that are part of the Christian tradition. This may be because such concepts have been obscured by other orthodox streams within Christianity.

Some mystical traditions also teach the value of memory, which is a conduit to the divine origin that we might otherwise have forgotten. For example, in Sufism, the name for the best known mystical tradition in Islam, remembering (dhikr) becomes a tool for connecting with the divine (Ludwig 2001, 442). The idea that we have a recollection (anamnesis/ἀνάμνεσις) derived from our pre-existing immortal souls is found in Plato's *Phaedo* 72–73, where human recollections are used as an argument for the immortality of the soul: "If it is true, Socrates, as you are fond of saying, that our learning is nothing else than the recollection, then this would be an additional argument that we must necessarily have learned in some previous time what we now remember. But this is impossible if our soul did not exist somewhere before being born in this human form; and so by this argument also it appears that the soul is immortal."[5]

This sort of epistemology also had a great influence in Christianity, and anticipates the psychology of Jung.

Anaya clearly prefers Jung over Freud. As he expressed it in an interview, "Well, all of Chicano literature, or a great deal of it, is talking about the reconciliation of self within the community, within the communal self, which is exactly what Jung says. You rediscover who you are individually in your collective memory, not in your individual memory. It's Freud who hung us up with the individual memory" (Dick and Sirias 1998, 46–47; see also Portillo-Orozco 1981). Some anthropologists of religion, however, would argue that Jung overemphasized the individual at the expense of the social self (Morris 1987, 166).

Jalamanta denies that he is against religions in general, except when they somehow violate the soul's harmony and peace (73). Anaya has always juxtaposed his system to the "dogmatism" of organized Christianity. However, an argument could be made that Anaya is no less dogmatic in his religious views, as expressed by Jalamanta. Jalamanta's statements do not differ much in structure, logic, or certitude from any doctrine taught by Christianity and the Catholic Church. As much as Jalamanta may wish to sound inclusive, he actually is quite exclusive of those that do not believe as he does, and he demonizes them in the same manner.

Thus, in the ceremony for the dead, the ritual he prescribes says that persons "must" pray in one of the sacred directions of the universe. But how does this "must" differ from any organized religion's prescriptions that one "must" also follow? Jalamanta objects to descriptions of God that might cause divisions and wars, but he does not explain why the divisions that he is causing with the Central Authorities should not also be an objection to his own descriptions of God.

His descriptions of God are no less dogmatic than anything taught by the Catholic Church. For example, the belief that the soul can become God is no less dogmatic than the belief that the soul cannot become God. Indeed, why is the one declaration not as dogmatic as the opposite declaration when both presume to be based on nonscientific grounds? If an appeal to some feeling or special power of perception is the criterion, then why can't the promoters of organized religion also make the same appeal for an opposite conclusion?

The anti-scientific stance of Jalamanta is also not new (see Harris 1992; Holton 1993). However, Anaya seems to think that scientific pronouncements are somehow more dogmatic than those of Jalamanta. Thus, Jalamanta asserts that "science cannot find the soul because its light is the light of love." But is it less dogmatic to proclaim that science cannot find the soul for the reason that Jalamanta provides? Jalamanta additionally bears an ironic stance toward written, as opposed to oral, traditions. He distrusts books. However, Anaya himself has participated in inscriptura-tion by the very act of writing his book.

In essence, some can well argue that Jalamanta's thinking, and that of Anaya by extension, is neither very consistent nor very self-critical when it comes to defining "dogma." Anaya seems to overlook the logic that all statements of the type "X is Y" usually exclude "X is not Y," and so any such statements are the basis of all dogma, whether it be in the form of organized religion or in the form of nonorganized religion or spirituality. Jalamanta also continues the anti-urban sentiments expressed in *Bless Me, Ultima* and *Heart of Aztlán*. For Anaya, modern civilization has eradicated the peaceful and more harmonious existence of more simple civilizations. Civilization has caused wars and misused knowledge (105). Robert B. Edgerton (1992), however, has critiqued extensively the idea of the pre-modern harmony of many aboriginal cultures (see also Albanese 1990).

Comparative summary

Piri Thomas and Rudolfo Anaya illustrate the search for religious mod-els outside of Christianity. In the case of Piri Thomas, his search in Islam leads him back to Christianity, at least temporarily. Thomas's attitude toward Islam, however, is best described as neutral in *Down These Mean Streets*. He attributes his reversion to Christianity not to some negative feature of Islam, but rather to his socio-religious habituation within Christianity. While Piri Thomas theorizes that God may be psychology and psychology is God, he does not seem interested in constructing a whole new religious system. So, in some ways, Thomas is a conservative, in that he is more interested in preserving his own existing traditions than in formulating new ones, at least systematically.

Anaya is interested in constructing a new religious system tailored to suit his needs. He expends much time and energy searching for features in world religions that he can bring to his own. In many ways, Anaya is prob-ably one of the most active integrators of Eastern religions in U.S. Latina/o literature. But as active as he might be, he and other U.S. Latina/o authors show no more than a passing knowledge of other reli-gions. Nonetheless, Anaya may be viewed as continuing a long Anglo-American tradition interested in mixing Eastern mysticism and indigenous religions (see Sharpe 1985). His construction functions as a specific response to what he views as dogmatic Catholicism, in particular. Accordingly, Anaya resembles the middle-class Gnostic New Ager described in Harold Bloom's *The American Religion*.

Notes

1. The most authoritative translation of Ibn Hisham's biography is that of Alfred Guillaume (1955).

2. Al-Bukhari (1997), 8/Book of Belief, 2/Darussalam Edition, 1:58.

3. Relevant Sanskrit terms are māyāyapahṛtajñāñā (Sargeant 1979, 345: "by illusion bereft of knowledge") and yogamāyasamāvṛtaḥ (Sargeant 1979, 355: "Yoga magic enveloped") in English transliteration.

4. Greek: αὐτὸς γὰρ ἐνηνθρῶπησεν, ἵνα ἡμεῖς Θεοποιηθῶμεν. Source: *Rouët De Journel* (1922, 261).

5. Greek: καὶ κατ ἐκεινόν γε τὸν λὸγον ὦ Σώκρατες, εἰ ἀληθής ἐστιν, ὂν σὺ εἴωθας θαμὰ λέγειν, ὅτι ἡμῖν ἡ μάθησις οὐκ ἄλλο τι ἢ ἀνάμνεσις τυγχάνει οὖσα, καὶ κατὰ τοῦτον ἀνάγκη που ἡμας ἐν προτέρῳ τινὶ χρόνῳ μεμαθκέναι ἃ νῦν ἀναμιμνησκόμεθα. τοῦτο δε ἀδύνατον, εἰ μὴ ἦν που ἡμῖν ἡ ψυχὴ πρὶν ἐν τῶδε τῷ ἀνθρωπίνῳ εἴδει γενέσθαι. ὥστε καὶ ταύτη ἀθάνατον ἡ ψυχή τι ἔοικεν εἶναι.

Chapter 7

Secularism

By "secularism," I refer to a mode of life and thought that does not presuppose the existence of, or relationship with, supernatural forces and/or beings. Many works by U.S. Latina/o literature manifest secular ideologies, which are usually juxtaposed with critiques of religion. For this reason, it is important to include attitudes toward secularism in our work. We could also see this chapter as a complement, in particular, to the chapters on Catholicism or Protestantism, as well as to other scholarship on secularism in literature (see Gordon's *Literary Atheism* 2002).

Socio-historical overview

Secularism is a variegated phenomenon. Perhaps the most common secular position is equated with "atheism," which we may divide into two types. The first, which we denominate as "passive atheism," sees no evidence for the existence of God and so lives without any reference to such an entity. Passive atheism can resemble deism, which though it believes in a creator, asserts that the creator neither relates personally to individual human beings nor takes an active role in the life of the universe. Accordingly, deists can live a life without much reference to a supernatural being, and so resemble frank atheists. Our second type, denominated as "positive atheism," argues that there is positive evidence against the existence of God.

Agnostics would argue that we do not know or cannot know if there is a God. As such, it can also resemble passive atheism in its practical consequences. However, it is possible for an agnostic to admit that he or she cannot know if there is a God, but will live as though there is one. As Buckley (1987, 14–15) reminds us, however, the word "atheist" (and agnostic) are best seen as dialectical. That is to say, their meaning can only be determined when theists affirm the particular idea of God they have in mind. Thus, if "God" is defined merely as a creator, it is possible to be merely an agnostic relative to that definition. However, if "God" is equated with the classical Christian omnipotent male deity, then the same individual could be an atheist relative to that definition if he or she believes such a god cannot exist. Today, many atheists and agnostics describe themselves as "secular humanists." The "secular" element refers to the nonreligious component, and "humanism" refers to the idea that the welfare of humanity (rather than serving the gods or afterlife) should be the focus of our worldview (Kurtz 2000, 35–36).

Although the first secular ideologies can be traced at least as far back as some Greek philosophers, it was in the Enlightenment that atheistic and agnostic ideologies came into greater fashion, at least among the intellectual elite of Western Europe. Here we may mention Denis Diderot (1713–1784), editor of the famous *L'Encyclopédie* and author of some skeptical and anti-clerical works, including *The Nun* (*La Religeuse*, 1796). Also important is Paul Henri-Dietrich Baron d'Holbach (1723–1789), a strident atheist who wrote the anti-Christian treatise, *Christianity Unveiled* (*Le Christianisme dévoilé* 1761). The Enlightenment *philosophes* often rejected the idea that human beings were originally depraved and needed some supernatural "salvation" (Anchor 1979, 7).

Karl Marx (1818–1883) figures prominently in the history of modern European atheism, as he believed that religion was part of an oppressive economic system that promised future and unattainable rewards in return for service and labor today (see further, McLellan 1987). Marx, in turn, was partly dependent on the ideas of Ludwig Feuerbach, (1804–1872), author of *The Essence of Christianity* (*Das Wesen des Christentums*, 1841). Feuerbach thought God was nothing more than a psychological projection of human needs, and developed a completely naturalistic philosophy of existence.

In early America, deism seemed more popular than outright atheism. Thomas Paine (1737–1809) took up the cause of deism in his *The Age of Reason*, published in parts between 1794 and 1807. Thomas Jefferson certainly would fit within the deistic camp (see Jayne 1998). The third

American president went so far as to remove all supernatural elements in his version of the Gospels. Jesus becomes a mere man, not a miracle worker and certainly not the Son of God. Other notable American atheists and agnostics include Robert Ingersoll (1833–1889), Thomas J. J. Altizer (1927–), Paul Kurtz (1926–), and Madalyn Murray O'Hair (1919–1995).

Latin America had its share of famous agnostics and atheists, some implementing anti-clerical measures (Meyer 1976). Indeed, the Mexican Constitution of 1917 contained a number of anti-clerical measures. President Plutarco Elias Calles (1924–1928) even suspended the Catholic practices, including Mass, baptism, and religious marriages. Such measures prompted an anti-government revolt, the so-called Cristero War, which exposed the failure of the government's dechristianization efforts (see Bantjes 1997; Meyer 1976). In Cuba, the historical linkage between Catholicism and imperialism led to the complete overthrow of the Catholic Church under Fidel Castro, though separation of church and state had been moving forward since the United States colonized the island (Pérez 1994, 155–156).

The reasons secular humanists give for their nonbelief in God can be complex. However, one common theme is the belief that religion is unable to deal with the problem of the origin and nature of evil. In philosophy, theodicy is the enterprise devoted to explaining how evil can coexist with God. For secular humanists there is no logical manner to resolve the problem (Pinn 1999). Kai Nielsen (1990), an atheistic ethicist, believes that basing any moral system upon God is an illusion, as the very notion of selecting God as a moral standard ultimately bespeaks a human selection.

In whatever manner secular humanists justify their beliefs, sociologists repeatedly have confirmed the relationship between education and secularism. Robert Wuthnow (1988, 168–169), who has tracked changes in American religion since the end of Word War II, comments: "Polls conducted in the mid-1980s have documented even more clearly the role of educational differences in the current divide between religious liberals and religious conservatives . . . Among college graduates only one person in three believes the Bible is absolutely true (contains no errors); among persons who have only attended high school the figure is closer to two-thirds."

According to Gallup and Castelli (1989, 77), 43 percent of Americans with no college believe in devils, but only 28 percent of college graduates do. Fifty-eight percent of persons with no college believe in angels, but only 42 percent of those with a college education do. Even if they do not become atheists, some 54 percent percent of Hispanic religious leaders reported that graduate school "had moved them toward more liberal religious beliefs" (Hernández and Davis 2001, 45). Scientists seem to form a particularly secularized group. Scientists have been consistent in their relatively high proportion of atheists. According to an authoritative report by Larson and Witham (1997, 435), 45.3 percent of scientists disbelieve in the existence of a personal god, a number similar to that reported in 1916 in one of the first systematic studies of religious beliefs among scientists.

According to *The World Almanac 2002* (684), there are over 150 million atheists in the world, but these numbers are very difficult to verify. It is likewise difficult to establish the number of self-described secular people in America. According to 1980s polls, some 94 percent of Americans expressed a belief in God, and we can infer that 6 percent do not (Gallup and Castelli 1989, 45).

Among Latinas/os, this may be reflected in some of the numbers reported by Rodolfo De La Garza et al. (1992, 37). In this tabulation of religious affiliations of Latinas/os is a category described as "other/no preference," and among them are 11.4 percent of Mexicans born in the U.S., 19.4 percent of Puerto Ricans born in the mainland, and 25.9 percent of Cubans born in the United States. Of course, "other" can mean almost anything from *santería* to Espiritismo, but we must assume that the category has also identified a few atheists and agnostics. The study by González and La Velle (1985, 31), who focus on self-identified Catholics and so eliminates most probable atheists, still finds .5 percent of persons surveyed expressing a disbelief in God. The Hispanic Churches in American Public Life summary places at 6 percent the number of Latinos "with no religious preference/other" (Espinosa, 15).

Needless to say, the Catholic Church is quite concerned about the level of secularism in the modern world. Much of *Gaudium et Spes* (1965), an important declaration issuing from Vatican II, is devoted to addressing atheism. It claims that atheism is not an original state of humankind ("*Atheismus . . . non es quid originarium*"; Flannery 1975, 919). The church sees atheism as part of man's unfortunate departure "from the noble state to which he is born" (920). Secular humanists, however, see religion as either an aberration or something that is indeed an unfortunate part of humanity's psycho-biological constitution. As our cases studies show, Latina/o authors have various approaches to secularism.

Case Study 1: *Pocho* (1959)

Often acknowledged as the first Chicano novel, *Pocho* emerged from the pen of José Antonio Villarreal (1924–), a native of Los Angeles. His parents hailed from Zacatecas, Mexico. Villarreal did not know English until he entered the first grade in Santa Clara, California, in 1930. He showed his literary side as early as the third grade when he began writing short stories and poems. He earned a bachelor's degree in 1950 at the University of California at Berkeley after serving in the Navy. He has taught at various institutions, including a stint in the 1970s (when he renounced his American citizenship) at the Universidad Autónoma de México. More recently, he has returned again to California, where he has taught at a number of institutions. Although he has published other works, *Pocho* remains his most important legacy.

Pocho tells the story of Juan Rubio and the disintegration of his family as he moves from Mexico to the United States. The central character is actually his young son, Richard Rubio, and the novel can be seen as a *Bildungsroman*. More importantly for our purposes, the novel involves a journey from religion to atheism. The story begins in Mexico during the throes of the Revolution of 1910. Juan Rubio is introduced as one of the exiles generated by that revolution (15). Rubio, who lived a life of debauchery in Mexico, makes his way to Los Angeles, where he begins to divest himself of his wild ways. He stops drinking and gambling and becomes more discreet in his philandering. He begins a stable relationship with a woman named Consuelo ("consolation"). The relationship between Consuelo and Juan Rubio results in the birth of what would be their only son, Richard, who is born near Brawley, California.

References to religion are numerous. Insofar as the people around Brawley are concerned, the narrator says, "although the people were religious, their poverty made them practical" (29). Burials among these immigrants were conducted by a former seminary student who was now agnostic, even if he was sensitive to praying according to the ways of his community (29).

In chapter 2, we find Richard Rubio on his way home from his first confession. Richard carries a picture of the Virgin Mary in one hand, but this picture has little value for him and functions more as a symbol of recognition for being the first in his age group to learn the catechism. But the catechism becomes a source of puzzlement for Richard (33): "The sky was his biggest problem these days. In the beginning, there was darkness—nothing, he was told, and accepted, before *God made the world. Who made the world? God made the world. Who is God? God is the creator of Heaven and Earth and of all things"* (33).

Although he "knows" this, the circularity becomes obvious, and Richard notes that "the answer to the second question was nothing more than the answer to the first" (33). Richard also keeps a Bible hidden. He likes to read it, but he believes that it is a mortal sin for him to read it (74). Richard's belief reflects his understanding of a Catholic prohibition, promulgated at the Council of Trent (1545–1563), against reading the Bible in a vernacular language and without the supervision of a cleric.

The common tension between sex and religion next becomes the focus. In one episode, Richard goes home and tells his mother of a conversation between himself and the priest (35–36). Richard has told the priest that he has "touched" his sister while they were playing. The priest immediately interprets Richard's remark as a reference to sexual interaction, and angrily warns Richard that touching his own sister is more of a mortal sin than touching another girl. So the priest prescribes penance, consisting of fifty Our Fathers and fifty Hail Marys. Richard, however, is left wondering how one mortal sin could be considered worse than any other mortal sin. Presumably both would have the same final consequence: eternal damnation.

His mother is horrified at the thought that Richard is answering in the affirmative because he understands the priest to be speaking about sexual activity. Richard explains that he does not play with Luz in the same way that he plays with a group of neighboring girls surnamed Mangini. Richard then tells his mother how the girls undress him and play with his genitals, even though he does not seem to understand the full implications of such activity, as he is still prepubescent.

His mother now screams in anger, telling him that he is not only filthy, but also in danger of dying that very night for his sins. She instructs him to go make his confessions to the priest early the next day (37). The experience of seeing his mother turn from a benign caretaker to a vicious inquisitor frightens Richard and prompts him to think further about the nature of God (37): "But if He was good and kind, why did He make darkness?" Richard suggests that God is responsible for the good and bad side of human beings.

Richard has a profound sense of guilt and often interprets events as due to sinning. Once, his mother is very sick, and he tries to comfort her. His mother tells him that the Virgin is taking care of her (39). But Richard rails against the Virgin and God because they made his mother suffer (39). He lies to his mother by telling her that he has eaten all of his meal. As his mother yells, he pulls her hands apart, breaking the rosary beads in her hand. Soon, Richard is hysterical and crying because he believes his skepticism and the broken rosary are part of the reason that his mother finds herself at the brink of death (39).

As Richard becomes more educated, his notions of God change. During a discussion about why he reads so much, his mother wonders what goal he has in mind. She assumes that his learning is to better himself and his children economically. But Richard tells her that he is learning for himself. This type of individualism is sinister for his mother. She says, "It is as if you were speaking against the Church" (64).

A discussion concerning God ensues, and Richard's mother tells him that he must trust in what God says. She advises that talking to God will provide the answers Richard needs. But Richard is now further away from orthodox Catholicism. He retorts that he believes now only part of what he is being told about God and that belief is fading fast because he can find no empirical evidence for God's existence every time he searches for him (65).

He sees God, not as the benevolent God of orthodox Christianity, but also as evil. He sees his parents' behavior as mirroring that of God's. His mother is grief-stricken at Richard's evolving skepticism. She exclaims, "You are the light of my life and I have already lost you" (66). Knowledge, it seems, is a dangerous thing.

Richard's movement away from Catholicism also involves deliberations about Protestantism. This is illustrated in a vignette about a brother and sister, whose last name is Madison, and who are new to the neighborhood. The boy is named Ronnie, a ten year old, and his sister is an eight year old named Mary. As the siblings approach the neighborhood children, a girl named Zelda greets them gruffly. She mocks the boy when he requests to play. One of the kids tells Zelda "my old lady says they're Protestants"(67).

Zelda wishes to initiate the new boy by taking off his pants. Richard tries to intervene, but he is eventually chased home by Zelda. His father tells him to go out there and fight Zelda. Richard proves to be no match for Zelda and ends up with a bloody nose. Ronnie's father, however, intervenes and Zelda keeps her distance. Ronnie's mother believes that this is anti-Protestant behavior. Ronnie announces that he wants to go into the ministry, though his father is skeptical (69).

In any event, Mary Madison likes Richard and strikes up a friendship with him. In one conversation, Richard tells her about all the bad things his Catholic teachers say about Protestants, including how Protestants are destined for Hell (71). His teachers warn against visiting Protestant churches. Likewise, Mary's mother believes that all Catholics are heathen. Thus, the friendship between Mary and Richard illustrates how children can overcome the theological differences that divide adults.

Pocho also features João Pedro Manõel, who arrives in Santa Clara when he is forty years old. He is from the Azores and of Portuguese descent. He rents a small shack and lives a mostly solitary life. When the townsfolk seek to initiate João into one of their religious societies, he declines. The narrator identifies him as an agnostic, even if he feared offending people by saying what he was (80). Don João, as he is called, becomes a favorite companion to Richard Rubio and a young girl named Genevieve Freitas. João soon confesses that he is attracted to men.

Richard frequently discusses religion with Don João. In one conversation, Richard tells Don João that he is worried about the "Immaculate Conception" (85), but Don João tells him that he is too young to worry himself with such issues. He counsels that it would be wrong for him to tell Richard what he should believe, as each person must figure things out for themselves. Richard rehearses some of the lessons he has learned, and these include not discussing sex with one's parents or religion with priests (85–86). Don João counsels Richard not to fear losing his faith, but to take this step at his own pace (86).

Although Richard is grateful to Don João for the advice, Richard is still afraid of the nagging doubts that he is having about religion. Don João is later tried for seducing and impregnating Genevieve Freitas, but he goes completely mad before a trial could begin. What hurts Richard the most is that "the prosecutor discovered that João Pete Mañoel did not believe in God, and in the Catholic town of Santa Clara that was perhaps worse than the seduction of Genevieve Freitas" (90).

We learn of attitudes toward Judaism in another episode that involves Ricky Malatesta, the kid at the top of the class in Richard's school. Ricky is an egotist, but he gains Richard's respect when he fights and loses to Zelda on five consecutive days. Ricky tells Richard that he wants to change his name to something that sounds less Italian. Ricky says, "I oughta get me a Jewish name, 'cause they make money. The bastards got all the money in the United States tied up!" (111).

Richard thinks this type of thinking is flawed and asks Ricky if he's ever even seen a Jew. Ricky tries to reverse matters by asking Richard if he has ever seen "a Yid." Richard says, "I see pictures of Jesus Christ all the time. He was a Jew." Yet, Ricky replies, "Yeah, but He was a good guy. That's why all the other Jews killed Him—anybody knows that—and besides

He's God, for Christ's sake" (111). Thus, Ricky represents a sort of mindless anti-Judaism infecting even well-schooled people.

As Richard grows into adolescence, he becomes obsessed with masturbation, and relishes telling the priest of his practice in the confessional. The priest insists that Richard is "insulting God," but Richard is already losing his fear of God (115–116). Richard's loss of faith is further chronicled in a conversation that begins when Richard's father asks why he is so late coming home. Richard responds that he must live his life. His father tells him that he has no life as an individual but lives in a communal manner. Richard tells his father that he is sick of living in a household where, among other things, he has to listen to his mother's beliefs about God (130). As the argument heats up, Juan Rubio appeals to theological fatalism and tells Richard that God wants them to live the way they do (131). Richard retorts, "Then there is something wrong with God" (131). Richard's father becomes terrified of the changes he sees in his son.

The demise of Juan Rubio's family continues when his wife no longer wishes to be a housekeeper and when his son no longer thinks the needs of the family should come before his own. Richard realizes that adjusting to American culture is part of the problem, and it is noted that "the transition from the culture of the old world to that of the new should never have been attempted in one generation" (135).

Richard's father eventually leaves the household altogether. Thereupon the mother suggests to Richard that they should all go to church so that things will get better (172). Richard finally sees an opportunity to proclaim his atheism: "No, Mamá. You go to your church and light the candles to your God. I am finished with such things . . . I have left the Church. It is now a long time since I have been to Mass, although I have believed all along. But now I find that I am through believing. I have not told you of this, because of what it would do to you—of what it is doing to you." His mother desperately demands a clarification of what Richard no longer believes, "What is this you do not believe? You do not believe in what?" Richard provides the definitive liberating reply: "I no longer believe in God" (172).

His mother argues that one cannot live a good life without Christianity, without religion. But Richard insists that this is a myth. He says, "I am good, and in my way I am a better Christian than most Christians I know" (173). However, Richard concedes that his mother needs her faith to live her life (173). At this point his mother knows she has lost both of her men.

As World War II begins, we find Richard still contemplating his future. He is willing to go to war, but he is not prepared to die. He likes living. He lives to find out about himself; individualism is the key to survival for him. At the end, Richard will never come back to his previous way of life. At this point, we remember some of the poignant words of Richard's father, who earlier said that he "was unaware that he was fashioning the last link of events that would bring him to America and the American way of life" (129). Narration tells it as such: "Had Juan Rubio been faced with the problem of explaining himself what had caused the imminent disintegration of his family, he would have been unable to do it" (135).

Critical discussion

Raymund Paredes (1982, 58–60) has criticized *Pocho* for promoting "an illusion against the weight of Chicano experience in this country." The illusion Paredes perceives is the hope that an individual can be evaluated on merit rather than ethnicity. However, insofar as religion is concerned, *Pocho*'s disillusionment with religion is a theme often repeated in U.S. Latina/o literature. Villarreal was very acute (*pace* Paredes) in outlining the reasons for this disillusionment.

One of the reasons Richard moves toward atheism is simply that he sees hypocrisy in religion. This coincides well with studies that cite perceived hypocrisy as a important reason for leaving religious institutions (Brinkerhoff and Mackie 1993, 253). Richard sees religion mostly as the cause of conflict and division among adults; he sees organized religion as intolerant. For Richard, there is no necessary link between being good and being religious. In fact, Richard argues that he may even be a better Christian without God. Ethics can be divorced from religion and may even improve without religion.

In sum, the story portrays atheism itself in a positive light, even though the transition from belief to disbelief is in many ways a destructive process. *Pocho* is indeed the chronicle of a Mexican family as it assimilates into American life. Even though it involves disintegration of their way of life in Mexico, that too can be in part a good thing. Entrance into the American way of life brings with it greater rights for women. It also comes with the freedom, should one choose, to be an atheist.

Case Study 2: . . . *And the Earth Did Not Devour Him* (1971)

As mentioned above, theodicy is the philosophical attempt to explain the existence of evil in light of the claim that there is a God. If there is an

157

all-good God, then he would not wish evil to exist. If he is all-powerful, then he could prevent or destroy evil. If one admits that evil does exist, then one can relate this to God's existence in at least four ways (see Geisler 1974, 328; McCloskey 1992):

1. God is all-powerful but not all-good.

2. God is all-good, but not all-powerful.

3. God is neither all-good nor all-powerful.

4. God does not exist at all.

In . . . *And the Earth Did Not Devour Him*, the story of a boy's lost year becomes, in part, an exploration of the fourth option, just as *Pocho* had been partly an exploration of the first option.

The landmark story, which won the prestigious Quinto Sol Prize, is written by Tomás Rivera. According to the biography written by Julián Olivares (1991, 13–46), whose edition of Rivera's works we are utilizing, Tomás Rivera was born in 1935 in Crystal City, Texas. His family consisted of migrant farm workers, who moved between Texas and northern states in search of work. Despite his impoverished upbringing, Rivera managed to earn an undergraduate degree in English education in 1958 from Southwest Texas State University. After receiving his master's degree in education from the same institution in 1964, Rivera earned a Ph.D. in romance literature from the University of Oklahoma in 1969. His ascent in academia was rapid, and he was chancellor of the University of California at Riverside at the time of his sudden death in 1984.

As Rivera (1991, 365) has noted in one of his critical essays, his authorial intention involves remembrance, discovery, and volition. For Rivera, remembrance is a basic form of Chicano literature. People remember, and those remembrances form the basis of the stories of the Chicano people. Rivera also says that he "deliberately used in [his] work young characters for the most part" (367) because the purest act of discovery is that of a child becoming aware of himself as a person. Likewise, the focus on the individual in respect to his/her environment is also another deliberate part of Rivera's writing. By telling a story about a particular individual, the nature of humanity can be discovered.

Those elements of Rivera's philosophy are combined in our featured story. The story is about the remembrance of a lost year by a particular

Chicano migrant working boy, who remains nameless. The setting of the story is 1945–1955, with the Korean War playing an important background. The story tells of the slave-like existence of Chicanos in the fields and the silence of God regarding their plight.

Almost from the beginning, the character sees many of his parents' beliefs as superstitions. His mother, for example, always leaves a glass of water under his bed for the spirits. Yet, "what his mother never knew was that every night he would drink the glass of water" (153). Telling her is something he might do when he grows up. His mother indeed is quite religious. She prays for the return of her older son from the Korean War. In return for her son's safe return from Korea, she makes a promise to pay homage to the Virgin de San Juan and Virgin of Guadalupe.

The boy explores the possibility that God does not exist. His skepticism becomes even more concrete when one night he decides to call the devil himself at exactly midnight. But when he calls the devil, the latter does not appear. The boy hypothesizes that "If there isn't a devil, maybe there also isn't . . ." (173). The apodosis of this conditional sentence is left as an ellipsis. The point might be that he does not really wish to say openly that perhaps there isn't a God. In fact, he again repeats his conditional statement, and adds "No, I better not say it. I might get punished" (174). There is still a sliver of belief left in him despite his growing skepticism.

Yet, the boy also says, "There is no devil, there is nothing" (174). He adds: "Those who summoned the devil went crazy, not because the devil appeared, but just the opposite, because he did not appear" (174). The implication seems to be that the discovery of the absence of Satan drove people crazy precisely because it means that God might not exist. Perhaps a world without God could be too much chaos for the human mind.

A short time later, the boy hears his parents clamoring for God's mercy. Prayers to God have not prevented his aunt and uncle's deaths from tuberculosis. His anger grows at seeing the impotence of his mother's rituals, and he discharges his anger in a spate of words (177):

What's to be gained from all that, Mother? Don't tell me you think it helped my aunt and uncle any. How come we're like this, like we're buried alive? Either the germs eat us alive or the sun burns us up. Always some kind of sickness. And every day we work and work. For what? Poor Dad, always working so hard. I think he was born working. Like he says, barely five years old and already helping his father plant corn. All the time feeding the earth and the sun, only to one day, just like that, get struck down by the sun. And there you are, helpless. And them, begging for God's help . . . Why, God doesn't care about us . . . I don't think there even is . . . No, better not say it, what if Dad gets worse. Poor Dad, I guess that at least gives him some hope . . . I tell you God could care less about the poor. Tell me, why must we live here like this? What have we done to deserve this? You're so good and yet have to suffer so much.

Here one can see many elements of biblical meditations of the nature of suffering. In other ways, the boy's complaints resemble those of the author of Ecclesiastes, one of the most radical thinkers and skeptics in the Bible (Crenshaw 1987, 23–28). The Ecclesiastes author questions the purpose of any human activity. Consider, for example, the following passage from Ecclesiastes 2:18-21:

I hated all my toil in which I had toiled under the sun, seeing that I must leave it to those who come after me—and who knows whether they will be wise or foolish? Yet they will be master of all for which I toiled and used my wisdom under the sun. This also is vanity. So I turned and gave my heart up to despair concerning all the toil of my labors under the sun, because sometimes one who has toiled with wisdom and knowledge and skill must leave all to be enjoyed by another who did not toil for it. This also is vanity and a great evil.

The complaints of the boy are reminiscent of the questions that the biblical Job poses as he grapples with his own suffering. Unbeknownst to Job, God has made a bet with Satan, who tests whether human beings are truly faithful to God (Job 1:10-12). Job, like the boy in our story, is full of questions. Compare, for example, Job's lament (6:30–7.7):

Is there any wrong on my tongue? Cannot my taste discern calamity? Do not human beings have a hard service on earth, and are not their days like the days of a laborer? Like a slave who longs for the shadow, and like laborers who look for their wages, so I am allotted months of emptiness, and nights of misery are apportioned to me. When I lie down I say, "When shall I rise?" But the night is long, and I am full of tossing until dawn. My flesh is clothed with worms and dirt; my skin hardens, then breaks out again. My days are swifter than a weaver's shuttle, and come to their end without hope. Remember that my life is a breath; my eye will never again see good.

The answer in Rivera's story is less clear than the answer in Job. In Job, suffering originates in the arbitrary decisions of God. Job never doubts that there is a God, but he does doubt that God is necessarily all good and just. The moral of Job's story may be that human beings have no right to know why God does anything.

160

In Rivera's story, the boy does something that Job never does—"He cursed God" (179). However, that curse also adds to his skepticism. If there were a God, the boy expects the earth to open up and swallow him as punishment for his curse. The narrator tells us (180):

> For a second he saw the earth opening to devour him. Then he felt his footsteps against the earth, compact, more solid than ever. Then his anger swelled up again and he vented it by cursing God. The fact that the earth did not swallow him is the final empirical confirmation that there is no God. This realization brings serenity to his life. The next day he kicks the earth again, and says, 'Not yet, you can't swallow me up yet. Someday yes, but I'll never know it.'

The last comment apparently refers to his final burial, which he believes will not involve any conscious afterlife.

A parallel story revolves around the existence of Santa Claus. The children are excited about Christmas, but they receive nothing. The mother has suffered an anxiety attack on the way to do her Christmas shopping and so brings back nothing. The solution suggested by the father is to tell the children that Santa Claus does not exist. The mother wants to tell them that if Santa does not bring them anything, it's because the Wise Kings, who come on January 6, will bring them things. However, January 6 arrives, and nothing is delivered. The children do not ask for explanations, as apparently they understand that neither Santa Claus nor the Wise Kings exist.

The boy's growing skepticism is accompanied by his growing cynicism about religious institutions. Catholic priests are not portrayed well in Rivera's work. For instance, the priest would charge five dollars for every car and truck he blessed for the people headed north (203). The priest uses that money to travel to Spain. Upon his return, the priest places postcards at the entrance of his church, depicting a very modern church. The postcards are meant to instill a desire for a more modern and grander church building, but the people begin to deface the postcards. Rivera concludes, "The priest was never able to understand the sacrilege" (203). One could interpret "the sacrilege" as the people's in defacing the postcards or as the priest's in using the postcards in trying to raise money from impoverished people.

Rivera's view of First Communion is a meditation on hamartiology, the set of teachings relating to sin. The boy sees First Communion as primarily a terrorist device, especially since "Mother had placed a picture of hell at the head of the bed" (182). His whole room, in fact, was decorated with depictions of Satan, something which led him to obsess about being saved from evil (182).

The process of instilling fear continues with the discourse of the nun who teaches the children about First Communion. She emphasizes that one cannot lie to God and that all actions are eventually to be discovered. Thus, one ought to confess thoroughly. Fear causes overcompensation in the boy's confession, and so he admits to two hundred sins even when he has just committed 150.

The implication of the vignette is that the boy could lie to the priest, with no apparent consequences. He feels a need to know more about everything, but thinks that "Maybe everything was the same" (185). Such a statement recalls Ecclesiastes 1:9: "What has been is what will be, and what has been done is what will be done; there is nothing new under the sun."

Protestants don't fare much better. Indeed, one vignette involves a Protestant minister who comes to town promising to bring a man who will teach them skills needed to escape field work. The man who comes, however, simply ends up spending his days in a trailer with the minister's wife and eventually runs away with her. The promises of Protestant ministers aren't subject to question either.

At the end of the story, the boy reminisces about his journey, "to discover and rediscover and piece things together. This to this, that to that, all with all" (220). The boy climbs a tree in his backyard and spots a palm tree in the horizon. He imagines someone looking back at him from that palm tree, and he waves "so that the other could see that he knew he was there" (220). In short, his self-discovery involves not the discovery of some relationship with God, but rather the discovery of the value of a relationship with other human beings.

Critical discussion

Tomás Rivera appears to be ambivalent about the value of religion. On the one hand, belief in God provides hope to some people (e.g., his father), even if based on lies or myths. The boy understands this and decides not to interfere with that aspect of religion. Alternatively, the boy's self-discovery involves a healthy skepticism about the existence of God. His problems are not solved with prayer. Rather meditation and remembrance are what eventually make him a satisfied human being. God, if God exists, is irrelevant to the boy's search for self.

But this doubt about the existence of God is also linked with the problems seen in organized religion. Like Oscar Acosta, Rivera portrays priests as greedy and out-of-touch with the people they are supposed to serve. Protestantism is no better. Sex and/or money drive ministers. Neither Catholicism nor Protestantism does much for the downtrodden and poverty-stricken members of humanity in these works.

Some of the symbolism appears to have religious overtones. For example, the boy goes out to the dump and is warned not to step where there is fire underneath (161). Such a scene invokes the image of subterranean hellfire—with the whole story pivoting on the threat that the earth may swallow him. It is interesting as well that both Rivera and José Villarreal allude to an image of the earth swallowing up those who displease God. The earth swallowing people up may ultimately derive from Mesoamerican ideas about the earth as a cosmic jaw (see Carrasco 1999, 164–187), though the motif occurs in the Bible as well (Num. 16:32).

Case Study 3: *The Comeback* (1985)

Ed Vega's *The Comeback* gives literary expression to the idea that God and religion are products of the human imagination. According to an interview (Hernández 1997, 197–210), Ed Vega, whose full name is Edgardo Vega Yunqué, was born in Ponce, Puerto Rico, in 1936. He and his family arrived in the mainland in 1949. After a stint in the Air Force (1954–1958), Vega earned an undergraduate degree in 1969 from New York University. He has taught at Hostos University, Hunter College, and the State University of New York at Old Westbury. Vega is also the author of *Mendoza's Dreams* (1987) and *Casualty Reports* (1991).

In many ways, *The Comeback* mirrors Ed Vega's own rejection of his religious upbringing. Although raised by a strict Baptist family, Vega states that at sixteen he was already an atheist (Hernández 1997, 198). One main reason he cites for his atheism is the restrictions imposed by the church on his adventurous sexual life. After Vega's arrival in the United States, his father established himself in a church that had been predominantly German Lutheran. When the Germans left, the church became mostly Latina/o. Despite his aversion to autobiographical writing expressed in the preface to *The Comeback* (xxi), Vega admits that this book does comment on his religious background (Hernández 1997, 199).

The central character of *The Comeback* is Armando Martinez, who is in a psychiatric ward at Stuyvesant Hospital, where a team of doctors attempts to cure him of an identity crisis. They believe he is really a Puerto Rican who has assumed the identity of a Euroamerican. Martinez believes himself to be a man named Frank Garboil, outlining a convoluted genealogy that includes Albanians and Eskimos. Garboil claims he is married to Joan Worthington Alcott, whose genealogy reaches back almost to the Mayflower, and who becomes pregnant with Peter, their first son, in 1961.

Garboil embarks on an identity change in 1970, while a professor of political science at Frick University (100). At that time, he wonders why he does not excel at sports, as some people think he should try hockey. So Garboil assumes the identity of a dead Latino Viet Nam veteran named Armando Martinez in order to secure a scholarship and become a college student. Garboil, now Martinez, excels as a hockey player. But after an argument with his hockey coach, Martinez experiences a head injury. He awakens to find himself at the Stuyvesant Hospital mental ward.

Meanwhile, Martinez's hockey exploits had made him a hero to a group of militant Puerto Ricans, who seek the independence of Puerto Rico.

This group becomes obsessed with liberating Martinez from the mental ward. The prime movers in this group are Maritza Soto and El Falcon, a mysterious man who has the ability to transform himself into a hawk. A detective named Juan Chota serves as an undercover officer who seeks to infiltrate the group and discover their plans.

The interactions among the characters in the story reveal a systematic critique of many religious traditions, and these critiques often involve sex.

This is the case in portrayals of Helen Christianpath, a missionary turned social worker in the mental institution. Christianpath was raised Protestant in the Midwestern town of Ravena, Kansas. A turning point in her life was when she saw her pastor, the Reverend Fleischer, urinating outside the church. After the he left for work in Africa, she saw angels, and says that only the memory of the pastor standing by that tree sustained her. She awaited his return (69) until she learned of his death. He was killed by a family of hippopotamuses as he undertook baptismal services in the Congo.

Another important commentary on religion occurs in the episodes detailing the interaction between F. William Kolodny, a private investigator, and John David Bacon, the president of Frick University, the Baptist institution where Garboil taught. Frick, the founder, was a religious heretic who manufactured contraceptives. He was run out of Massachusetts by opposing members of his church (208). A divinity school graduate, Bacon is a Baptist. He is so self-centered that he thanks the Almighty only as an afterthought. Kolodny was raised with a girl's name (Frances), and is obsessed with squeezing women's breasts in public.

Kolodny often dreams he is making love to a dead fish with twelve breasts (303). This imagery recalls the use of the fish as a symbol of Christianity and twelve as the number of apostles.

Kolodny pretends to be a newspaper man in order to investigate and expose the president of Frick (267), who has been using Garboil's salary line to recruit players. Bacon has also unsuccessfully begged Garboil to stay at his institution. When Kolodny calls to set up an appointment with Bacon, the latter becomes frightened. Bacon calls upon God's name, goes to the bathroom, and has a few drinks of bourbon. In response to Bacon's call, God appears in the bathroom. God looks like a stereotypical redneck, with bib overalls, a straw hat, and a blade of grass between his teeth.

God is annoyed that Bacon seems so pusillanimous, and he starts a long sermon admonishing Bacon. God tells Bacon all the good things he's done for his athletic prowess, and adds, "And dammit, boy. I never once told you nothing about what to do with your pecker" (270). When Bacon tries to speak up, God hushes him and continues (270–271):

> Do you think I like to explode volcanoes and have molten rock cover whole villages so that five minutes later it looks like Hell after a Saturday night party? I don't like it one bit, son, but I have to get some release. I don't drink, don't smoke, don't take no kinda dope . . . Son, I don't even mess around with Mary anymore. I've just lost the ole urge, even though it puts me in a hell of a spot. She's starting to spread rumors about me being anti-semitic because of that whole thing over in Europe with that maniac, Hitler. What am I supposed to do? How are people going to learn any respect. A volcano here, a tidal wave there . . . a massacre, a pogrom, an assassination, a war and once in a while a miracle to give the people some hope. I'm running out of tricks, boy.

Bacon finds the conversation encouraging, so he enlists a theater professor to impersonate Garboil to fool Kolodny. Talking with God results in more immoral behavior.

Bacon also has a peculiar way of combining Scripture with sex. Bacon's wife, Jo Ellen, tells another woman that, on her wedding night, David Bacon (178): "knelt between my thighs . . . He began praying. The Lord is my Shepherd, I shall not want. He maketh me to lie down in green pastures; He leadeth me beside still waters. He restoreth my soul: he leadeth me in the paths of righteousness for his name's sake. Yea, though I walk through the valley of the shadow of death, I will fear no evil: for thou art with me; thy rod and thy staff they comfort me." Jo Ellen says that because certain phrases (e.g., "rod") of this sacred Psalm acquire sexual connotations, she has an enormous orgasm.

Catholicism also comes under criticism. The narrator highlights the fact that a Catholic girl named Angela Piscatelli does not practice the sexual abstinence she proclaims. Later Garboil speaks about how "the Catholic Church should come out in favor of gay rights since there were avowed, albeit celibate, homosexual priests in their midst" (384). Again, the use of vocabulary is quite interesting, as "avowed" could also be an allusion to the vows that priests take. Mullvaney, another detective in the story, attempts to free himself, as a Catholic, from the guilt of masturbation. The Catholics also throw aspersions on Protestants, as when there is a reference to that "Protestant dingbat down at City Hall" (415).

Far Eastern religions are not exempt from criticism. During a failed attempt to spring Garboil from the hospital, the Puerto Rican militants use nitrous oxide. This causes Dr. Kohonduro, another staff member in the hospital, to have a religious vision, in which he sees himself as a cobra amidst a mass of orchids (408). He sat in a lotus position repeating a mantra and uniting with the universe, and then "saw his penis as a huge cobra from which orchids were being sprayed upwards into the heavens" (408).

The spiritualist traditions of Latinos are not spared satire either. Earlier in the story, Maritza, the Puerto Rican militant, proclaims that spiritualists "don't do anything but rip people off" (7). Nonetheless, Chota, the undercover detective, goes to see Doña Ursula Porrata, a spiritualist, for help against El Falcon. She believes that this hawk is the devil's messenger. Since the devil "likes to see virgins raped," one needs a female white virgin pigeon to trap the hawk (189). Chota purchases a dove named Pepe, who turns out to be quite aggressive. A ceremony then is performed in Doña Ursula's apartment. The ceremony requires Chota to sit in a fetid, smelly tub, filled with all sorts of revolting ingredients. The ceremony fails, and the pigeon flies about wildly, seemingly possessed. El Falcon escapes unharmed. Yet, Doña Porrata concludes that a *brujo* (sorcerer) named Yunqé might be able to help.

Judaism is not represented well in the character of David Friedenberg, a childhood friend of Garboil. When Garboil decides to change his identity to become a hockey player, he contacts Friedenberg, who is a New York bookie. Friedenberg, who thinks Garboil is Jewish, casts all sorts of aspersions on other races. He tells Garboil that "These Japs are smart as hell and vengeful" (248), which is a stereotype often directed at Jews. Friedenberg also speaks of the "Wall Street, gentile bastards that control all the legit money," which seems to imply that Jews control illegitimate money (250). Friedenberg also speaks about "Arab creeps" who killed his childhood sweetheart, Belle Howitzer (254).

But it is in the final chapter that the book's atheism is most cleverly expressed. The Cervantesque chapter heading gives us a clue, "The protagonist and his lady fair come face to face with their maker . . ." (459). Garboil has actually managed to escape from the mental hospital. He has been told about his unwitting role in the experiment of a government secret agency. He was born a Puerto Rican, but much of his non-Puerto Rican identity had been manufactured for him after he had lost his memory in an accident in Viet Nam. Garboil joins up with Maritza Soto, and tells her that he wants to learn how to be a real Puerto Rican. They go see a man named Vega (same name as the author), who might have the answers.

Vega tells both characters facts about themselves that they find amazing. They ask how he knows these things. The answer is simple: He, as the author of their story, is their creator. He can make reality into anything he wishes. He tells Garboil to tell Maritza, "A vivid imagination is good for only two things. One is the writing of fiction and the other is going crazy" (462). Aside from advice on how to deal with the politics of Puerto Rican independence, Vega denounces any thought of martyrdom for Puerto Rico (474):

> All of that crap is predicated on Christ on the Cross indoctrination . . . What more of a contradiction would you want? But at the same time, how fitting that the Church help people martyr themselves. Perfect. The hypocrisy is overwhelming . . . Martyrdom for the sake of the state is political cant and no less Christian, except that it's couched in Marxist terms. Forget it. Enslavement to doctrine. If you want that kind of life, you can have it. I don't want it. I believe in people and their capacity to unite and do good. Do you understand?

After exploring a number of options with their "maker," Maritza and Garboil garner the assurance that they will not vanish. Maritza, however, wants to be something other than invisible. Vega suggests that they can be "crypto-Puerto Ricans. Like Frank [Garboil] was for a long time. Like the crypto-Jews of Spain after they were supposedly kicked out. Not invisible but camouflaged. Keeping our traditions alive and continuing to work for independence" (478). After this conversation, both Maritza and Garboil seem satisfied with their answers and retire to a sleeping room. They drift into a peaceful sleep, but not before they hear "the steady tapping of a typewriter down the hall . . ." (479).

Critical discussion

Vega's secular humanist philosophy is evident throughout the book. Every religious tradition is found to be flawed in some way. God himself is portrayed as an interloper from the South. Moreover, Vega parallels the thought of Feuerbach, mentioned at the beginning of this chapter, and other atheists who hold that God is simply a human creation. Nothing can illustrate this more than the idea that the human author is the creator of every character, including God, found in the book. The human author has deified himself. Moreover, the author's statement that he believes "in people and their capacity to unite and do good" parallels that of Humanist Manifesto I (1933), article fourteen, "The goal of humanism is a free and universal society in which people voluntarily and intelligently cooperate for the common good" (American Humanist Association 1973, 1).

Of course, there are also inconsistencies in interpreting the human author as creator. Vega, after all, has not totally created himself, and some of his characters are based in reality. Sometimes, he contradicts himself. For example, he indicates in his preface that he finds autobiographical writing to be repulsive, yet states that at least part of this book is autobiographical. Thus, one would have to either conclude that Vega is contradicting himself, or that he uses contradiction as a conscious literary expression (a là Gloria Anzaldúa). Vega probably does not represent most Latinos but is best seen as part of an elite group of educated Latinos who have abandoned organized religion or religion altogether. They actually have adopted ideas found in educated Anglo-Saxon culture, which is more secular than the large majority of Anglos or Latinos.

Case Study 4: *The Rag Doll Plagues* (1992)

This book is unusual because it bears many aspects of science fiction, a genre that is not often associated with Latina/o literature. At the same time, the book illustrates how secular ideas have been subtly integrated into Latina/o literature without express uniform hostility to religion. The author, Alejandro Morales, is renowned in a number of different areas of creative activity. Currently, he is a professor in the department of Spanish and Portuguese at the University of California at Irvine. He received a master's degree (1971) and a Ph.D. (1975) in Spanish from Rutgers University. Perhaps his best known work is *Caras Viejas y Vino Nuevo* (1975), which was translated into English in 1981. More recently he published *Waiting to Happen* (2001), which heavily integrates religion. He is sufficiently well-known to have a book devoted to his work (Gurpegui 1996).

In a telephone communication on May 2, 2002, Morales described himself as a Catholic and a religious person. However, he also admits that his version of Catholicism is not necessarily congruent with the orthodox view. He prays to different deities, including ancestral spirits and Mesoamerican deities. Moreover, he also has room for secular scientific solutions to problems—some problems are best solved by science, even if some problems are also caused by science. Likewise, religion can be helpful and it can be problematic. For Morales, the term "religion" connotes an organized, hierarchical, and patriarchal entity; he prefers the term "spirituality" to describe his personal views.

The Rag Doll Plagues spans three distinct periods, with different generations of physicians as the central characters. The first period is set in colonial Mexico, where a plague known as "*La Mona*" (the doll) is ravishing the country. As the book opens, a physician named Gregorio Revueltas is arriving in Mexico City in 1788. He has been sent by the King of Spain to help stamp out this mysterious plague. As Dr. Revueltas enters Mexico City on a carriage sent for him by Don Juan Vicente, the viceroy of New Spain, he sees a culture that repulses and attracts him. He sees Indians, and wonders if they even have souls. He is against using *curanderos* (folk medicine practioners) and comments that "They had to be prevented from practicing their evil craft" (16).

But he sees the brutality of the Americas first hand, as Indians help transport his carriage across the river. One Indian, who falls under the weight, is crushed by the wheels of the carriage and is left to die as if he were an animal. Yet, for all his feeling of superiority, Revueltas understands his mission as God-given as well as economically beneficial to the empire. In short, he begins as a true imperialist.

Revueltas's main assistant in Mexico is Father Jude, a monk who is horribly disfigured from an encounter with French pirates in the Caribbean. His face resembles a skull because his nose and upper lips have been sliced away. Only a stinking hole remains where his nose once stood. Father Jude was saved by Mayan Indians, who nursed him back to health. He also learned folk medicine by living with a *curandero* for five years.

Father Jude also seems to offer a window into the morals of Catholicism in colonial Mexico, as when he casually offers Dr. Revueltas the service of prostitutes in case he needs "sexual alleviation" (22). Revueltas, however, is not interested. Father Jude tells Dr. Revueltas that *La Mona* (The Doll) manifests itself in ugly bruising that begins at the extremities and eventually consumes the patient. The plague has begun in the countryside and is moving toward the capital. The disease does not discriminate by "sex, race, age or rank" (21). The cachetic corpses left resemble pliable rag dolls, and hence the name of the plague. It is clear that this plague must be stopped before it depopulates Mexico and brings the Spanish colonial empire to an end (21).

The churches of colonial Mexico City were the primary points of urban organization. Yet, the churches co-existed with bordellos, which were a special object of Father Jude's ministry. Lewd acts were practiced openly, and Dr. Revueltas sees oral sex being performed right at the entrance to one of the bordellos. The spatial organization of colonial Mexico will be used as a contrast to the spatial organization seen in places that feature prominently in subsequent chapters.

Dr. Revueltas tries as best he can to stamp out the plague. However, neither prayer nor native medicine seems to help. Father Jude is afraid that using indigenous medicine will bring a charge of witchcraft by the Holy Office (33). Brutal amputations have been tried, but they also have failed. He despairs and exclaims at one point, "God, was there no beauty here? No peace, no joy? No love in New Spain?" (43).

The sufferings cause Dr. Revueltas to have visions. In one of these visions, an old man of about fifty, and a young man, eighteen to twenty years old, approach him as he stands outside a small adobe room. These characters seem to represent different sides of him; the young man is also named Gregorio. He sees a serpent coiled around Gregorio's body, while a man and a woman pray in Dr. Revueltas's room to the Virgin of Guadalupe. The old man, named Papá Damián, promises to be Revueltas's guide.

As the story of Dr. Revueltas nears its end, we find him transformed by the suffering he has seen. He writes a report recommending that the persecution of *curanderos* cease. He suggests that *curanderos* are better at saving lives than Catholic priests (40). While folk medicine cannot stop the plague, it does no worse than amputations in easing the pain of the afflicted.

More importantly, Revueltas has come to love Mexico and its people. He has shed most of his imperialistic attitude and adopted a new stance based on caring for the downtrodden. He even surrenders the betrothed he left behind in Spain. As that story ends, we see him holding Monica Marisela, a child he saves from the very womb of her dying mother, Marisela, the mistress of the viceroy of Mexico. The mother dies from the plague. Dr. Revueltas adopts Monica Marisela as his own, and together they place flowers on Father Jude's grave, who dies peacefully in his sleep. Marisela represents the future hope of the Mexican masses (Morales, telephone comm. May 2, 2002).

The second part of *The Rag Doll Plagues* is titled "Dehli," after a poor neighborhood of Orange County, California. This story is set in the 1970s, and the main character is Gregory, a descendant of the Dr. Revueltas of colonial Mexico. Gregory works at the Santa Ana Clinic, which caters to indigent populations, including many Mexican Americans from the *barrio*. Gregory falls in love with an Anglo girl named Sandra Spears, who is an aspiring stage actress and loves Mexico. Sandra's family is very wealthy; her father has even given her a twelve-cylinder Jaguar automobile as a gift.

As in colonial Mexico, churches helped to establish the demographic geography of Orange County. Gregory says, "There were two churches that seemed to be important in my life. One was Our Lady of Mount Carmel, the Simons Church, where Father Charles attended to his 'wild savages' . . . I spent practically a fourth of my youth participating in activities organized by the Catholic Church" (73–74).

Gregory tells us that "The second important church was the United Anglican Church of Whittier" (74). This is where Sandra's family goes. In the church, Sandra's uncle (mother's brother) is getting married to an Asian girl. The father makes a bigoted remark about mixed marriages but is quickly rebuffed by his wife. The wedding serves to remind Gregory of his position vis-à-vis this Anglo world; he sees himself as ugly compared to Sandra. At this wedding he also contemplates her breasts, which "became temples where the mysteries of blood and desire resided" (74).

The episode at the Anglo church shows a reversal in the status of the Revueltas family as they have migrated into the United States. While Gregory's ancestor, Dr. Revueltas, once saw the Indians as his inferiors, now Dr. Revueltas's own progeny is seen as declassé in an Anglo world. Another parallel is that Gregory has visions of an old man. In another vision, he sees Sandra's face transformed into two great serpents. Unlike his ancestor, Gregory decides not to save a fetus about to be born to a dying drug-addicted mother. Dr. Flink, who is identified as Jewish, convinces Gregory that it is better that the child not be born.

As the story progresses, we learn that Sandra is a hemophiliac, a condition she first tried to hide from Gregory. She loses a child because of her disease. Nonetheless, she is able to stage a play, titled "Blood Wedding," that becomes very successful in attracting Chicano youths. The play is about how love and passion inevitably drive some people to their own death (89). Eventually, the play becomes so successful that the white politicos of Orange County shut it down for fear that their space will be overrun by inhabitants of the Mexican *barrios*.

Later, Sandra is involved in an automobile accident in her Jaguar and nearly bleeds to death. She discovers that she has AIDS, probably as a result of a blood transfusion. People become hesitant to work with her on plays. She now needs more care than ever from Gregory. The AIDS plague, just like the *La Mona* plague in colonial Mexico, helps to symbolize the plague of racism of the society (Morales, telephone comm. May 2, 2002). But Gregory, like his ancestor, also neglects his beloved for the sake of his patients. Once, when visiting the grave of his father, his mother asks, "When was life really ours?" (110). Gregory ponders this and says: "We were not who we were, in the past, in the present, in the future . . . My lonely collective face was everyone's face" (110–111).

Gregory decides to take Sandra to Mexico City. He stops by the Jesuit Seminary and encounters Señora Jane, the librarian. She has saved thousands of books that had once been destined for destruction by the Catholic Church. Among the books are the writings of the colonial Dr. Revueltas. She gives Gregory and Sandra a tour of the place, and they see the graves of Dr. Revueltas, Father Jude, and Monica Marisela. Doña Jane explains that this is holy ground, where the sick come to be cured by the spirits of the people buried there.

Shortly thereafter, Sandra begins her final days on earth. But the women of the Jesuit seminary tell her not to fear death. Gregory explains that death and decay are part of the cosmic order and are to be loved rather than disdained (119).

Gregory sees Papá Damián helping Sandra and praying to the Virgen de Guadalupe. *Curanderas*, who were not afraid of Sandra's illness, also helped with a variety of cures, including the use of mysterious "luminous rocks from the heavens" (126). In the final death scene, we see Don Clemente, another spiritual guardian who has a jaguar. He is to watch for the coming of Death. We also see Papá Damián. Sandra finally expires, surrounded by her loved ones (129).

The third section of the book is titled "LAMEX," the name of a futuristic part of an entity called the Triple Alliance, composed of parts of what used to be the United States, Canada, and Mexico. Lamex stretches from the center of Mexico to the Pacific Coast of what used to be the United States. The central character is also named Gregory, and his grandfather was the Gregory we encountered in the 1970s. Gregory, the medical director of the Lamex Health Corridor, lives in the late twenty-first century in a city called Temecula, which is categorized as a "Higher Life Existence" city. As the story opens, people of Temecula are going to see a play called "Ramona," which portrays "Indian, Mexican and Spanish cultures two hundred years ago in the region" (133).

Most Mexicans now live in a sector called the Middle Life Existence. This improvement comes about because 90 percent of the military forces of the Triple Alliance are Mexicans. The Mexican population of Los Angeles is about twenty-five million. Whites are irrelevant there, and the main alliance now is between Mexicans and Asians, with a high degree of intermarriage and economic cooperation. Around 2020 the United States-Mexico border had been abolished and *maquiladoras* (special border factories) seemed to be everywhere in that region.

Gregory is concerned about a plague that is raging in Chula Vista, a city in the Lower Life Existence, a sector for the underclass. Gregory notes that Chula Vista has an ironic name, as it means "beautiful view." Lower Life Existence cities are built around prisons. Rehabilitation has been abandoned as a strategy for managing criminals, so the families of prisoners, known also as "Lumpen," settled around the prison to form these communities.

Gregory is assisted by Gabriela "Gabi" Chung, who is partly bionic. She has a hand, whose fingertips are equipped with laser surgical instruments and "knowledge cylinders" (136). She is part of a trend in which the "world had turned against humanity" in favor of computerized people. Papá Damián and Gregory's grandfather also assist Gregory as sorts of cyber-ghosts who transcend time and store more historical data than normal computers (136). He also prays to God for help in combating the plague.

Plagues now are generated by pollution. Huge masses of filth have even taken on a life of their own in the Pacific and must be guarded by ships of the Triple Alliance. The plagues are spontaneous, appearing anywhere at any time. The emanations caused by polluted masses can travel through the air, killing thousands at a time. One woman they encounter is swelling up like a balloon. Gabi extracts some liquid from her that turns out to contain plutonium oxide. They now must help dispose of these contaminated bodies.

The plague has also infected a Higher Life Existence city called Los Cinco Cielos, where the wealthy are dying. However, Gregory has discovered a medical oddity that proves helpful. In examining a soldier from Mexico City, Gregory finds a low white cell count that should mean the soldier is dead. Yet, the soldier seems perfectly healthy. Further research in Mexico reveals that the blood of people from Mexico City had mutated to the point they could survive in the most highly polluted environments (165). Transfusions from these individuals may help cure sick people.

Gregory and Gabi return to Los Angeles to try out their theory. Although there is some resistance at first, Gregory's experiments result in success. Gregory realizes that this mutated Mexican blood, previously regarded as inferior, now was a gift to the world (181).

However, the most challenging case comes when he meets Elena Tarn, the first directorate of the Triple Alliance. She has a daughter named Udina, who is very ill. Tarn asks Gregory to help cure her. He draws samples from the soldier in whom the mutated blood was first discovered. The treatment works, so the soldier and all those having the precious blood are treated like royalty. Mexicans from Mexico City become in such demand that people in the Los Angeles areas must produce proof that they are natives of Mexico City. Anglos and others now want to intermarry with Mexico City Mexicans in order to improve their progeny's chance of survival. Gregory provides the following summary that applies to the whole book (195):

> In the past, it was Mexican Indian blood that was sacrificed to the sun forces; it was Mexican blood that was spilled during the conquest; it was Mexican blood that ran during the genocidal campaign of the Spanish Colonial period; it was Mexican blood that stained the bayonets during the war of Independence and the Mexican Revolution of 1910; it was Mexican blood that provided the cheap labor to California during the first half of the nineteenth century and that now provided the massive labor force in the maquiladora factory belt; it was Mexican blood that provided the millions of men and women that constituted more than ninety percent of the Triple Alliance military forces. It was Mexican blood that guaranteed a cure and prevention from lung disorders. In a matter of time Mexican blood would run in all the population of the LAMEX corridor. Mexican blood would gain control of the land it lost almost two hundred and fifty years ago.

The story ends with Gregory enjoying his success and living in Tarn's fortress, which he calls the Library. Gabi has committed suicide by electrocuting herself when she realizes that her robotic arm is being rejected by her human body. In the end, Gregory tells us that he is no longer himself, but that he has been transfigured into all of his ancestors.

Critical discussion

The book is obviously a commentary on Mexican American history, but it also bears many subtle implications concerning religion. In the colonial period, churches formed the center of human geography. People were religious, but religion did nothing to stamp out the plague of that time. God was nowhere to be seen. In the middle period, churches served to divide populations into races and classes. In the final period, human geography, particularly in the Lower Existence sector, is not centered around churches, but rather around prisons. This symbolizes the movement away from organized religion that Morales (telephone comm. May 2, 2002) sees for the future.

In the third, futuristic period, we also see that salvation, especially for Mexicans, is not to be found in religion at all. In the third period, the savior of humanity is not God or the blood shed by Jesus. Rather it is Mexican blood that has acquired mutated immunobiological properties. Thus, the book has completely abandoned any notion of Christian soteriology.

God is nowhere to be found in Gregory's final explanation for what stops the plague at Lamex. Even the visions that were previously interpreted as supernatural are now interpreted as scientifically explainable time travel.

The science fiction element is unique in relation to the corpus of U.S. Latina/o literature. Science fiction is a genre with a name attributed to Hugo Gernsback (1929). Definitions are difficult to establish, but Moskowitz (1963, 11) provides one, "Science fiction is a branch of fantasy identifiable by the fact that it eases the 'willing suspension of disbelief' on the part of its readers by utilizing an atmosphere of scientific credibility for its imaginative speculations in physical science, space, time, social science and philosophy" (for other definitions, see also Hillegas 1979). We may even provide a more succinct definition: science fiction is a creative genre that significantly integrates, or centers on, the possibilities and consequences of science and technology.

The genre of science fiction has been a prime bearer of religious messages. Important studies of the relationship between religion and science fiction have been contributed by Frederick A. Kreuziger (1986). Anthologies of scholarly studies include those edited by Robert P. Reilly (1985) and Robert E. Meyers (1983). Mayo Mohs (1971) provides an anthology of science fiction stories with a religious element. Morales's novel might be compared with Walter M. Miller's *A Canticle for Leibowitz*, first published in 1959, which deals with a future holocaust interspersed with a role for the Catholic Church. Morales's notion that Hispanics and Asians will be the most important ethnic groups of the "American" future echoes a number of current scholarly studies (see Hamamoto and Torres 1997).

In any case, Morales attempts to blend the relatively recent genre of science fiction with what is often termed as "magical realism," which is characterized by the insertion of fantastic and magical events in a matter-of-fact style into otherwise prosaic narratives. The genre is represented by, among other authors, Gabriel García Marquez in *One Hundred Years of Solitude* [*Cien años de soledad*]. Euroamerican scholars often uncritically assume magical realism to be the "definitive style of Latin America" (Poey 29; see also Zamora and Faris 1995).

In sum, Morales has a mixed attitude toward secularism. While he is not an atheist, he sees problems with religion. He sees room for scientific solutions to future problems. God is sometimes irrelevant, as in curing the plague in Lamex. Science replaces orthodox Christian soteriology, but the former may bear both good and bad consequences for humanity and for the Mexican people.

Case Study 5: *How the García Girls Lost Their Accents* (1991)

Julia Alvarez is the only Dominican American writer in our study. In this novel, we have a representation of passive secularism from a female viewpoint, especially in the character of Yolanda, who is the alter ego of Julia Alvarez. According to biographical sources (e.g., Rosario-Sievert 1997; J. Alvarez 1998), Julia Alvarez was born in New York City in 1950, though she spent much of her youth in the Dominican Republic. Her father was a physician who was forced from the Dominican Republic in 1960 because of his opposition to Rafael L. Trujillo (1891–1961), the military dictator of that country. Alvarez details some of these struggles in her book on the García girls. Alvarez was trained in American colleges, earning a bachelor of arts degree from Middlebury and a master of fine arts from Syracuse University in 1975. She has spent much of her time teaching at Middlebury College (Vermont), where she is listed as a professor of English.

How The García Girls Lost Their Accents is principally about four sisters (from oldest to youngest): Carla, Sandra, Yolanda, and Sofia (Fifi). They are the daughters of Carlos García, a physician, and Laura (de la Torre), a homemaker. The daughters are described as growing up "in the late sixties" (28). As has often been the case in other books by women authors (e.g., by Castillo, García), the Alvarez's views on religion are manifested as the characters speak about themselves.

The book is divided into three parts, told in reverse chronological order, 1989–1972, 1970–1960, and 1960–1956. Episodes take place in both the United States and in the Dominican Republic. The book opens with a chapter on Yolanda's birthday, being celebrated in the Dominican Republic. At this time, Yolanda has been away from that country for five years. Her aunts are commenting on her Americanization, among other things. Very little of any conversation has to do with religion, except for a stray comment by Tía Flor about attending "novena" (5).

Yolanda's stance toward Catholicism is also revealed in her ideas about sex. She has difficulty finding a partner who understands her "peculiar mix of Catholicism and agnosticism" (99). In an episode where she attempts to explain her hesitancy to sleep with a boyfriend, Yolanda says "By then, I was a lapsed Catholic; my sisters and I had been pretty well Americanized since our arrival in this country a decade before, so really, I didn't have a good excuse" (87). What she is really concerned about is getting pregnant. She is on birth control, and has resolved to trade in her "immortal soul for a blues kind of soul" (102). For her, it is a "sin" for a man to think he could sleep with a woman just because he brought her wine five years after leaving her (103).

Yolanda is very concerned about discovering her body. While she was growing up in the Dominican Republic, she and her sister Sofía had exposed themselves to their male cousin. At that point she recalls the religious instructions of a nun, who told her that her body was a temple. The nun also alluded to how God had clothed Adam and Eve after they had sinned in the Garden of Eden (234). When she is older and has moved to America, Yolanda brings *Our Bodies Our Selves*, a book about women's bodies, into the house. When still older she sometimes speaks to her lover about "the Great Mother and the holiness of the body and sexual energy being eternal delight" (48).

Carla also uses religion for wish fulfillment. In one instance, the family is celebrating their first anniversary in the United States. Carla wonders what her family will wish for now, and she exclaims, "Dear God . . . Let us please go back home." The narrator notes, perhaps satirically, that Carla "could not get used to this American wish-making without bringing God into it" (150).

The viewpoint of Haitian voodoo is expressed through the eyes of Sofía. She speaks about Chucha, the family's Haitian maid, in the last days before the move to the United States. Chucha, who represents yet another immigrant in the book, begins working for the family after appearing on their doorstep one day. She is described as being "blue-black." In the last days before the Garcias depart, Chucha does some "farewell voodoo . . . Chucha always had a voodoo job going, some spell she was casting or spirit she was courting or enemy she was punishing" (219). Laura gives Chucha, who sleeps in a coffin, her own room because the other maids are afraid of her powers. Chucha also narrates from her own viewpoint, describing her loving feelings for the departed family, even though she remembers "the insolence and annoyance of young girls with no faith in the spirits" (224).

Sandra seems to be quite religious while on the island. She recalls one episode where she is celebrating Christmas Eve in the National Cathedral. She sees some of the icons that were made by a crazed Dominican married to a German immigrant. Despite the odd talents of the human creator, these icons move her spiritually. In particular, she is drawn to a figure of the Virgin, in which Sandra finds her own likeness.

One example of Sofia's religious attitudes is seen in the story of her love affair with a German chemist named Otto. She meets him while on a "church trip" in Perú (59). Sofia, the only sister without a college degree, likes to talk about men. Upon her return to America, her father grows suspicious about the loss of her virginity. He finds proof in her correspondence filled with "unmentionable things" done with Otto (29). The father confronts her, "Has he deflowered you? That's what I want to know . . . Are you dragging my good name through the dirt, that is what I would like to know!" (30). Absent is any reference to religion. The father is explicitly concerned only with his own reputation, not with the breaking of any religious rules about sex.

The mother, Laura, reflects a mixture of traditionalism and benign flexibility. She does not "believe in sex for girls" (46). She enrolls them in Catholic School, fearing public schools because they teach evolution (152). Yet, the most elaborate chapter ("Daughter of Invention") about the mother reveals her secularization. The narrator notes that Carlos takes the girls to the Statue of Liberty on his free Sundays, but Laura believes that "Down in housewares were the true treasures women were after" (133). Going to church on Sundays seems irrelevant or a low priority for both parents.

Critical discussion

Alvarez's book exemplifies the belief that Americanization leads to secularization and a movement away from the family's Dominican

Catholicism. Of course, Dominicans don't follow orthodox teachings uniformly. Thus, González and La Velle (1985, 46) report that only 58.3 percent of Dominican Catholics "believe firmly" that artificial contraception is wrong. Seventy-five percent of Dominicans believe abortion is wrong, but 84.3 percent of those born in Cuba believe so. Some 79 percent of Dominican Catholics believe in intercession by saints, compared to 86 percent of those born in Cuba (39).

The Garcia girls do receive religious instruction in the Dominican Republic. But this education has very little effect on their behavior. Yolanda exposes herself to her cousin, despite the warnings given to her by the nun. Agnosticism concerning divine powers already begins in the Dominican Republic for at least some of the girls. We see Chucha complaining that the girls don't seem to believe in the spirits. Presumably, Catholics might believe in these spirits, even if regarded as demonic.

Nonetheless, the movement away from Catholicism, and even into agnosticism, becomes more pronounced as the girls become more Americanized. This abandonment of Catholicism seems to be manifested first and foremost in sexual practices. Yolanda, for example, hesitates to have sex, not because she fears breaking some divine law, but because she is afraid of pregnancy. Practicality replaces religious morality. Religious experimentation expands in the United States. We also see at least one daughter experimenting with goddess religions as part of her feminist development.

But most of the time, the family indulges in the secular consumerism that is American society. Visits to department stores or American monuments are more important than visits to church on Sundays. Religion is almost absent from the father's injunctions (honor is more important), and it is very weak with the mother's injunctions. The girls use "God" rhetorically and as a sort of good-luck charm. Religion no longer functions as an institutionalized systematic approach to life. In this book we have an example where the lack of discussion of religion speaks volumes about secularization.

Comparative summary

Justo L. González (1990, 26) states that "Among Hispanics, there is a growing tendency toward radical secularization and bitterness. This secularization, however, is not due to the intellectual difficulties with which academic theologians often deal but rather to the existential difficulty that the gospel of love is not translated into actual good news." González is partially correct. Our survey shows that secularism has many shades and many levels among U.S. Latina/o authors.

In *Pocho*, the wholesale rejection of religion by Richard Rubio is portrayed as a consequence of education and Americanization. Secularization seems total and hostile toward religion. In Tomás Rivera's work, atheism is portrayed as the result of the struggle with the problem of evil, manifested particularly by the struggle of Chicano migrant workers. His work has been perceived as more concerned with communitarian values than with the individualism seen in *Bless Me, Ultima* or in *Pocho* (Calderón 1991, 112). Ed Vega has a more systematic attack on religious traditions, finding all of them wanting. Instead, Vega deifies the human author and himself, thus putting into literary form what Feuerbach had put into philosophical form.

The Rag Doll Plagues also has a mixture of secularism and religion. Science, not consumerism, becomes the savior in the future. Soteriology has been biologized, but there is still some uneasiness with this secularization. In *The García Girls*, one finds a more flexible and passive attitude. Secularization, even if the result of Americanization, is not total and it is not particularly bitter or radical. Rather it results in a "peculiar mixture of Catholicism and agnosticism," at least for Yolanda. But the other family members don't seem as religious as they were in the Dominican Republic. Consumerism and individualism have become the new ultimate concern.

Within the larger corpus of U.S. Latina/o literature, one may note Aristeo Brito's *The Devil in Texas*, which has demythologized the devil into a metaphor for the racism and oppression of Mexican Americans. Essays by Richard Rodriguez (1983, 1992) also display secularist tendencies. In sum, U.S. Latina/o literature bears more secularist tendencies than overtly pro-Catholic ones. As such, U.S. Latina/o authors share attitudes found within American-educated elite society.

Chapter 8

Comparative Synthesis

D iscussion of religion permeates U.S. Latina/o literature. Since this study is not comprehensive, it is not proper to provide very precise or inflexible statistics about the findings. We are more impressionistic than scientifically precise here, more Monet and less a photograph. However, there is enough of a sample to yield useful comments about general attitudes toward religious traditions found in the corpus of literature studied here. We can also issue some educated observations about the religious themes that interest U.S. Latina/o writers.

The profile of U.S. Latina/o religion

As noted in our introduction, Samuel P. Huntington (2004), argues that American culture, which he identifies as "Anglo-Protestant" in nature, is being threatened by the growing Latino population. According to Huntington, Latinos do not share the main Anglo-Protestant core values such as individualism and the value of the English language. However, the study of religion in U.S. Latina/o literature shows that Huntington's fears, which are probably shared by many Americans, are misplaced. The U.S. Latina/o religious experience follows some of the normal developments one has seen in the longer history of relationships between empowered and under-empowered groups in America and elsewhere.

The fact that U.S. Latina/o religious traditions will change America is probably not in doubt. However, as opposed to the often violent way in which Anglo-Protestant culture changed native American and Latino cultures (e.g., the Mexican-American War, the colonization of Puerto Rico and Cuba), the religious traditions of U.S. Latinas/os are quite decidedly changing America in a nonviolent mode in which market and demographic forces play a more significant role. By studying U.S. Latina/o literature, Americans who share Huntington's discomfort may see that the interaction between Latino and Anglo-American traditions, far from being threatening, can be viewed as one of the more peaceful changes in culture that has been experienced in history.

The distinctive character of the U.S. Latina/o religious experience lies, first and foremost, in the particular triadic mixture of cultures that have interacted for the last five hundred years of Latin American history. Prior to 1492, European and Native American peoples had never mixed. Prior to 1492 Native Americans and Africans had never mixed. The U.S. Latina/o religious experience may be seen as the manifestation of the many ways in which Europeans, Africans, and Native Americans dealt with this triadic interaction after the Latin American experience became part of the preeminent imperial power that came to be known as the United States. Indeed, most U.S. Latinos became part of the United States at about the time when the United States was expanding southward and westward.

The religious experience of Latin America has been central to the construction of Latina/o literature. The fact that Catholicism has been the dominant European tradition in the Americas for the last five hundred years means that most U.S. Latina/o authors still reflect that Catholic experience in their writing. Protestantism, which is a newer tradition, is not as dominant in literature and will probably have a very checkered future in U.S. Latina/o literature. On the one hand, it is seen as a Euroamerican tradition and not a Latin American one. Thus, Protestantism may be seen as a sign of assimilation in literature. On the other hand, Protestantism faces more competition in the United States than Catholicism did for most of its history among U.S. Latinos. Therefore, overt Protestantism will probably not affect the literature to the extent that Catholicism did for much of U.S. Latino history.

However, many Anglo-Protestant norms and values identified by Huntington are reflected in U.S. Latina/o literature. These include the importance of individualism and the use of the English language. Most Latina/o authors are quite individualistic and use the English language predominantly to express themselves. At the most general level, therefore, we see a sort of reversal: The Euroamerican canon began as distinctively Protestant and has moved toward the inclusion of more Catholic and non-Christian authors, but the U.S. Latina/o canon has moved from a Catholic identity to a more religiously pluralistic identity that has assimilated many Anglo-Protestant norms, even if it does not espouse Protestantism overtly.

The religious configurations in different Latina/o subgroups has also affected U.S. Latina/o literature. We see, for example, that the interaction of indigenous and Catholic traditions are manifested most strongly in Mexican American literature. Cuban American, Dominican, and Puerto Rican literature, on the other hand, has more frequent reference to African religious traditions, as is evident in the work of Tato Laviera, Julia Alvarez, and Cristina Garcia. And, in all cases, how those traditions have been interacting with Euroamerican culture is a central theme. Attitudes toward this interaction have usually been negative insofar as Latinos have seen their religious traditions devalued in America.

The interaction of Latina/o sub-groups that formerly had lived quite independently of each other is another feature of the U.S. Latina/o religious experience. For example, it is in the United States that Cuban and Puerto Ricans have interacted with each other and with Mexican Americans in new ways and at new levels of intensity. We see this reflected in Ana Castillo's allusions to *santería* in *So Far From God*. The work of Tato Laviera mixes Cuban *santería* with Puerto Rican spiritism. James Roberto Curtis offers an Euroamericanized view of African traditions in *Shangó*.

The interaction of Latina/o sub-groups in the United States has prompted the construction of a pan-ethnic "Latino" identity. Of course, the fact is that there is no such thing as a homogeneous "Latino" identity. Such a pan-ethnic identity is always under construction and is subject to the vicissitudes of politics and economics, among other factors. To the extent that many Latinos will see a political and economic advantage in a pan-ethnic identity, then such an identity will thrive. To the extent that such a pan-ethnic identity is seen to suppress nationalistic identities, then there may always be an uneasy co-existence between pan-ethnicity and nationalistic identities.

It is just as important to note it is in the United States that many persons of Afro-Caribbean descent have confronted a "black" identity as configured by African Americans and Euroamericans. American notions of "race" are sometimes linked to how religion is viewed by Latinos. Piri

Thomas experimented with Islam precisely because he saw that religion as more affirming of his racial identity. Likewise, Cristina Garcia's *Dreaming in Cuban* shows how *santería* and race are interconnected.

U.S. Latinas/os have experienced both continuity and change as the traditions born in Latin America have become part of the United States.

In the case of U.S. Latinas/os, it is clear that even the most systematic attempts to erase indigenous roots never were entirely successful. Thus, folk indigenous practices were retained regardless of how the Catholic hierarchy tried to erase them. Nor can even the largest institutions and empires ever achieve complete geographical coverage. Thus, many places were only nominally Christian or Catholic even if the inhabitants might declare themselves otherwise. The fact that Catholicism never permeated all of Latin America explains, in part, why U.S. Latinas/os are often seen as not being very familiar with orthodox tenets of Catholicism or with the decisions outlined by Vatican II. However, most Euroamericans are also not that familiar with the orthodox tenets or documents of their institutions. Gallup and Castelli (60) report that "eight in ten Americans say they are Christians, but only four in ten know Jesus, according to the Bible, delivered the Sermon on the Mount." There has always been a level of disconnect between the elite and the populace.

The larger population of Latinas/os still reflect their Catholic heritage insofar as the various versions of the Virgin Mary are a very distinctive part of their devotion and symbolism. The Virgin of Guadalupe, for instance, is seen as an "essential" part of Mexican American identity by certain theologians (e.g., Andrés Guerrero). On the other hand, Protestantization is changing the very nature of what counts as the "essence" of a Latina/o identity. Catholicism or devotion to the Virgin of Guadalupe will probably not be the essential feature of Mexican American identity in the future. Rather Mexican American identity, like that of many other Latina/o sub-groups, will continue to evolve as it interacts with Euroamerican cultures.

Despite these distinctive aspects of the U.S. Latina/o religious experience, the interaction between Latinos and Euroamericans is not unlike what has been occurring since the dawn of recorded history in the ancient Near East. Some scholars note how flexible religious traditions can become when incorporated into empires. When the Romans destroyed the Jewish temple, for example, sacred space was reconceptualized by Jewish and Christian authors. Instead of emphasizing a geographical location, Paul emphasized that each body was now a temple (1 Cor. 3:16). The author of Revelation (21:22) argued that a temple would, in fact, not be necessary in the future because God himself would be the temple. Jews throughout history have struggled with the extent to which their identity is retained or lost within larger societies.

As is the case with under-empowered groups, U.S. Latinos are caught in a classic struggle between assimilation and the maintenance of their cultures. Since an important aspect of culture is religion, then it is not surprising that Latinos who seek to express themselves through literature will often comment on how religion offers a barometer of assimilation. Thus, it is difficult to understand Gloria Anzaldúa's affirmation of an Aztec religious identity in *Borderlands* unless one also understands that she is resisting assimilation to broader Euroamerican religious traditions. Nonetheless, her struggle is very "American" insofar as she values the individual's right to shape religion. Her focus on "borderlands" is actually a continuation of Frederick Jackson Turner's ideas about how the frontier has shaped American identity. Likewise, Julia Alvarez's *How the Garcia Girls Lost Their Accents* shows how assimilation to American culture is accompanied by secularization and abandonment of her family's Catholic culture.

In sum, the U.S. Latina/o religious experience shares much with the experience of many under-empowered groups throughout history. In America, U.S. Latino religious experience is changing the larger American society in a peaceful manner that should be less threatening than the way in which Euroamerican culture has sought to change Latino religious experience. Education and Protestantization are probably the most important factors in the extent to which Latinas/os retain many of the beliefs and practices that had been seen as "essential" parts of their identity in the past five hundred years. As shown more thoroughly below, U.S. Latino literature offers an important window into how Latino religious traditions are changing as more Latinos become educated.

The profile of U.S. Latina/o authors

As has been argued before, U.S. Latina/o authors represent the broader Latina/o community only in part. Catholic heritage has played a great part in the lives of Latina/o authors, and this is reflected in the amount of space given to Catholicism in the literature. The fact that few discuss Islam or Eastern religions at great length also would be consonant with the religious profile of the overall Latina/o population. The fact that African traditions are found among Caribbean writers more than they are found in

Mexican American authors reflects what might be said of those respective ethnic groupings on a broader scale.

But there are also major differences between U.S. Latina/o authors as a group and Latina/o communities at large. U.S. Latina/o authors form an elite educated group of Americans. Most authors have a college education, often with degrees in literature (see also Calderón 1991, 99; Soldatenko 1998). Most authors are well traveled. Many authors are college professors or have been college professors (e.g., Acosta, Alvarez, Anzaldúa, Curtis, Hinojosa, Morales, Rivera, Villarreal). At least two are or were lawyers (Acosta and Ruiz). Most authors have at least read about other religions. These are not the educational experiences of most Latinas/os. Given the educationally privileged nature of U.S. Latina/o writers, it would be difficult to sustain the thesis that any Chicana/o or U.S. Latina/o writer is part of a "Third World Continuum," something reflected in the work of Debra Castillo (1992; see also Rebolledo 1995, 2–3).

The fact is that most Latina/o authors strongly share the trends we see among college-educated Anglo-Americans. For example, among the general American population, the view of God as "father" ranges from 71 percent for those with less than a high school education to 48 percent of those with a college education (Roof and Roof 1984, 202). God as "master" drops from 63 percent to 44 percent for the same groups (202). The images of God as "father" and "master" are certainly rejected by Anzaldúa and Castillo, but they are also criticized by Acosta, T. Rivera, Ruiz, and Villarreal to some extent. We can do a similar analysis using other religious beliefs.

It is equally untenable to generalize that "All Latinos are metaphysicians" with "no pragmatic Yankee views" on religion (see Shorris 1992, 363). Sometimes there is more Yankee New England than there is authentic Aztlán among U.S. Latina/o authors. We must remember that even Alvarez sometimes describes herself as a "Vermont writer." Anzaldúa's *Borderlands* may be considered an updating of Frederick Jackson Turner's *The Frontier in American History*, which also speaks of a "mixed race" and glorifies individualism (see Turner 1920, 23, 30). Rivera (1991, 368) acknowledges the influence of O. E. Röllvaag, the Norwegian-American author who wrote about the miserable life of Norwegian immigrant farmers in *Giants in the Earth* (1927). U.S. Latina/o authors, in fact, show just as much or even more continuities with Anglo-American and European religious traditions than they do with authentic indigenous or African traditions of any type.

Likewise, most U.S. Latina/o authors are very critical of institutionalized religion, as is the case with most Americans featured in books such as Robert Bellah's *Habits of the Heart* (see also Bellah, 1998). Religion is seen primarily as individual and "experiential," something that the celebrated psychologist of religion William James thought was particularly "American." James ([1982], 31) said, "Religion . . . shall mean for us the feelings, acts, and experiences of individual men in their solitude, so far as they apprehend themselves to stand in relation to whatever they may consider the divine."

Many Latina/o authors have a more "generalized belief system," as was noted in a study of changing funeral patterns among Mexican Americans (Williams 1987, 210). Harold Bloom (1992, 32), the literary critic who has written on American religion, argues that "The American religion . . . [which] masks itself as Protestant Christianity, has ceased to be Christian." Bloom might likewise argue that U.S. Latina/o authors, just like most Anglo-American authors and the Anglo-American populace, have ceased to be orthodox Christians. Some might even be described as having a "religion without God" (see Billington 2002).

The broader Hispanic community has not gone as far. True, only about 40 percent of Americans go to a church on a weekly basis, whereas only 29 percent of college graduates attend a church weekly (Gallup and Castelli 1989, 35). Among Catholic Latinas/os, however, attendance one or more times per week is over 50 percent (González and La Velle 1985, 72). There are differences among Latina/o sub-groups; for example, Puerto Rican Catholics have very low rates of attendance (73). Even Hispanic college-educated Catholics attend Mass on Sunday/Holy days at a rate of 54.7 percent (75). However, if church attendance is the measure of commitment to institutionalized religion, then U.S. Latina/o authors whose works manifest dissatisfaction with organized worship (e.g., Anaya, Alvarez, Castillo, Anzaldúa, Acosta, Rivera, Villarreal) seem more like college-educated Anglo-Americans than like Hispanics or even like educated Hispanics in general.

Americans indeed have gravitated away from denominational affiliations to buffet-style religions centered on the self, on the individual. This is quite in line with American traditions that reach at least as far back as Thoreau and Whitman (see also Bruce-Novoa 1990, 78). Many U.S. Latina/o authors also reflect what some might regard as very Anglo middle-class or elitist preoccupations with Jungian psychology and archetypes (e.g., Anzaldúa, Anaya).

The rise in religious pluralism among Americans finds a resonance in U.S. Latina/o authors. In 1947, only 6 percent of Americans identified themselves as anything other than Protestant, Catholic, or Jewish. This trichotomous pattern was enshrined in Will Herberg's *Protestant-Catholic-Jew* (1955). By 1987, about 13 percent of American adults identified themselves as something other than these three (Gallup and Castelli 1989, 24). Likewise, we see a lot of Latina/o authors identifying themselves as other than a strict Catholic or Protestant (Anaya, Anzaldúa, Vega, Rivera, Villarreal, Castillo).

We find a disproportionate number of authors who professed, at one time or another, some form of atheism, agnosticism, or no religion (e.g., Alvarez, Curtis, Vega, T. Rivera, Ruiz, Villarreal). But only 7.4 percent of Hispanic Catholics surveyed by González and La Velle (1985, 31) indicated a lack of belief in God, and all of these had a graduate-school education. Secularized authors are indeed not representative of the Latina/o community.

The types of books that have been part of the U.S. Latina/o canon also attest to a middle-class American view of religion. Nicky Cruz, a zealous Protestant Christian, is not part of the canon, even if his writing differs very little from that of Piri Thomas, who is part of the canon. No books in our corpus are thoroughly pro-orthodox Catholic; fewer books are pro-orthodox Protestant. Few, if any, books criticize indigenous or African religions in an overt way. Curtis, who comes closest to a negative view of Mayombe, does so in an almost unwitting manner. Thus, Latina/o authors and the academy, for the most part, are anti-orthodox and exclude orthodox views from the canon.

From the viewpoint of a scholar of religion, few Latina/o authors show a thorough familiarity with any religion that they discuss. This is actually typical of most college-educated Americans, who might at most take an introductory course in world religions. Some authors indeed have very superficial prejudices, such as Anzaldúa's ideas about the "Old Testament." Others have read perhaps introductory textbooks, but are not familiar with the complexities of even Christian theology (e.g., Anaya). Others perpetuate Euroamerican stereotypes about indigenous traditions, especially in making the urban/imperialistic/patriarchal/graphocentric Aztecs paradigmatic of indigenous traditions (e.g., Anzaldúa, Anaya).

Some do seem to have read a bit more than the average American—e.g., Ed Vega and James Curtis—even though the latter's view of Mayombe might be disputed by Mayomberos. Insofar as religion is concerned, most U.S. Latina/o authors resemble middle-class educated Anglo-Americans more than they resemble the majority of Latinas/os. As noted already, we await the results of *Hispanic Churches in American Public*

Life. This survey will help test more of our speculations about how Latino authors compare with broader religious communities of Hispanics.

The author as religious reformer

Sixto García (1994, 5), a scholar of Latina/o theology, argues that a Hispanic theologian could be viewed as a "thinker, actor, poet, and prophet of the community." It is true that religious reformations are often wrought by influential writers. We may think of Luther and his ninety-five theses (1517), Saint Paul and his epistles, or Moses and his law. Whether they think of themselves as religious reformers or not, many of the Latina/o authors in our corpus parallel at least a few of the characteristics that some historians have ascribed to revolutionaries and reformers.

In a celebrated study of revolutions, Crane Brinton (1965) observed that revolutions were often lead by the educated and elite classes. Many revolutions began not because people had so little, but because they grew to expect more after a period of prodigious prosperity. Perhaps the best example was the American Revolution. In his study of the social background of the signers of the Declaration of Independence, Brinton (1965, 102) noted, "Of its fifty-three signers thirty-three held college degrees in an age when few ever went to college . . . There were five doctors, eleven merchants, four farmers, twenty-two lawyers, three ministers. Nearly all were affluent." Even if many of our authors started out impoverished, they would compare well with our "Founding Fathers" in terms of education and occupation, as our above unscientific survey shows.

We cannot claim that all of our authors are out to reform. Curtis seems more interested in providing an entertaining novel about *santería* than in reforming Catholicism. Hijuelos certainly does not seem a radical reformer. Nicky Cruz does not wish to reform his own institutionalized religion, but rather wishes to spread it and draw people away from religions he deems demonic. Alvarez seems more like a passive agnostic than a condemnatory reformer. But there are authors who probably desire a change in institutionalized religion. For example, Ruiz's *Happy Birthday Jesús* cannot be seen as anything but a plea for change.

Among the most vociferous "reformers" in the Latina/o corpus is Acosta. He preached reform; he wrote about reform; he lived for protests outside of churches. He was also an instructor of religion, even if only as a sort of stunt. Other "reformers" (e.g., Anaya, Anzaldúa, Castillo, Laviera, E. Rivera, T. Rivera) are quite vocal, even if not as radically activist as Acosta. Even if reformation is not their goal, the relatively wide distribution of their books offers readers alternatives to institutionalized religion. Whether they actually succeed in attracting converts is another matter.

Basic attitudes

Since our study has been attitudinal in focus, it now behooves us to summarize how U.S. Latina/o authors reflect attitudes toward the religious traditions that they inherited from Latin America, as well as the attitudes toward religious traditions encountered in the United States. Recall that we see the U.S. Latina/o religious experience as, in part, the ongoing denouement in America of a triadic interaction of European Catholic Christianity with African and indigenous traditions that began in Latin America. Upon incorporation into the American empire, many Latinos encountered Protestantism and important non-Christian religious traditions for the first time.

Indigenous religions are mostly represented positively. Anzaldúa, in *Borderlands*, sees Nahuatl religions, particularly those that center on goddesses, as part of her salvation from institutional and repressive Catholicism. Anaya in *Bless Me, Ultima* sees some indigenous traditions as good (emphasis on nature), and some as not so good (e.g., the golden carp, who brings destruction). Besides Nicky Cruz, it is difficult to find an author who is wholly negative about indigenous religions (or non-Christian religions).

African traditions are mostly represented positively. In fact, Tato Laviera uses Afro-Caribbean religions as an antidote to Catholicism. He believes that his people ought to return to those African traditions. Cristina García, though more secular, seems sympathetic to Afro-Caribbean religions. James Curtis has a mixed attitude, seeing Mayombe as more malevolent than *santería*, even if the motives arise out of a sort of literary utilitarianism.

Catholicism is almost universally criticized, ridiculed, or rejected. Acosta preaches against the institutional preference of Catholicism for the rich and elite at the expense of the poor. Rivera's "First Communion" shows that Catholicism does not always help overcome the racism that exists between Irish and Puerto Ricans. *Happy Birthday Jesús* focuses on the idea that Catholicism creates sociopaths through its nearly institutionalized ritual sexual abuse. Castillo's *So Far from God* provides a critique of the patriarchal nature of Catholicism. Hijuelos's *Mr. Ives' Christmas* is the only one in our set to see the Church as having a generally positive effect. Hijuelos does not dwell on any problems that the Church causes for race relations, the poor, individuals, or Latinas/os.

Vatican II, if meant to make Catholicism more attractive in the modern world, has not been successful, if one judges by U.S. Latina/o authors. The changes have simply not gone far enough for someone like Anzaldúa or Castillo, and probably never will go far enough for them. Liturgical changes have still not brought about changes in the proportion of Hispanic Catholic leaders. The misuse of money, so vehemently denounced by Acosta, would probably not be seen as any better today in light of recent scandals. Certainly, the sexual ethics of Catholicism are not appealing or being followed by many lay Catholics, and even less by our authors' characters. Only Hijuelos shows some sympathy for pre-Vatican II days (in the person of Ives's son).

Most writers have a negative attitude toward Protestantism. It is seen as comical, foreign, and disingenuous in Hinojosa's *Klail City*. Protestantism is seen only as a temporary fix in Thomas's *Savior, Savior, Hold My Hand*. But the most salient example of how Protestantism is still rejected by U.S. Latina/o authors is the virtual exclusion of Nicky Cruz, a zealous Pentecostal Protestant, from the canon. Otherwise, Protestantism, despite its growing significance, is still not as much a factor as Catholicism in U.S. Latina/o literature.

Judaism is portrayed in a mixed fashion. *The Autobiography of a Brown Buffalo* seems to spout forth many anti-Jewish stereotypes that Acosta may have assimilated from his Catholic or Gentile background. Other authors and characters manifest equally scattered anti-Jewish sentiments (e.g., Lourdes in *Dreaming in Cuban*). Nicholasa Mohr is quite positive, particularly as she sees the possibility of compromise and friendship between Judaism and Christianity. In "Xerox Man," Ilan Stavans, a Jewish Latino, concentrates on some Jewish themes with an enigmatic or ambivalent attitude.

With the presumed exception of Nicky Cruz, Islam and Eastern Religions are seen either neutrally or positively. Piri Thomas experiments with Islam in *Down These Mean Streets*, abandoning that religion only for reasons of custom, not for anything particularly undesirable about Islam. Eastern religions contain elements that Anaya, in *Jalamanta*, finds attractive. Other authors or characters see no objection to experimenting with Eastern religions (e.g., Caroline in *Mr. Ives' Christmas*).

Secularism is much more of a powerful movement in U.S. Latina/o literature than is probably realized by scholars. Wholesale rejection of religion was/is part of the real life of Acosta, Ruiz, and Vega. Usually, secularization is a reaction against what is deemed to be repressive or unsatisfactory institutional and theological structures. *Pocho* sees atheism as a consequence of increased education and assimilation. Tomás Rivera sees atheism as a consequence of an unsatisfactory account of evil in Christian theology. Vega's *The Comeback* implies that all religions are human creations. Alvarez's *García Girls* manifests a mixture of passive secular impulses along with religious ones. Morales's *The Rag Doll Plagues* sees secular-scientific solutions to human problems as inevitable, even if not wholly desirable.

Major themes and symbols

The discussion of religion in U.S. Latina/o literature, as in literature in general, appears in the context of literary forms and genres. Many Latinas/os still see autobiography as a primary vehicle for their writings, so outline their religious evolution in the context of becoming self-aware.

Themes of struggle between Latina/o and Anglo identities are quite strong, with religion often coming into play in efforts to assert or regain a Latina/o identity. Many integrate what is termed "magical realism" and other literary forms associated with Latin America to express their literary heritage. Such personal writing is also a key to understanding religion in U.S. Latina/o literature.

The portrayal of God in our corpus is eclectic and American in some ways. In classical Christian doctrine, God is an infinite, eternal, and perfect Spirit, who is also the omnipotent, omniscient, benevolent Creator of the universe. He exists as a Trinity of Father, Son, and Holy Spirit. This is not necessarily the god of many U.S. Latina/o authors. We find God to be a "New Age" heliocentric energy in Anaya's *Jalamanta*. Tato Laviera's favorite deities are African *orishas*. In *Bless Me, Ultima*, Anaya wonders what the world would be like if God were a woman. Anzaldúa virtually recreates a pantheon of Aztec goddesses to serve her needs. Vega, in *The Comeback*, makes himself the creator of his literary universe. Only Nicky Cruz maintains a relatively orthodox and institutional vision of God as founded in his understanding of the Bible. The forgiving God of Hijuelos's *Mr. Ives* is perhaps more traditionally Hispanic than that of most authors.

The Bible, the prime locus of divine revelation in orthodox Christianity, is not a very important authority for characters found in U.S. Latina/o literature. There are quotes and allusions to the Bible in almost every Latina/o author we have featured. However, very few authors build entire works around biblical passages or books such as is the case with Vicente Leñero's *The Gospel of Lucas Gavilán* (1979), which rewrites the entire book of Luke from a modern Mexican secular perspective (see Lustig 1989; Avalos 1996). Piri Thomas, in *Savior, Savior, Hold My Hand*, explicitly criticizes Paul's view of slavery when he discovers what that biblical author really says. The Bible, for the most part, is the source of literary inspiration rather than divine revelation or moral authority.

As such, U.S. Latina/o authors are participating, wittingly or unwittingly, in the shift that has occurred in biblical scholarship in the last century or more. Indeed, modern critical scholarship sees the Bible less as a source of divine moral authority and more as a literary and political document. One can also argue that our authors are more Catholic than Protestant in their diminished appeal to the Bible. Historically, the Bible has had secondary importance for Catholic laypersons in terms of direct access, and Tridentine orthodoxy discouraged individual laypersons from reading the Bible unsupervised. The Bible was often heard rather than read by individual Catholics in pre-Vatican II days.

Nonetheless, there are a handful of biblical stories that are repeatedly adapted in U.S. Latina/o literature. Perhaps the most favorite biblical story is that of Jesus, whose life and character finds parallels in many U.S. Latina/o works, including *Happy Birthday Jesús* and *So Far From God*. The story of the creation of Adam and Eve is also a favorite. We find allusions to Paradise in *BMU*. Conflicts between the sexes in *So Far From God* have the biblical story of Adam and Eve in the background. Other biblical themes include Noah's flood (*BMU*), and the apocalypse (*BMU*, *Rag Doll Plagues*).

Prime modes of revelation in U.S. Latina/o literature seem to be dreams, anamnesis, and visions. Dreams are certainly important in Anaya's *Bless Me, Ultima*. They offer explanations of things Antonio has seen, and also illuminate prophecies. Remembrance and dreams are a great revelatory vehicle in *Dreaming in Cuban*. The visions of Mr. Ives in Hijuelos's novel are also very important to the spiritual development of that character. Experience itself is a mode of revelation, as in Tomás Rivera's work. Connecting with the inner divine self, rather than with the Christian orthodox God, is much more important in Anzaldúa or Anaya's writing.

The idea of direct access to God in our inner selves is sometimes denominated as "mysticism," and its roots run very deep in U.S. Latina/o literature.

Bronislaw Malinowski once claimed that sex "plays an astonishingly insignificant part in religion" (1948, 24). However, sexuality is a prime lens through which Catholicism and other religions are critiqued or discussed in U.S. Latina/o literature. Since so many works are autobiographical in genre, it is no surprise that puberty becomes the point of departure for most confrontations with Catholicism and religion in general. In *Happy Birthday Jesús*, masturbation causes great feelings of depression, owing to Church teachings. The devaluation of homosexual orientations is problematic for Anzaldúa and Castillo. Sexual exploitation and clerical hypocrisy is outlined by almost every author. Most authors depict characters who either break taboos or do not deem them relevant. On a broader scale, U.S. Latina/o authors comment on the sexual aspects of non-Christian religions, as is the case with *santería* in Curtis's *Shangó* and in Vega's view of Hinduism/Buddhism in *The Comeback*.

The role of the human body is also quite important in discussions of religion. Many of the complaints against Catholicism by Anzaldúa and Castillo center on that institution's repression and devaluation of the female body (see also Alarcón 1989). Ronald Ruiz sees the repressive control of Catholicism over natural human bodily needs (e.g., autoeroticism) as the cause of sociopathy. Many female authors make a point of sacralizing menstrual blood to counter Christian ideas of the impurity of women's blood (see also Buckley and Gottlieb 1988; Branham 2002).

Not surprisingly, gender plays an important role in how religion is discussed, as well. Female authors focus much more on critiques of patriarchal structures than do male authors. Thus, Castillo's *So Far From God* uses a sororal matrix to launch a pointed attack on male-dominated religions, be they Catholic or indigenous. For Castillo, all religions are evaluated by the role that they assign to women. Anaya seems concerned about women's viewpoints in *Bless Me, Ultima* but by the time he pens *Jalamanta* the main religious instructor is again a male figure associated with the sun.

Health care is yet another locus of contention between the laity and institutional Catholicism. Folk healing is usually touted as an example of indigenous traditions that should be respected, and even promoted, today. Folk healing is additionally a critique of modern scientific medicine in many instances (*The Rag Doll Plagues*). Anaya, Castillo, and Morales depict unjust persecution of folk healers. At the same time, few if any U.S. Latina/o authors ever highlight the reported dangers of folk medicine. For example, Trotter (1985; see also 1991) reports a significant number of children with lead poisoning resulting from the use of "folk" remedies for *empacho*, a sort of catch-all name for various digestive symptoms. Nevertheless, for some Hispanic authors, the folk healer has become a hero in the face of modern science and institutional religions.

In 1887, José Martí (1999, 60) said, "Man grows. Behold how he has outgrown churches and chosen the sky as the only temple worthy of sheltering his deity." But U.S. Latina/o authors have gone beyond simply seeing "the sky" as sacred space. Anzaldúa strives to sacralize her human body. In *BMU* we see the contrast between the llano and the town as symmetrical between spiritual purity and sin. In *The Cockroach People*, we see sacred space reversed, as the Chicano Mass takes place outside the sacred space of the Basilica. At least one author, James Curtis, who is an academic geographer, structures domestic space to express aspects of *santería*. In *Mr. Ives' Christmas*, we see that spiritual experiences are extended beyond the boundaries of the physical church and into the streets of Manhattan. Indeed, almost all our authors emphasize that sacred space is not coterminous with a physical or institutional "church" (on sacred space, see J. Z. Smith 1987).

The sacramental system, so defining of orthodox Catholicism, is a common theme in U.S. Latina/o literature. The First Communion, in particular, is a focal point of the life of characters ranging from Richard Rubio in *Pocho* to Santos in E. Rivera's "First Communion." The Eucharist can be a terroristic and repressive instrument to control people, as is outlined by Ruiz's *Happy Birthday Jesús*. Baptism also plays an important theme in *Bless Me, Ultima* though not as much as First Communion. The associated practice of confession is likewise a target of criticism. It is seen as a means of intelligence in a sort of totalitarian society. Sometimes it is a means for priests to gain sexual gratification. Confession can function paradoxically to increase sins.

The literary expression of an opposition to Catholicism, in particular, sometimes is embodied in "counterliturgies." These are meant to oppose the orthodox liturgy or to offer an alternative. Tato Laviera's poem is structured as a mass, but with African deities and practices instead. We see counterliturgy in Acosta's *Revolt*, where a protest in front of the Basilica substitutes tortillas for the host. An instance outside of our corpus may be found in Judith Ortiz Cofer's poem, "Cada Dia" in *Terms of Survival* (1995, 31), which rewrites the Lord's Prayer from a feminist and humanistic perspective.

Hamartiology, the doctrine of sin, is an important corollary of any discussion of Catholicism, and Christianity in general. Some find the idea of sin to be outdated and simply part of a repressive social system (so Anzaldúa, Castillo, Ruiz, Villarreal). Other authors target the hypocrisy of teachings on sin. All allude to the idea that most Catholics ignore teachings on sin. And some find the whole theology of sin to be an incentive to sin. If a thousand deadly sins receive the same penalty, then there is no disincentive to commit one thousand sins once you commit one.

Forgiveness is surprisingly not as prominent a topic as might be expected. About 88 percent of the general Hispanic Catholic group surveyed by González and La Velle (1985, 28) believed in a forgiving God. *Mr. Ives' Christmas* centers on a forgiving God, but this is the exception. In *Bless Me, Ultima* the Christian God is very unforgiving. The gods associated with the golden carp are not much better. Likewise, T. Rivera's portrayal of God is not one of benevolence. Ed Vega's God seems to enjoy making people suffer and is not very forgiving. The women authors don't center much on forgiving goddesses. Anzaldúa's goddesses are as much bent on violence as engaged in nurturing. Castillo's view of the divine does not entail much forgiveness, either.

Soteriology, the doctrine of salvation, figures very prominently in our corpus. Very few of the authors still maintain a Christian soteriology, in which God incarnate sacrifices himself, thus bringing redemption from the sinful condition obtained at the Fall in the Garden of Eden, and an eternal afterlife. Soteriology in Morales's *Rag Doll Plagues*, for example, rests in mutated Mexican blood, not in the blood of Christ. For Acosta, salvation is not supernatural, but rather centers on bettering the conditions of the oppressed on earth. For Alvarez, Anzaldúa, and Castillo, as feminists, women need to be saved from the oppressive patriarchal structures of Catholicism. Other authors believe that we need to be saved from the very idea of sin itself, which can cause sociopathologies (so Ruiz).

Religious conflicts are important themes in many works. Conflicts between Catholics and Protestants are mentioned in *Bless Me, Ultima* as when Horse argues that Red is going to hell because he's not Catholic. The conflict between Eastern pantheistic ideas and orthodox Western religions is part of the plot of *Jalamanta*. Mohr speaks about divisions between Jews and Christians precipitated by adults. Cristina García speaks of the persecution of *santería* in Cuba. Castillo and Anzaldúa highlight conflicts between patriarchal and matriarchal religions. Solutions for these conflicts are not as easy to discern.

From a literary viewpoint, our authors often use diet to highlight religious conflicts or differences. Diet is one of the first religious differences identified in Mohr's stories about Jewish characters. Food figures prominently in stories about *santería* because different deities have favorite things to eat—these foods become integrated into any story that presumes acquaintance with these African traditions. Thus, we find Pilar at a cafeteria selecting apples and bananas (for Shangó) in *Dreaming in Cuban*. We find James Curtis describing the food left at the crime scene in *Shangó*. And, of course, we find food as part of discussions of the theophagous and cannibalistic nature of the Eucharist in Rivera's "First Communion." Acosta, in *The Revolt of the Cockroach People*, sees tortillas as an indigenous substitute for the Christian Eucharistic host.

Color is a primary symbol associated with discussions of *santería*. We find all sorts of color symbolism used to outline Rosa's identity as Shangó; for example, she drives a red and white car. In *Dreaming in Cuban*, Herminia lives in a red and white house; and blue is associated with Yamayá and Cecilia. Black is associated with malevolence as well as with the "other." In *Shangó* and *Dreaming in Cuban*, the most mysterious religions are associated with the blackest people, betraying a Eurocentric stance.

We could continue with many more themes, but we hope that we have provided sufficient evidence of the rich array of religious commentary that can be found in literary form. For now, let us suggest more themes that could be explored by other scholars. Certainly, we need a larger number of female voices to delve more deeply into gender and religion. The place of Latina/o literature within the larger scope of European philosophy is a desideratum. The influence of postmodernism and critical legal and race theory can be integrated with the study of religion in U.S. Latina/o literature (on critical race theory, see Delgado and Stefancic, 2001). Possibly, a whole study might be done on how Latina/o authors view children's conceptions of religion.

Conclusion

U.S. Latina/o literature is not only of Latin American extraction, but also very much a part of Anglo-American literary and religious traditions. The ambivalent and conflicted attitude toward religious pluralism and mixture in Latina/o literature is a hallmark of the American experience. We see such ambivalence and conflict almost every time under-empowered groups have been incorporated into larger empires. We saw it when Jews meditated on their identity in the Babylonian, Persian, and Roman empires, among many others. We saw it when Irish Catholics encountered a Protestant British empire. On a broader scale, the ambivalent and conflicted attitude toward religious pluralism and mixture found in U.S. Latina/o literature repeats a theme in human history.

But we cannot forget that the study of religion and U.S. Latina/o literature is being birthed as you read these words. I, of course, cannot claim to be a sole accoucheur. We need more studies of religion in U.S. Latina/o literature. We need at least one monograph on religion and Latina literature. No Latina/o studies program can think of itself as even adequate unless it includes study of the religion of Latinas/os and of the ways in which literature reflects or does not reflect their religious experiences. All authors are commenting on religion or manifesting an attitude toward religion, whether they realize it or not—at the keyboard of every author is a commentator on religion. I will count myself successful if I stimulate further research and expansion of the Latina/o corpus that will be analyzed for its religious content.

Appendix 1

Summary of Attitudes

The following is a summary of attitudes toward religions expressed by authors we have featured.

Positive = mostly positive; negative = mostly negative; ambivalent = instances where the author has strong positive and negative views or declares himself or herself to be ambivalent. A work in parenthesis designates works by authors with more than one featured work. Some authors may appear in categories in which they were not featured (e.g., Cruz is presumed to be negative toward any non-Christian religion).

INDIGENOUS
Positive: Anaya, Anazaldúa
Ambivalent: ?
Negative: Cruz

AFRICAN
Positive: Laviera, García
Ambivalent: Curtis
Negative: Cruz

CATHOLICISM
Positive: Hijuelos
Ambivalent: Hinojosa
Negative: Acosta, Anaya, Castillo, Cruz, E. Rivera, T. Rivera, Ruiz, Vega, Villarreal

PROTESTANTISM
Positive: Cruz
Ambivalent: Thomas (*Savior, Savior, Hold My Hand*)
Negative: Hinojosa

JUDAISM
Positive: Mohr, Stavans
Ambivalent: Stavans?
Negative: Acosta (*The Autobiography of a Brown Buffalo*), Cruz

ISLAM
Positive: Thomas (*Down These Mean Streets*)
Ambivalent: Thomas (*Down These Mean Streets*)
Negative: Cruz

EASTERN RELIGIONS
Positive: Anaya (*Jalamanta*), Hijuelos
Ambivalent: None
Negative: Cruz

SECULARISM
Positive: T. Rivera, Vega, Villarreal
Ambivalent: Morales, Alvarez
Negative: Anaya (*Jalamanta*), Cruz

Appendix 2

A Canonical Comparison

Works Selected by Olmos and Augenbraum (2000, 201)
Works Selected for This Study

OLMOS AND AUGENBRAUM	THIS STUDY'S "CANON"
Julia Alvarez, *How the Garcia Girls Lost Their Accents*	X
Rudolfo Anaya, *Bless Me, Ultima*	X
Sandra Cisneros, *The House on Mango Street*	X
Cristina García, *Dreaming in Cuban*	X
Piri Thomas, *Down These Mean Streets*	X

Appendix 3

A Canonical Comparison

Authors Selected by Augenbraum and Stavans (1993)
Authors Selectd for This Study

AUGENBRAUM AND STAVANS (1993)	THIS STUDY'S "CANON"
Oscar "Zeta" Acosta	X
Julia Alvarez	X
Rudolfo Anaya	X
Gloria Anzaldúa	X
Nash Candelaria	
Denise Chávez	
Sandra Cisneros	
Jesús Colón	
Genaro González	
Oscar Hijuelos	X
Rolando Hinojosa	X

Nicholasa Mohr X

Judith Ortiz-Cofer

Americo Paredes

Patricia Preciado Martin

Edward Rivera X

Tomas Rivera X

Richard Rodriguez

Gary Soto

Piri Thomas X

J. L. Torres

Alma Villanueva

Helena Maria Viramontes

Ed Vega X

José Antonio Villarreal X

Glossary

A

Advaita: In Hinduism, the idea that God and the universe are identical.
Aiye: Yoruba term for the earth.
Altarcitos: Small altars usually found in homes.
Anamnesis: The act of remembrance.
Antigua, mi Diosa : The Ancient, my Goddess.
Apsu: In Babylonian mythology, the watery abyss that is present at the beginning of creation.
ashe: In Yoruba religious tradition, divine force or power.
Atman: In Hinduism, the soul or self.
Attitudinal: relating to attitudes.

B

Babalawo, a priest in *santería*.
Barrio: neighborhood.
Bhagavad Gita: One of the sacred scriptures of Hinduism.
Botanica: a store that sells santería supplies and herbs.
Brahman: In Hinduism, the Supreme all-pervading God.
Brujeria: witchcraft.
Brujos de fufu: sorcerers who use fufu (a banana mixture) in spells.

C

Cabildos: Social and ethnic clubs associated with Afro-Cubans.

Centros: Gathering places for practitioners of Spiritism.

Chicano: Name, derived from the latter part of Me-xicano, for a U.S.-born individual who wishes to assert their Mexican identity.

Cihuacoatl: an Aztec earth-mother goddess.

Coatlalopeuh: An aztec goddess central for Anzaldúa.

Coatlicue: "Serpent skirt," Aztec goddess and mother of Huitzilopochtli.

Conquistadores: Spanish conquerors.

Corridos: A genre of Mexican narratives or poems set to music and particularly popular in the borderlands.

Cuautlaohuac: Aztec goddess.

Cubano: Cuban.

Curandera/o: folk healer.

Curanderismo: folk healing.

D

De facto: (Latin) in fact.

De su genocidio: from their genocide.

Deus absconditus: (Latin) The hidden God.

Dhikr: "Remembrance;" which in mystical Islamic traditions is associated with the idea that memory is a means to connect with the divine.

Diosa: goddess.

E

El Bautismo del Espiritu Santo: Baptism of the Holy Spirit; the hallmark of a Pentecostal spiritual experience believed to be characterized by speaking in tongues.

El espiritual o estetico: Aesthetic spirit, as envisioned by José Vasconcelos.

El intelectual o politico: intellectual or political.

Ella: her.

Enuma elish: The Babylonian creation epic dating from at least the second millennium B.C.E.

Eschatology: doctrines about the end of the world.

Espiritus malos: evil spirits.

Essentialist: One who believes that a particular characteristic is part of the essence of an entity.

Evangelion: The Gospel.

Ex opere operato: (Latin) In Catholic theology, the teaching that the sacraments are "effective by virtue of performance."

F

Fuereño: An outsider.

G

Genizah: Repository for unusable Jewish sacred literature.

H

Hadith: In Islam, the traditions that preserve Muhammad's teachings outside of the Quran.
Halakah: (Transcribed Hebrew, literally "way" or "path"); In Judaism, a genre of literature specializing in legal rulings; the entire corpus of rules by which Jews must abide.
Hamartiology: The doctrines pertaining to sin.
Ḥajj: In Islam, pilgrimage to Mecca at least once in the believer's lifetime.
hoc est: (Latin) "this is."

I

Ifá: Yoruba divination system.
Ile: A *santería* shrine.
Ile-Ifá: In Yoruba religious tradition, a heavenly primordial place.
indigenismo: Attitude or philosophy related to recovery and celebration of indigenous identities.
inter alia: (Latin) "among other things."

J

Jíbaro: a Puerto Rican peasant.

K

Kamasutra: A Hindu erotic manual.
Kosi, iku, kosi arun, kosi araye: Yoruba sacred chant.
Kyrie eleison: (Transliterated Greek) "Lord, have mercy."

L

La Llorona (loca): "The wailing madwoman;" In Mexican and Mexican-American folklore, the figure who eternally wails her murder of her children.
La Madrina: godmother.
La Mona: the doll.
La raza final: In Vasconcelos' racial ideology, the ultimate race.
Latina/o (plural: Latinas/os): Term for a person living in the United States who traces his or her roots to the Spanish-speaking countries of Latin America.
Liberation Theology: Theology that centers on the needs and liberation of the oppressed.
Llano: the range, the wilderness.
Lucumi: One of the names for the Yoruba, and sometimes used as a name for *santería*.

M

Mahdi: Islamic messicanic figure.

Maquiladora: A border factory that is part of a system of trans-national manufacturing.

material o guerrero: material or warrior; in Vasconcelos's racial ideology, one of the periods of social history.

Matzo: Unleavened bread used at the Jewish feast of Passover.

Māyāyapahṛtajñāñā: (Transcribed Sanskrit) name for an illusion; a false appearance.

Mayombe: An African religious tradition of the Bantu-speaking people.

Mazehual: A humble Chichimeca social class.

Mestizaje: Mixture, especially between Mesoamerican and European peoples.

Mestizo/a: a person of mixed European and Native American ancestry.

Modus vivendi: (Latin) mode of co-existence.

mujer mala: evil woman.

Mujerista: Relating to womanist, feminist philosophy and mode of life.

N

Nuyorican: Combination of New York and Puerto Rican; A person who integrates a New York and Puerto Rican identity.

O

Obatala: Yoruba/*santería* god of creation, King of the white cloth.

Obi: Yoruba divination system utilizing coconuts.

Ogun: Yoruba god of metal, and rival of Shangó.

Olodumare: The Supreme Being in Yoruba religious tradition.

Orisha: General name for Yoruba/*santería* deities.

Orun: Heaven in Yoruba religious tradition.

Ota: Sacred stone in *santería*.

P

Pace: (Latin) despite; with due respect.

Padre: Father; a priest.

Pantheism: The idea that everything is part of God.

Philosophes: Term for French philosophers, especially during the Enlightenment era.

Plan del espiritu: Spiritual plan, especially as it relates to the Mexican people of the United States.

Prabha: (Transcribed Sanskrit) light of the sun and/or moon.

Prenda: Ceremonial kettle associated with Shangó in James Curtis's book.

R

Reglas: Forms of Afro-Cuban worship.
Regla de Ocha: Alternate name for *santería*.
Regla Lucumi: Alternate name for *santería*.
Retablos: Wooden painted panels, usually containing religious themes.

S

Ṣalat: in Islam, ritual prayer five times a day while facing Mecca.
Santería: Afro-Cuban religious traditons that integrates Yoruba and Catholic elements.
Santero/a: A practioner of *santería*.

Ṣawm: In Islam, fasting from dawn to sunset during the month of Ramadan.
Shahada: In Islam, the proclamation that there is only one God, Allah, and Muhammad is his prophet.
Shamanism: Tradition, derived historically from Siberian peoples, associated with supernatural forces and beings that can be controlled by a specialist called a Shaman.
Shangó: In Yoruba/Afro-Cuban religious traditions, the god of thunder and lightning, and rival of Ogun.
Shankara: Hindu philosopher who advocated the doctrine of advaita (see above).
Shul: Yiddish term for a Jewish synagogue.
Soteriology: The study of salvation; the set of ideas pertaining to salvation.
Sufi: mystical tradition in Islam.
Systematic Theology: A treatise which discusses systematically the major themes of Christian theology.

T

Talmud: A compilation, completed around 500 C.E., of Jewish oral "Law."
Tipo étnico superior: In Vasconcelos's racial ideology, a superior ethnic group.
Tlazolteotl: An Aztec goddess of purification.
Tonantsi: For Anzaldua, an Aztec goddess translated as "Our Lady Mother," and alternate name for Tonantzin.
Tonantzin: An honorific Nahuatl term that can be applied to a goddess.
Transubstantiation: In Catholic teaching, the doctrine that the host and wine in Communion become the true body and blood of Christ.
Tres estados sociales: In Vasconcelos' racial ideology, three evolutionary periods of social history.
Tsichtinako: Goddess of the Acoma Indians of the American Southwest.

U

Ummah: in Islam, the Muslim community.

V

Vatican II: The most recent (1962–1965) of the major Councils of the Catholic Church that addressed many major aspects of liturgy and doctrine.
veri homines (Latin): "truly men/human beings."
Virgin of Guadalupe: The most important figure of Mexican Catholicism.

Y

Yemayá: The Yoruba/*santería* the goddess of the sea.
Yogamāyasamāvṛtaḥ : In Hinduism, a sort of spiritual veil.
Yoruba: Ethnic group, primarily from Nigeria, that brought traditions that became part of *santería* in Cuba.

Z

Zakat: The giving of alms, one of the five pillars of Islam.

Bibliography

I. Works featured as case studies

Acosta, Oscar Zeta. 1989. *The Autobiography of a Brown Buffalo*. New York: Vintage Books. First published in 1972. San Francisco: Straight Arrow Books.

———. 1989. *The Revolt of the Cockroach People*. New York: Vintage Books. First published in 1973. San Francisco: Straight Arrow Books.

Alvarez, Julia. 1991. *How The García Girls Lost Their Accents*. New York: Plume.

Anaya, Rudolfo. 1972. *Bless Me, Ultima*. Berkeley: TQS Publications. Twenty-first printing, 1991.

———. 1996. *Jalamanta: A Message from the Desert*. New York: Warner Books.

Anzaldúa, Gloria. 1987. *Borderlands/La Frontera: The New Mestiza*. San Francisco: Aunt Lute Books.

———. 1999. *Borderlands/La Frontera: The New Mestiza*. 2nd ed. San Francisco: Aunt Lute Books.

Castillo, Ana. 1993. *So Far From God*. New York: Plume.

Cruz, Nicky. 1992. *Run, Baby, Run*. Revised Edition. Green Forest, Ark.: New Leaf Editions. First published in 1968.

Curtis, James Roberto. 1996. *Shangó*. Houston: Arte Público Press.

Garcia, Cristina. 1992. *Dreaming in Cuban*. New York: Ballantine Books.

Hijuelos, Oscar. 1995. *Mr. Ives' Christmas*. New York: HarperCollins.

Hinojosa, Rolando. 1987. *Klail City*. Houston: Arte Público Press.

Laviera, Tato. 1992. *La Carreta Made a U-Turn*. 2nd ed. Houston: Arte Público Press.

Mohr, Nicholasa. 1986. *El Bronx Remembered*. Houston: Arte Público Press.

Morales, Alejandro. 1992. *The Rag Doll Plagues*. Houston: Arte Público Press.

Rivera, Edward. 1982. *Family Installments: Memories of Growing Up Hispanic*. New York: Penguin.

Rivera, Tomás. 1991. *. . . And the Earth Did Not Devour Him*. In *Tomás Rivera: The Complete Works*, ed. Julián Olivares, 151–220. Houston: Arte Público Press. First published in 1971.

Ruiz, Ronald L. 1994. *Happy Birthday Jesús*. Houston: Arte Público Press.

Stavans, Ilan. 2000. "Xerox Man." In *The Essential Ilan Stavans*, ed. Ilan Stavans, 301–307. New York: Routledge.

Thomas, Piri. 1967. *Down These Mean Streets*. New York: Vintage.

———. 1972. *Savior, Savior, Hold My Hand*. Garden City, New York: Doubleday.

Vega, Ed. 1985. *The Comeback*. Houston: Arte Público Press.

Villarreal, José Antonio. 1959. *Pocho*. New York: Doubleday.

II. Other literary works and anthologies mentioned

Alarcón, Francisco X. 1992. *Snake Poems: An Aztec Invocation*. San Francisco: Chronicle Books.

Alurista. 1971. *Floricanto en Aztlán*. Los Angeles: Chicano Cultural Center, University of California.

Alvarez, Julia. 1995. *In the Time of the Butterflies*. New York: Plume.

———. 1997. *¡Yo!* New York: Plume.

———. 1998. *Something to Declare*. New York: Plume.

Anaya, Rudolfo. 1976. *Heart of Aztlán*. Albuquerque: University of New Mexico Press.

———. 1979. *Tortuga*. Albuquerque: University of New Mexico Press.

Athanasius, *De incarnatione verbi dei*. In *The Ante-Nicene Fathers* eds. Alexander Roberts and James Donaldson, 4:65. 1885–1887. 10 volumes, Reprint: Peabody, Massachusetts: Hendrickson Press, 1994.

Augenbraum, Harold, and Ilan Stavans, eds. 1993. *Growing Up Latino: Memoirs and Stories*. Boston: Houghton Mifflin.

Baker, Houston A. Jr. 1982. *Three American Literatures: Essays in Chicano, Native American, and Asian-American Literature for Teachers of American Literature*. New York: Modern Language Association.

Baym, Nina, Ronald Gottesman, Laurence Holland, David Kalstone, Francis Murphy, Hershel Parker, William H. Pritchard, and Patricia B. Wallace. 1989. *The Norton Anthology of American Literature*. 3rd ed. Shorter. New York: W. W. Norton and Company.

Brito, Aristeo. 1990. *The Devil in Texas/El Diablo en Texas*. Tempe, Arizona: Bilingual Press/ Editorial Bilingüe. First published in 1976.

Carlyle, Thomas. 1831 "Characteristics." In *The Harvard Classics*, ed. Charles W. Eliot, Volume 25: 319–356. New York: Collier, 1937. Original publication in *The Edinburgh Review* (1831).

Castillo, Ana. 1986. *The Mixquiahuala Letters*. Tempe, Arizona: Bilingual Press/Editorial bilingüe.

Cather, Willa. 1927. *Death Comes for the Archbishop*. Reprint, New York: Vintage Classics Edition, 1990.

Cervantes, Miguel de. 1997. *Don Quijote de la Mancha*, ed. Florencio Sevillo Arroyo and Elena Varela Merino. 2 volumes. Madrid: Editorial Castalia. Edited reprint of editions of 1605 and 1615.

Cisneros, Sandra. 1984. *The House on Mango Street*. New York: Vintage.

———. 1991. *Woman Hollering Creek and other Stories*. New York: Vintage.

Cofer, Judith Ortiz. 1990. *Silent Dancing: A Partial Remembrance of a Puerto Rican Childhood*. Houston: Arte Público Press.

———. 1995. *Terms of Survival*. 2nd ed. Houston: Arte Público Press.

Elbert, Sarah. 1997. *Louisa May Alcott on Race, Sex and Gender*. Boston: Northeastern University Press.

Emerson, Ralph Waldo. 1983. *Essays and Lectures*. Reprint in The Library of America. New York: Literary Classics of the United States.

Escandón, María Amparo. 1999. *Esperanza's Box of Saints*. New York: Scribner.

211

Fernandez, Roberto G. 1988. *Raining Backwards*. Houston: Arte Público Press.

García, Cristina. 1997. *The Aguero Sisters*. New York: Alfred A. Knopf.

Gómez, Alma, Cherríe Moraga and Mariana Romo-Carmona. 1983. *Cuentos: Stories by Latinas*. Latham, New York: Kitchen Table/Women of Color Press.

González, Rodolfo "Corky." 2001. *Message to Aztlán: Selected Writings*. Edited by Antonio Esquibel.16–29 Houston: Arte Público.

Gutierrez, Gustano. 1972. *Teología de la liberaction: Perspectivas*. Salamanca: Ediciones Sígueme.

Kovacs, Maureen Gallery. 1989. *The Epic of Gilgamesh*. Stanford: Stanford University Press.

Leñero, Vicente. 1979. *El Evangelio de Lucas Gavilán*. Barcelona: Seix Barral.

———. 1991. *The Gospel of Lucas Gavilán*. Translated by Robert Mowry. Lanham, MD: University Press of America.

Márquez, Gabriel García. 1986. *Cien años de soledad*. Mexico City: Editorial Diana. First published in 1967.

Martí, José. 1999. *Reader: Writings on the Americas*, ed. Deborah Schookal and Mirta Muñiz. Melbourne: Ocean Press.

Mascaró, Juan. 1962. *The Bhagavad Gita*. London: Penguin.

McCourt, Frank. 1996. *Angela's Ashes*. New York: Touchstone.

Méndez M., Miguel. 1991. *Peregrinos de Aztlán*. Tempe, Arizona: Bilingual Press/Editorial Bilingüe. 1974. Tucson: Editorial Peregrinos.

Miller, Barbara Stoler. 1986. *The Bhagavad-Gita: Krishna's Counsel in Time of War*. New York: Bantam Books.

Miller, Walter M. 1997. *A Canticle for Leibowitz*. New York: Bantam Books. First published in 1959.

Mohr, Nicholasa. 1993. *In Nueva York*: Houston: Arte Público Press.

Moraga, Cherríe and Gloria Anzaldúa, eds. 1981. *This Bridge Called My Back:Writings by Radical Women of Color*. New York: Kitchen Table: Women of Color Press.

Morales, Alejandro. 2001. *Waiting to Happen*. San Jose: Chusma House Publications.

Plato. *Republic*. 1930–1935. Translated by Paul Shorey et al. Two volumes. Loeb Classical Library. Cambridge: Harvard University Press.

———. 1982. *Phaedo, Apology, Crito, Phaedo, Phaedrus*. Translated by H. N. Fowler. Loeb Classical Library. Cambridge: Harvard University Press.

Rechy, John. 1991. *The Miraculous Day of Amalia Gómez*. New York: Arcade.

Rodriguez, Richard. 1983. *Hunger of Memory: The Education of Richard Rodriguez*. New York: Bantam.

———. 1992. *Days of Obligation: An Argument with My Mexican Father*. New York: Penguin.

Rölvaag, O. E. *Giants in the Earth*. 1957. Translated by Lincoln Colcord and O. E. Röllvaag. New York:Harper and Row. Reprint of 1927 edition.

Sanchez, Ricardo. 1995. *Canto y Grito mi Liberación*. Pullman: Washington State University Press.

Sargeant, Winthrop. 1979. *The Bhagavad Gita*. New York: Doubleday.

Segundo, Luis. 1974. *Liberación de la teología*. Buenos Aires: Ediciones: Carlos Lohlé, 1975

Sierra O'Reilly, Justo 1981. *La hija del judío*. Mexico City: Consejo nacional para el fomento de la Educación. First published in 1848–1849.

Villaseñor, Victor. 1991. *Rain of Gold*. New York: Delta.

Whitman, Walt. 1986. *Leaves of Grass*. Ed. Malcolm Cowley. London: Penguin. Reprint of 1855 edition.

III. General bibliography

Abalos, David T. 1986. *Latinos in the United States: The Sacred and the Political*. Notre Dame: University of Notre Dame Press.

Bibliography

Abusch, Tzvi. 2001. "The Development and Meaning of the Epic of Gilgamesh: An Interpretive Essay." *Journal of the American Oriental Society* 121: 614–622.

Acuña, Rodolfo. 1972. *Occupied America: The Chicano's Struggle Toward Liberation*. San Francisco: Canfield Press.

———. 1994. *Occupied America: A History of Chicanos*. 4th edition. New York: Longman.

Alarcón, Norma. 1989. "The Sardonic Powers of the Erotic in the Work of Ana Castillo." In *Breaking Boundaries: Latina Writing and Critical Readings*, ed. Asunción Horno-Delgado and Nancy Saporta Sternbach, 94–10. Amherst: University of Massachusetts Press.

Albanese, Catherine L. 1990. *Nature Religion in America: From the Algonkian Indians to the New Age*. Chicago: University of Chicago.

Alberigo, Giuseppe and Joseph A. Komonchak, eds. 1996. *The History of Vatican II. Volume 1: Announcing and Preparing Vatican Council II: Toward a New Era in Catholicism*. Maryknoll, New York: Orbis Books.

———. 1998. *History of Vatican II. Volume 2: The Formation of the Council's Identity: First Period and Intercession, October 1962–September 1963*. Maryknoll, New York: Orbis Books.

———. 2000. *History of Vatican II. Volume 3: The Mature Council, Second Period and Intersession, September 1963–September 1964*. Maryknoll, New York: Orbis Books.

Al-Bukhari, *Shahih Al-Bukhari*. 1997. Translated by Muhammad Muhsin Khan. 9 volumes. Riyadh, Saudi Arabia: Darussalam Publishers and Distributors.

Alter, Robert and Frank Kermode. 1987. *The Literary Guide to the Bible*. Cambridge: Harvard University Press.

Alvar, Manuel. 1976. *Diario del Descubrimiento*. 2 volumes; Gran Canaria: Cabildo Insular de Gran Canaria.

American Humanist Association. 1973. *Humanist Manifestos I & II*. Amherst, New York.

Anawalt, Patricia. 1982. "Understanding Aztec Human Sacrifice." *Archaeology* 35, no. 5 (September/October):38–45.

Anchor, Robert. 1979. *The Enlightenment Tradition*. Berkeley: University of California Press. Reprint of 1967 edition.

Anti-Defamation League. 2002. *Anti-Semitism in America 2002*. New York: Anti-Defamation League. Viewed June 18, 2002 at http://www.adl.org/anti_semitism/2002/as_survey.pdf

Aparicio, Frances R. and Susana Chávez-Silverman, eds. 1997. *Tropicalizations: Transcultural Representations of Latinidad*. Hanover, New Hampshire: Dartmouth College Press.

Aquino, María Pilar, Daisy L. Machado and Jeanette Rodriguez. 2002. *A Reader in Latina Feminist Theology: Religion and Justice*. Austin: University of Texas Press.

Arce-Valentín, Reneiro. 1996. *Religión: Poesía del mundo venidero. Las implicaciones teológicas en la obra de José Martí*. Quito: Consejo Latinoamericano de Iglesias.

Arreola, Daniel D. and James Curtis. 1993. *The Mexican Border Cities: Landscape Anatomy and Place Personality*. Tucson: University of Arizona Press.

Augenbraum, Harold and Margarite Fernández Olmos, 2000. *U.S. Latino Literature: A Critical Guide for Students and Teachers*. Westport, Connecticut: Greenwood Press.

Avalos, Hector. 2005. "Liberation Theology." In *Encyclopedia Latina: History, Culture, And Society In The United States*. ed. Ilan Stavans. Danbury, CT: Grolier.

———. ed. 2004. *Introduction to the U.S. Latina and Latino Religious Experience*. Boston: Brill.

———. 2003. "Deconstructing 'Nahualismo' in Mexican-American Theology," *Journal of Hispanic/Latino Theology* 10, no. 4 (May): 45–63.

———. 2001. "Maria Atkinson and the Rise of Appalachian Pentecostalism in the U.S. Mexico-Borderlands." *Journal of Religion and Society* 3; at http: moses//creighton.edu/JRS/2001/2001-5.html.

———. 1996. "The Gospel of Lucas Gavilán as Postcolonial Biblical Exegesis."*Semeia* 75: 87–105.

———. 1996. "Columbus as Biblical Exegete: A Study of the *Libro de Las Profecias*," In *Religion in the Age of Exploration: The Case of Spain and New Spain*, ed. B. Le Beau and M. Mor, 59–80. Omaha: Creighton University Press.

———. 1996. "Evangelicals." In *The Latino Encyclopedia*. eds. Richard Chabrán and Rafael Chabrán, 2.560–563. Six volumes New York: Marshall Cavendish.

———. 1996. "Protestantism." In *The Latino Encyclopedia*. eds. Richard Chabrán and Rafael Chabrán, 5.1307–1310. Six volumes New York: Marshall Cavendish.

———. 1999. *Health Care and the Rise of Christianity*. Peabody, Massachusetts: Hendrickson Press.

Bachofen, Johann Jakob. 1967. *Myth, Religion, and Mother Right. Selected Writings of J. J. Backhofen*. Translated by Ralph Mannheim. Princeton: Princeton University Press. Originally published in 1861.

Bagby, Ihsan, Paul Perl and Bryan T. Froehle. 2001. *The Mosque in America: A National Portrait*. Washington: Council on American-Islamic Relations.

Baker, Houston A. ed. 1982. *Three American Literatures: Essays in Chicano, Native American, and Asian-American Literature for Teachers of American Literature*. New York: The Modern Language Association.

Bantjes, Adrian A. 1997. "Idolatry and Iconoclasm in Revolutionary Mexico: The De-Christianization Campaigns, 1929–1940." *Mexican Studies/Estudios Mexicanos* 13, no. 1 (Winter):87–120.

Barnard, Ian. 1997. "Gloria Anzaldúa's Queer Mestisaje." *MELUS: The Journal of the Society for the Study of the Multi-Ethnic Literature of the United States*, 22, no. 1 35–53.

Barnes, Thomas, Thomas H. Naylor, and Charles W. Polzer. 1981. *Northern New Spain: A Research Guide*. Tucson: University of Arizona Press.

Barnet, Miguel. 1997. "La Regla de Ocha: The Religious System of Santería." In *Sacred Possessions: Vodou, Santería, Obeah and the Caribbean*, ed. Margarite Fernandez Olmos and Lizabeth Paravisini-Gebert, 79–100. New Brunswick, New Jersey: Rutgers University Press.

Barrera, Mario. 1988. *Beyond Aztlan: Ethnic Autonomy in Comparative Perspective*. Notre Dame: University of Notre Dame Press.

Bejarano, Margalit. 1996. *La comunidad hebrea de Cuba: La memoria y la historia*. The Abraham Harman Institute of Contemporary Jewry. Jerusalem: Hebrew University Press.

Bellah, Robert N. 1998. "Is There a Common American Culture?" *JAAR* 66:3 (Fall): 613–625.

Bellah, Robert N., Richard Madsen, William M. Sullivan, Ann Swidler and Steven M. Tipton. 1985. *Habits of the Heart: Individualism and Commitment in American Life*. New York: Harper & Row.

Bernheimer, Charles, ed. 1995. *Comparative Literature in the Age of Multiculturalism*. Baltimore: The Johns Hopkins University Press.

Bettinger-López, Caroline. 2000. *Cuban-Jewish Journeys: Searching for Identity, Home, and History in Miami*. Knoxville: The University of Tennessee Press.

Betto, Frei. 1990. *Fidel and Religion: Conversations with Frei Betto*. Translated by Mary Todd. Melbourne: Ocean Press.

Billington, Ray. 2002. *Religion without God*. New York: Routledge.

Binder, Wolfgang. 1985. *Partial Autobiographies: Interviews with Twenty Chicano Poets*. Erlanger Studien 65/1. Erlangen: Verlag Palm & Enke Erlangen.

Blom, Gerdien. 1997. "Divine Individuals, Cultural Identities: Post-Identitarian Representations and Two Chicana/o Texts." *Thamyris: Mythmaking from Past to Present* 4, no. 2 (Autumn): 295–324.

Bloom, Harold. 1992. *The American Religion; The Emergence of the Post- Christian Nation*. New York: Touchstone.

Borg, Marcus. 1999. *Jesus and Buddha: The Parallel Sayings*. Berkeley: Seastone Press.

214

Bottéro, Jean. 1992. *Mesopotamia: Writing, Reason, and the Gods*. Translated by Z. Bahrani and M. van de Mieroop. Chicago: University of Chicago Press.

Bowden, Henry Warner. 1991. *Church History in an Age of Uncertainty: Historiographical Patterns in the United States 1906–1990*. Carbondale and Edwardsville: Southern Illinois University Press.

Branche, Jerome. 1995. "Anzaldúa: El Ser y la Nación." *entorno* 34(invierno):39–44.

Branham, Joan R. 2002. "Bloody Women and Bloody Spaces." *Harvard Divinity Bulletin* 30, no. 2 (Spring):15–22.

Brathwaite, Edward Kamau. 1974. "The African Presence in Caribbean Literature." *Daedalus* 103, no. 2 (Spring):73–109.

Brett, R. L. 1997. *Faith and Doubt: Religion and Secularization in Literature from Wordsworth to Larkin*. Macon, Georgia: Mercer University Press.

Brinkerhoff, Merlin B. and Marlene M. Mackie. 1993. "Casting Off the Bonds of Organized Religion: A Religious-Careers Approach to the Study of Apostasy." *Review of Religious Research* 34, no. 3(March):235–258.

Brinton, Crane. 1965. *The Anatomy of Revolution*. New York: Vintage Books.

Broda, Johanna, Davíd Carrasco, and Eduardo Matos Moctezuma. 1987. *The Great Temple of Tenochtitlan: Center and Periphery in the Aztec World*. Berkeley: University of California Press.

Brown, Lyle C. and William F. Cooper. 1980. *Religion in Latin American Life and Literature*. Waco, Texas: Markham Press.

Bruce-Novoa, Juan. 1990. *Retrospace: Collected Essays on Chicano Literature*. Houston: Arte Público Press.

Buckley, Michael J.S.J. 1987. *At the Origins of Modern Atheism*. New Haven: Yale University Press.

Buckley, Thomas and Alma Gottlieb. 1988. *Blood Magic: The Anthropology of Menstruation*. Berkeley: University of California Press.

Burkhart, Louise M. 1993. "The Cult of the Virgin of Guadalupe in Mexico." In *South and Meso-American Native Spirituality.From the Cult of the Feathered Serpent to the Theology of Liberation*, ed. Gary H. Gossen, 198–227. New York: Crossroad.

———. 2001. *Before Guadalupe: The Virgin Mary in Early Colonial Nahuatl Literature*. Institute for Mesoamerican Studies Monograph 13. Albany: State University of New York at Albany; distributed by University of Texas Press at Austin.

Burns, Jeffrey M. 1994. "The Mexican Catholic Community in California." In *The Mexican Americans and the Catholic Church 1900–1965*, ed. Jay P. Dolan and Gilberto Hinojosa, 129–233. Notre Dame History of Hispanic Catholics in the U.S. Volume 1. Notre Dame: University of Notre Dame Press.

Busto, Rudy. 1998. "The Predicament of Nepantla: Chicana/o Religions in the 21st Century." *Perspectivas: Hispanic Theological Initiative Occasional Papers Series* 1 (Fall):7–21.

Cabrera, Lydia. 1971. *El Monte*. Miami: Coleccion de Chicherekú.

———. 1986. *Reglas de Congo: Mayombe Palo Monte*. Miami: Ediciones Universal.

Cadena, Gilbert and Lara Medina. 1996. "Liberation Theology and Social Change: Chicanas and Chicanos in the Catholic Church." In *Chicanas and Chicanos in Contemporary Society*, ed. Roberto M. De Anda, 99–111. Boston: Allyn and Bacon.

Calderón, Hector. 1991. "The Novel and the Community of Readers: Rereading Tomás Rivera's *Y no se lo tragó la tierra*." In *Criticism in the Borderlands: Studies in Chicano Literature, Culture, and Ideology*, ed. Héctor Calderón and José David Saldívar, 97–113. Durham: Duke University Press.

———. and José David Saldivar, ed. 1991. *Criticism in the Borderlands Studies in Chicano Literature, Culture, and Ideology*. Durham: Duke University Press.

Cantú, Roberto. 1979. "Degradación y regeneración en *Bless Me, Ultima*: El chicano y la vida nueva." In *The Identification and Analysis of Chicano Literature*, ed. Franciso Jiménez, 374–388. New York: Bilingual Press.

———. 1990. "Apocalypse as an Ideological Construct: the Storyteller's Art in *Bless Me, Ultima*." In *Rudolfo Anaya: Focus on Criticism*. ed. César A. González-T., 13–63. La Jolla, California: Lalo Press.

Capps, Walter H. 1995. *Religious Studies: The Making of a Discipline*. Minneapolis: Fortress Press.

Cardoza-Orlandi, Carlos F. 1995. "Drum Beats of Resistance and Liberation: Afro-Caribbean Religions, the Struggle for Life and the Christian Theologian." *Journal of Hispanic/Latino Theology* 3, no. 1 (August):50–61.

Carmack, Robert M., Janice Gasco and Gary H. Gossen. 1996. *The Legacy of Mesoamerica*. Prentice Hall: Upper Saddle River, New Jersey.

Carnes, Tony, and Anna Karpathakis, eds. 2001. *New York Glory: Religions in the City*. New York: New York University Press.

Carr, Irene Campos. 1993. "Flicker, Flame, Butterfly Ablaze." *Belles Lettres* (Spring):19–20.

Carrasco, Davíd. 1982. "A Perspective for a Study of Religious Dimensions in Chicano Experience: *Bless Me, Ultima* as a Religious Text. *Aztlán* 13, nos. 1 and 2 (Spring and Fall):195–220.

———. 1992. *Quetzalcoatl and the Irony of Empire: Myths and Prophecies in the Aztec Tradition*. Chicago: University of Chicago Press.

———. 1999. *City of Sacrifice: The Aztec Empire and the Role of Violence in Civilization*. Boston: Beacon Press.

Carroll, Michael P. 2002. *The Penitente Brotherhood: Patriarchy and Hispano-Catholicism in New Mexico*. Baltimore: The Johns Hopkins University Press.

Carter, Stephen L. 1993. *The Culture of Disbelief*. New York: Basic Books.

Castillo, Ana. 1996. *Goddess of the Americas: Writings on the Virgin of Guadalupe*. New York: Riverhead Books.

Castillo, Debra. 1992. *Talking Back: Toward a Latin American Feminist Literary Criticism*. Ithaca: Cornell University Press.

———. 1995. "Postmodern Indigenism: 'Quetzalcoatl and All That'." *Modern Fiction Studies* 41, no 1: 35–73.*Catechism of the Catholic Church*. 1994. United States Catholic Conference; Mahwah, New Jersey: Paulist Press.Chavez, César E. 1968. "The Mexican American and the Church."*El Grito* 1. no. 4 (Summer):9–12.

Chow, Rey. 1995. "In the Name of Comparative Literature." In *Comparative Literature in the Age of Multiculturalism*, ed. Charles Bernheimer, 97–116. Baltimore: The Johns Hopkins University Press.

Cinader, Martha and Matthew Finch. 1998. "Ana Castillo Interview." *http://216.71.173.167/ AuthorInterviews/anacastillo.html* . Viewed on June 14, 2002.

Coe, Michael D. 1993. *The Maya*. Fifth Edition. New York: Thames and Hudson.

Cohen, Jeremy. 1999. *Living Letters of the Law: Ideas of theJew in Medieval Christianity*. Berkeley: University of California Press.

Coleman, Kristy. 2001. "Matriarchy and Myth." *Religion* 31:247–263.

Conrad, Geoffrey W. and Arthur A. Demarest. 1984. *Religion and Empire:The Dynamics of Aztec and Inca Expansionism*. Cambridge: Cambridge University Press.

Crenshaw, James L. 1987. *Ecclesiastes: A Commentary*. Philadelphia: The Westminster Press.

Crone, Patricia and Michael Cook. 1977. *Hagarism: The Making of the Islamic World*. Cambridge: Cambridge University Press.

Curry, Mary Cuthrell. 2001. "The Yoruba Religion in New York." In *New York Glory: Religions in the City*, ed. Tony Carnes and Anna Karpathakis, 74–87. New York: New York University Press. Curtis, James Roberto. 1980. "Miami's Little Havana: Yard Shrines, Cult Religion and Landscape." *Journal of Cultural Geography* 1, no. 1:1–15.

———. 1982. "Santeria: Persistence and Change in an Afrocuban Cult Religion." In *Objects of Special Devotion: Fetishes and Fetishism in Popular Culture*, ed. Ray B. Browne, 336–351. Bowling Green, Ohio: The Bowling Green University Popular Press.

Daly, Mary. 1985. *Beyond God the Father: Toward a Philosophy of Women's Liberation*. Boston: Beacon Press. First published in 1973.

Davis, Kenneth. 1994. "The Hispanic Shift: Continuity Rather than Conversion." *Journal of Hispanic/Latino Theology* 1, no. 3 (May):68–79.

Dayton, Donald W. 1987. *Theological Roots of Pentecostalism*. Peabody, Massachusetts: Hendrickon Press.

De Anda, Roberto M. 1996. *Chicanas and Chicanos in Contemporary Society*. Boston: Allyn and Bacon.

Deck, Alan Figueroa. 1994. "Latino Theology: The Year of the 'Boom.'" *Journal of Hispanic/Latino Theology* 1, no. 2 (February): 51–63.

De La Garza, Rodolfo O., Louis DeSipio, F. Chris Garcia, John Garcia, and Angelo Falcon. 1992. *Latino Voices: Mexican, Puerto Rican, and Cuban Perspectives on American Politics*. Boulder, Colorado: Westview Press.

De La Torre, Miguel A. 2004. *Santería: The Beliefs And Rituals Of A Growing Religion In America*. Grand Rapids: Eerdmans.

———. 1999. "Masking Hispanic Racism: A Cuban Case Study." *Journal of Hispanic/Latino Theology* 6, no. 4 (May):57–74.

——— and Edwin D. Aponte. 2001. *Introducing Latino/a Theologies*. Maryknoll, New York: Orbis.

Delgado, Richard and Jean Stefancic. 2001. *Critical Race Theory: An Introduction*. New York: New York University Press.

Deloria Jr., Vine. 1994. Foreword to *The Dreamseekers: Native Visionary Traditions of the Great Plains*, by Lee Irwin. Norman: University of Oklahoma Press.

Díaz-Stevens, Ana María. 1993. *Oxcart Catholicism on Fifth Avenue: The Impact of Puerto Rican Migration upon The Diocese of New York*. Notre Dame: University of Notre Dame Press.

———. 1996. "In the Image and Likeness of God: Literature as Theological Reflection." In *Hispanic/Latino Theology: Challenge and Promise*, ed. Ada María Isasi-Diaz and Fernando F. Segovia, 86–103. Minneapolis: Fortress.

——— and Anthony M. Stevens-Arroyo. 1998. *Recognizing the Latino Resurgence in U.S. Religion: The Emmaus Paradigm*. Boulder: Westview Press.

Dick, Bruce and Silvio Sirias, eds. 1998. *Conversations with Rudolfo Anaya*. Jackson: University Press of Mississippi.

Dimont, Max I. 2001. *The Jews in America: The Roots, History and Destiny of American Jews*. Chicago: Olmstead Press.

Dolan, Jay P., and Gilberto Hinojosa, ed. 1994. *The Mexican Americans and the Catholic Church 1900–1965*. Vol. 1 of *Notre Dame History of Hispanic Catholics in the U.S.* Notre Dame: University of Notre Dame Press.

——— and Jaime R. Vidal, eds. 1994. *Puerto Rican and Cuban Catholics in the U.S. 1900–1965*. Notre Dame History of Hispanic Catholics in the U.S. Volume 2. Notre Dame: University of Notre Dame Press.

——— and Allan Figueroa Deck, S.J. eds. 1994. *Hispanic Catholic Culture in the U.S.: Issues and Concerns*. Notre Dame History of Hispanic Catholics in the U.S. Volume 3. Notre Dame: University of Notre Dame Press.

Draz, M. A. 2000. *Introduction to the Qur'an*. London: I.B. Tauris.

Drinan, Robert F. S.J. and Jennifer I. Huffman. 1993. "Religious Freedom and the *Oregon v. Smith* and *Hialeah* Cases." *Journal of Church and State* 71 (Winter):19–35.

Dussel, Enrique. 1995. *The Invention of the Americas: Eclipse of "The Other" and the Myth of Modernity*. New York: Continuum Press.

Eagleton, Terry. 1983. *Literary Theory: An Introduction*. Minneapolis: University of Minnesota Press.

Edgerton, Robert B. 1992. *Sick Societies: Challenging the Myth of Primitive Harmony*. New York: Free Press.

Eisler, Riane. 1987. *The Chalice and the Blade: Our History, Our Future*. San Francisco: Harper and Row.

Elizondo, Virgilio. 1978. *Mestizaje: The Dialectic of Cultural Birth and the Gospels*. Three volumes. San Antonio: Mexican American Cultural Center.

———. 1988. *The Future is Mestizo: Life where Cultures Meet*. Bloomington: Meyer-Stone.

Eller, Cynthia. 2000. *The Myth of Matriarchal Prehistory: Why an Invented Past Won't Give Women a Future*. Boston: Beacon Press.

Elzey, Wayne. 1976. "The Nahua Myth of the Suns: History and Cosmology in Pre-Hispanic Mexican Religions." *Numen* 23, no. 2 (August):114–135.

Erickson, Vincent O. 1988. "*Buddenbrooks*, Thomas Mann, and North German Social Class: An Application of Literary Anthropology." In *Literary Anthropology: A New Interdisciplinary Approach to People, Signs, and Literature*, ed. Fernando Poyatos, 95–125. Amsterdam: John Benjamins Publishing Company.

Espín, Orlando O. 1994. "Popular Catholicism among Latinos." In *Hispanic Catholic Culture in the U.S.: Issues and Concerns*. ed. Jay P. Dolan and Allan Figueroa Deck, S.J., 308–359. Notre Dame History of Hispanic Catholics in the U.S. Volume 3. Notre Dame: University of Notre Dame Press.

Espinosa, Gastón, et al. 2003. "*Hispanic Churches in American Public Life: Summary of Findings,*" *Interim Reports* 2003.2 (January 2003), available at http://www.hcapl.org/HCAPL _Summary_of_Findings_English.pdf

Flannery, Austin, O.P. 1975. *Vatican II: The Conciliar and Post-Conciliar Documents*. Collegeville, Minnesota: The Liturgical Press.

Flores, Edmundo. 1983. "Science and Technology in Mexico; Toward Self-Determination." *Science* 219, no 4591:1398–1401.

Flores, Juan. 1993. "Puerto Rican Literature in the United States: Stages and Perspectives." In *Recovering the U.S. Hispanic Literary Heritage*, ed. Ramón Gutiérrez and Genaro Padilla, 53–68. Houston: Arte Público Press.

———, John Attinasi, and Pedro Pedraza, Jr. 1981. "*La Carreta Made a U-Turn*: Puerto Rican Language and Culture in the United States." *Daedalus* 110, no. 2 (spring):193–217.

Flynn, Elizabeth A. and Patrocinio P. Schweickart. 1986. *Gender and Reading Essays on Readers, Texts and Contexts*. Baltimore: The Johns Hopkins University Press.

Fox-Genovese, Elizabeth. 1995. "Between Elitism and Populism: Whither Comparative Literature." In *Comparative Literature in the Age of Multiculturalism*, ed. Charles Bernheimer, 134–142. Baltimore: The Johns Hopkins University Press.

Francis, Mark. R. 2000. "Hispanic Liturgy in the U.S.: Toward a New Inculturation." *Journal of Hispanic/Latino Theology* 8, no. 2 (November):33–53.

Fregosi, Paul. 1998. *Jihad in the West: Muslim Conquests from the 7th to 21st Centuries*. Amherst, New York: Prometheus.

Frei, Hans W. 1974. *The Eclipse of Biblical Narrative: A Study in Eighteenth and Nineteenth Century Hermeneutics*. New Haven: Yale University Press.

Frymer-Kensky, Tikva. 1992. *In the Wake of the Goddesses: Women Culture and Biblical Transformation of Pagan Myth*. New York: Free Press.

Gagnier, Regenia. 1991. "Feminist Autobiography in the 1980s," *Feminist Studies* 17, no. 1 (Spring):135–148.

Gallup, George and Jim Castelli. 1989. *The People's Religion: American Faith in the 90's*. New York: Macmillan.

García, Ismael. 2001. "The Future of Hispanic/Latino Theology: The Gifts Hispanics/Latinas Bring to the Table." *Journal of Hispanic/Latino Theology* 9, no. 1 (August):46–57.

García, Sixto. 1992. "A Hispanic Approach to Trinitarian Theology: The Dynamics of Celebration, Reflection, and Praxis." In *We Are a People! Initiatives in Hispanic American Theology*, ed. Robert Goizueta, 107–132. Minneapolis: Fortress Press.

Garnsey, Peter. 1996. *Ideas of Slavery from Aristotle to Augustine*. Cambridge: Cambridge University Press.

Garrison, Vivian. 1974. "Sectarianism and Psychosocial Adjustment: A Controlled Comparison of Puerto Rican and Pentecostals and Catholics." In *Religious Movements in Contemporary America*, ed. Irving G. Zaretzky and Mark P. Leone, 298–329. Princeton: Princeton University Press.

Geisler, Norman L. 1974. *Philosophy of Religion*. Grand Rapids, Mich.: Zondervan Publishing House.

George, Andrew. 1999. *The Epic of Gilgamesh*. London: Penguin.

Gillespie, Susan D. 1989. *The Aztec Kings: The Construction of Rulership in Mexica History*. Tucson: University of Arizona Press.

Gimbutas, Marija. 1982. *The Goddesses and Gods of Old Europe Myths and Cult Images*. Berkeley: University of California Press.

Goizueta, Roberto S. 1994. "La Raza Cósmica? The Vision of José Vasconcelos." *Journal of Hispanic/Latino Theology* 1, no. 2 (February):5–27.

———. 1995. "The Preferential Option for the Poor: The CELAM Documents and the NCCB Pastoral Letter on U.S. Hispanics as Sources for U.S. Hispanic Theology." *Journal of Hispanic/Latino Theology* 3, no. 2 (November):65–77.

———. 1996. "Bartolomé de las Casas, Modern Critic of Modernity: An Analysis of a Conversion." *Journal of Hispanic/Latino Theology* 3, no. 4 (May):6–19.

González, Justo L. 1990. *Mañana: Christian Theology from a Hispanic Perspective*. Nashville: Abingdon.

González, Roberto O. and Michael La Velle. 1985. *The Hispanic Catholic in the United States: A Socio-Cultural and Religious Profile*. New York: Northeast Catholic Pastoral Center for Hispanics.

González-T., César A. ed. 1990. *Rudolfo Anaya: Focus on Criticism*. La Jolla, California: Lalo Press.

Gordon, David J. 2002. *Literary Atheism*. New York: Peter Lang. Gossen, Gary H. ed. 1993. *South and Meso-American Native Spirituality. From the Cult of the Feathered Serpent to the Theology of Liberation*. New York: Crossroad.

Graff, Gerald. 1987. *Professing Literature: An Institutional History*. Chicago: University of Chicago.

Greeley, Andrew M. 1988. "Defection Among Hispanics." *America* (July 30):61–62.

———. 1997. "Defection Among Hispanics." *America* (September 27):12–13.

Greenleaf, Richard E. 1994. "The Persistence of Native Values: the Inquisition and the Indians of Colonial Mexico." *The Americas* (January):351–376.

Guillaume, Alfred. 1955. *The Life of Muhammad: A Translation of Ibn Ishaq's Sirat Rasul Allah*. London/Karachi: Oxford University Press.

Guerrero, Andrés G. 1987. *A Chicano Theology*. Maryknoll, New York: Orbis.

Gumerman, George J. 1991. *Exploring the Hohokam: Prehistoric Desert Peoples of the American Southwest*. Amerind Foundation New World Studies Series 1. Albuquerque: University New Mexico Press.

Gurpegui, Jose Antonio, ed. 1996. *Alejandro Morales: Fiction Past, Present and Future Perfect*. Tempe, Arizona: Bilingual Press/Editorial Bilingüe.

Gutiérrez, Ramón. 1991. *When Jesus Came, the Corn Mothers Went Away: Marriage, Sexuality, and Power in New Mexico, 1500–1846*. Stanford: Stanford University Press.

Gutiérrez, Ramón and Genaro Padilla. 1993. *Recovering the U.S. Hispanic Literary Heritage*. Houston: Arte Público Press.

Hall, Lynda. 1999. "Writing Selves Home at the Crossroads: Anzaldúa and Chrystos (Re)Configure Lesbian Bodies." *ARIEL: A Review of International English Literature* 30, no. 2 (April):99–117.

Bibliography

Halsell, Grace. 1989. *Prophecy and Politics: The Secret Alliance Between Israel and the U.S. Christian Right*. New York: Lawrence & Hill.

Hamamoto, Darrell Y. and Rodolfo D. Torres, ed. 1997. *New American Destinies: A Reader in Contemporary Asian and Latin Immigration*. New York: Routledge.

Harap, Louis. 2003. *The Image of the Jew in American Literature*. Syracuse: Syracuse University Press. Reprint of 1978 2nd ed..

Harris, James F. 1992. *Against Relativism: A Philosophical Defense of Method*. La Salle, Il:Open Court.

Hedley, Jane. 1996. "Nepantlist Poetics: Narrative and Cultural Identity in the Mixed-Language Writings of Irena Klepfisz and Gloria Anzaldúa." *Narrative* 4, no. 1 (January):36–54.

Heidel, Alexander. 1949. *The Gilgamesh Epic and Old Testament Parallels*. Chicago: University of Chicago Press.

———. 1951. *The Babylonian Genesis*. Chicago: University of Chicago Press.

Herberg, Will. 1955/1960. *Protestant-Catholic-Jew*. Revised edition. Garden City, New York: Doubleday.

Hernández, Carmen Dolores. 1997. *Puerto Rican Voices in English: Interviews with Writers*. Westport, Connecticut: Greenwood Press.

Hernández, Edwin I. and Kenneth G. Davis. 2001 "The National Survery of Hispanic Theological Education." *The Journal of Hispanic/ Latino Theology* 8, no. 4 (May):37–59.

Hernton, Calvin. 1969. *Sex and Race in America*. New York: Grove Press.

Heyck, Denis Lynn Daly, ed. 1994. *Barrios and Borderlands: Cultures of Latinos and Latinas in the United States*. New York: Routledge.

Hillegas, Mark R. 1979. "The Literary Background of Science Fiction." In *Science Fiction: A Critical Guide*, ed. Patrick Parrinder, 2–17. Longman: London.

Hinojosa, Gilberto M. 1994. "Mexican-American Faith Communities in Texas and the Southwest." In *The Mexican Americans and the Catholic Church 1900–1965*, ed., Jay P. Dolan and Gilberto Hinojosa, 11–125. Notre Dame History of Hispanic Catholics in the U.S. Volume 1. Notre Dame: University of Notre Dame Press.

Hirsch, David H. and Nehama Aschkenasy, ed. 1984. *Biblical Patterns in Modern Literature*. Brown Judaic Studies 77. Chico, California: Scholars Press.

Ibn Hishâm, 'Abd al-Malik. *al-Sîrat al-Nabawîyah li-Ibn Hisham*. Four volumes; Beirut, Lebanon: Dar al-Kotob al-Ilmiyah, 2000.

Hodgson, Marshall G. S. 1974. *The Ventures of Islam: Conscience and History in a World Civilization*. 2 volumes. Chicago: The University of Chicago Press.

Hoge, Dean R., Kenneth McGuire, Bernard F. Stratman and Alvin A. Illig. 1981. *Converts, Dropouts, and Returnees*. New York: The Pilgrim Press.

Hollenweger, Walter J. 1997. *Pentecostalism: Origins and Developments Worldwide*. Peabody: Hendrickson Press.

Holton, Gerald J. 1993. *Science and Anti-Science*. Cambridge: Harvard University Press.

Huntington, Samuel P. 2004. *Who Are We? The Challenges to America's National Identity*. New York: Simon & Schuster.

Isasi-Díaz, Ada María. 1996. *Mujerista Theology: A Theology for the Twenty-First Century*. Maryknoll, New York: Orbis.

——— and Fernando F. Segovia, eds. 1996. *Hispanic/Latino Theology: Challenge and Promise*. Minneapolis: Fortress.

——— and Yolanda Tarango. 1992. *Hispanic Women: PropheticVoice in the Church*. Minneapolis: Fortress Press.

——— and Fernando F. Segovia, 45–62. Minneapolis: Fortress. Olmos, Margarite Fernandez and Lizabeth Paravisini-Gebert. 1997. *Sacred Possessions: Vodou, Santería, Obeah and the Caribbean*. New Brunswick, New Jersey: Rutgers University Press.

James, Janet Wilson, ed. 1980. *Women in American Religion*. Philadelphia: University of Pennsylvania Press.

James, William. 1982. *The Varieties of Religious Experience*. New York: Penguin Books. Reprint of 1902 edition.

Jara, René and Nicholas Spadaccini, eds. 1992. *Amerindian Images and the Legacy of Columbus*. Minneapolis: University of Minnesota Press.

Jasper, David. 1989. *The Study of Literature and Religion: An Introduction*. Minneapolis: Fortress.

Jayne, Allen. 1998. *Jefferson's Declaration of Independence: Origins Philosophy, and Theology*. Louisville: The University Press of Kentucky.

Jiménez, Francisco, ed. 1979. *The Identification and Analysis of Chicano Literature*. New York: Bilingual Press/Editorial Bilingüe.

Kanellos, Nicolás. 1993. *Short Fiction by Hispanic Writers of the United States*. Houston. Arte Público Press.

———. 1993. *Reference Library of Hispanic America*. 3 volumes. Detroit: Gale Research Service.

———. 2002. *Herencia: The Anthology of Hispanic Literature in The United States*. New York: Oxford.

Karttunen, Frances. 1983. *An Analytical Dictionary of Nahuatl*. Norman: University of Oklahoma, 1983.

Kaufman, Terrence. 1976. "Archaeological and Linguistic Correlations in Mayaland and Associated Areas of Mesoamerica." *World Archaeology* 8, no 1:101–18.

Keating, AnaLouise. 2000. *Gloria Anzaldúa: Interviews/Entrevistas*. New York: Routledge, 2000.

Keefe, Susan E. and Amado M. Padilla. 1987. *Chicano Ethnicity*. Albuquerque: University of New Mexico Press.

Keller, Gary D., Rafael J. Magallán, and Alma M. Garcia, eds. 1989. *Curriculum Resources in Chicano Studies: Undergraduate and Graduate*. Tempe, Arizona: Bilinguial Revew/Press.

Kevane, Bridget. 2003. *Latino Literature in America*. Westport, CT.: Greenwood Press.

Kinealy, Christine. 1995. *This Great Calamity: The Irish Famine 1845–52*. Boulder, Colorado: Roberts Rinehart Publishers.

Kirk, Pamela. 1998. "Sor Juana Inés de la Cruz: Precursor of Latin American Feminism." *Journal of Hispanic/Latino Theology* 5, no. 3 (February):16–38.

Klein, Charlotte. 1978. *Anti-Judaism in Christian Theology*. Translated by Edward Quinn. Philadelphia: Fortress Press.

Klemke, Elmer D. ed. 1992. *To Believe or Not to Believe: Readings in the Philosophy of Religion*. Fort Worth: Harcourt Brace Jovanovich College Publishers.

Kreuziger, Frederick A. 1986. *The Religion of Science Fiction*. Bowling Green, Ohio: Bowling Green State University Popular Press.

Kurtz, Paul, 1983. *In Defense of Secular Humanism*. Amherst, New York: Prometheus Press.

———. 2000. *Humanist Manifesto 2000: A Call for a New Planetary Humanism*. Amherst, New York: Prometheus Books.

Larson, Edward and Larry Witham. 1997. "Scientists are Still Keeping The Faith." *Nature* 386 (3 April):435–436.

Larue, Gerald. 1996. *Freethought Across the Centuries: Toward a New Age of Enlightenment*. Amherst, New York: Humanist Press.

Lattin, Vernon E. 1979. "The Quest for Mythic Vision in Contemporary Native American and Chicano Fiction." *American Literature* 50, no. 4 (January):625–640.

Leal, Luis. 1985. *Aztlán y México: Perfiles literarios e históricos*. Binghamton, New York: Bilingual Press.

———. 1997. "Into the Labyrinth: Chicano Literature in Search of a Theory." *Aztlán* 22, no. 2 (Fall):107–119.

León, Luis. 1999."The Poetic Uses of Religion in *The Miraculous Day of Amalia Gómez*." *Religion and American Culture* 9, no. 2 (Summer):205–231.

221

————. 2004. *La Llorona's Children: Religion, Life, and Death in the U.S.-Mexican Borderlands.* Berkeley: University of California Press.

León-Portilla, Miguel. 1992. "Have We Really Translated the Mesoamerican 'Ancient World'?" In *On the Translation of Native American Literatures*, ed. Brian Swann, 313–338. Washington: Smithsonian Institute Press.

————. 1993. "Those Made Worthy by Divine Sacrifice: The Faith of Ancient Mexico." In *South and Meso-American Native Spirituality: From the Cult of the Feathered Serpent to the Theology of Liberation*, ed. Gary H. Gossen, 40–64. New York: Crossroad.

Lincoln, C. Eric. 1994. *The Black Muslims in America.* 3rd ed.. Grand Rapids, Michigan: Eerdmans.

Liptzin, Solomon. 1966. *The Jew in American Literature.* New York: Bloch Publishing Company.

Lorde, Audre. 1981. "An Open Letter to Mary Daly." In *This Bridge Called My Back: Writings by Radical Women of Color.* eds. Cherríe Moraga and Gloria Anzaldúa, 94–97. New York: Kitchen Table: Women of Color Press.

Luccock, Halford E. 1934. *Contemporary American Religion and Literature.* Chicago: Wilbert Clark & Company.

Ludwig, Theodore M. 2001. *The Sacred Paths: Understanding the Religions of the World.* 3rd ed.. Upper Saddle River, N.J.: Prentice Hall.

Luis, Willliam. 1997. *Dance Between Two Cultures: Latino Caribbean Literature Written in the United States.* Nashville: Vanderbilt University Press.

Lustig, Wolf. 1989. *Christliche Symbolik und Christentum im spanischamerikanischen Roman des 20. Jahrhunderts.* Main: Peter Lang.

Lux, Guillermo and Maurilio E. Vigil. 1979. "Return to Aztlan: The Chicano Rediscovers his Indian Past." In *The Chicanos: As We See Ourselves*, ed. Arnulfo D. Trejo, 1–17. Tucson: University of Arizona Press.

Malachy, Yona. 1978. *Fundamentalism and Israel: The Relation of Fundamentalist Churches to Zionism and the State of Israel.* Jerusalem: Institute of Contemporary Jewry at the Hebrew University of Jerusalem

Maldonado, David Jr. ed. 1999. *Protestantes/Protestants:Hispanic Christianity within Mainline Traditions.* Nashville: Abingdon.

Maldonado, Robert D. 1995. "¿La Conquista? Latin American (*Mestizaje*) Reflections on the Biblical Conquest." *Journal of Hispanic/Latino Theology* 2, no. 4 (May):5–25.

Malinowski, Bronislaw. 1948. *Magic, Science, and Religion and Other Essays.* Boston: Beacon Press.

Marín, Gerardo and Raymond J. Gamba. 1993. "The Role of Expectations in Religious Conversions: The Case of Hispanic Catholics." *Review of Religious Research* 34, no. 4 (June):357–371.

Marrero, Maria Teresa. 1997. "Historical and Literary Santería: Unveiling Gender and Identity in U.S. Cuban Literature." In *Tropicalizations: Transcultural Representations of Latinidad.* ed. Frances R. Aparicio and Susana Chávez-Silverman, 139–159. Hanover, New Hampshire: Dartmouth College Press.

Marriott, David. 2000. *On Black Men.* New York: Columbia University Press.

Martin, Michael. 1990. *Atheism: A Philosophical Justification.* Philadelphia: Temple University Press.

Matibag, Eugenio. 1996. *Afro-Cuban Religious Experience: Cultural Reflections in Narrative.* Gainesville: University Press of Florida.

————. 1997. "Ifá and Interpretation: An Afro-Caribbean Literary Practice." In *Sacred Possessions: Vodou, Santería, Obeah and the Caribbean*, ed. Margarite Fernandez Olmos and Lizabeth Paravisini-Gebert, 151–170. New Brunswick, New Jersey: Rutgers University Press.

Matthiessen, Francis O. 1941. *American Renaissance: Art and Expression in the Age of Emerson and Whitman.* New York: Oxford.

McCloud, Aminah Beverly. 1995. *African American Islam.* New York: Routledge.

Mazrui, Ali A., ed. 1999. *Africa since 1935*. General History of Africa 8. Paris: UNESCO.

McCloskey, H. J. 1992. "God and Evil." In *To Believe or Not to Believe: Readings in the Philosophy of Religion*, ed. Elmer D Klemke, 465–481. Fort Worth: Hartcourt Brace Jovanovich College Publishers. First published in *The Philosophical Quarterly* 10, no. 39 (1960).

McCutcheon, Russell T. 2001. *Critics not Caretakers: Redescribing the Public Study of Religion*. Albany: State University of New York Press.

McLellan, David. 1987. *Marxism and Religion*. New York: Harper & Row.

Mejido, Manuel J. 2001. "A Critique of the 'Aesthetic' Turn in U.S. Hispanic Theology: A Dialogue with Roberto Goizueta and the Positing of a New Paradigm." *Journal of Hispanic/Latino Theology* 8, no. 3 (February):18–48.

Merkley, Paul Charles. 1998. *The Politics of Christian Zionism 1891–1948* London: Frank Cass Publishers. Meyer, Jean A. 1976. *The Cristero Rebellion: The Mexican People Between Church and State 1926–1929*. Cambridge: Cambridge University Press.

Meyers, Robert E. ed. 1983. *The Intersection of Science Fiction and Philosophy: Critical Studies*. Westport, Connecticut: Greenwood Press. Mielziner, Moses. 1968. *Introduction to the Talmud*. New York: Bloch.

Mignolo, Walter D. 1992. "When Speaking was Not Good Enough: Illiterates, Barbarians, Savages, and Cannibals," In *Amerindian Images and the Legacy of Columbus*, ed. René Jara and Nicholas Spadaccini, 312–345. Minneapolis: University of Minnesota Press.

Mirandé, Alfredo and Evangelina Enríquez. 1979. *La Chicana: The Mexican-American Woman*. Chicago: The University of Chicago Press.

Moctezuma, Eduardo Matos. 1988. *The Great Temple of the Aztecs: Treasures of Tenochtitlan*. London: Thames & Hudson.

Mohs, Mayo. 1971. *Other Worlds, Other Gods: Adventures in Religious Science Fiction*. Garden City, New York: Doubleday. Monk, Maria. 1969. *Awful Disclosures of Maria Monk, or The Hidden Secrets of a Nun's Life in a Convent Exposed*. London: Canova Press. First published in 1836.

Morales Blouin, Egla. 1979. "Símbolos y motivos Nahuas en la literatura chicana," In *The Identification and Analysis of Chicano Literature*, ed. Franciso Jiménez, 179–190. New York: Bilingual Press.

Morello-Frosch, Marta. 1984. "*One Hundred Years of Solitude* by Gabriel Garcia Marquez or Genesis Rewritten." In *Biblical Patterns in Modern Literature*, ed. David H. Hirsch and Nehama Aschkenasy, 155–163. Brown Judaic Studies 77. Chico, California: Scholars Press.

Morris, Brian. 1987. *Anthropological Studies of Religion: An Introductory Text*. Cambridge: Cambridge University Press.

Moskowitz, Sam. 1974. *Explorers of the Infinite: Shapers of Science Fiction*. Westport, Connecticut: Hyperion Press. 1963. Cleveland, New York: World Publishing Company.

Muhammad, Elijah. 1957. *The Supreme Wisdom: Solution to the So-Called Negroes's Problem*. Volume 1. Atlanta: M.E.M.P.S.

———. 1994. *History of the Nation of Islam*. Atlanta: Secretarius M.E.M.P.S. Publication.

Murphy, Joseph M. 1993. *Santería: African Spirits in America*. Boston: Beacon Press.

Nelson, Wilton M., ed. 1989. *Diccionario de historia de la Iglesia*, Miami: Editorial Caribe.

Neusch, Marcel. 1982. *The Sources of Modern Atheism: One Hundred Years of Debate over God*. Translated by Matthew J. O'Connell. New York: Paulist Press.

Neusner, Jacob. 1982–89. *The Talmud of the Land of Israel: A Preliminary Translation and Explanation*. Chicago: University of Chicago Press.

———. 1970. *The Formation of the Babylonian Talmud*. Leiden: Brill.

Nicholoff, James B. 1994. "Indigenous Theology and Andean Resistance to Spanish Colonial Rule: The Rebellion of Túpac Amaru (1780–1782)." *Journal of Hispanic/Latino Theology* 2, no. 1 (August):5–27.

Nicholson, Henry B. 1971. "Religion in Pre-Hispanic Central Mexico." In *Archaeology of Northern Mesoamerica, Part 1*. ed. Ignacio Bernal and Gordon E. Elkholm, 395–446. Handbook of Middle American Indians, Volume 10: Austin: University of Texas Press.

Nielsen, Kai. 1990. *Ethics Without God*. Amherst, New York: Prometheus Press.

Niezen, Ronald. 2000. *Spirit Wars: Native North American Religions in the Age of Nation Building*. Berkeley: University of California Press.

Noll, Mark. A. 1986. *Between Faith and Criticism: Evangelicals: Scholarship, and the Bible in America*. San Francisco: Harper & Row.

Noll, Richard. 1994. *The Jung Cult: The Origins of a Charistmatic Movement*. Princeton: Princeton University Press.

———. 1997. *The Aryan Christ: The Secret Life of Carl Jung*. New York: Random House.

Ohanneson, Joan. 1980. *Woman: Survivor in the Church*. Minneapolis: Winston Press.

Olazagasti-Segovia, Elena. 1996. "Judith Ortiz Cofer's *Silent Dancing: The Self-Portrait of the Artist as a Young, Bicultural Girl*." In *Hispanic/Latino Theology: Challenge and Promise*, ed.

Ozment, Steven. 1980. *The Age of Reform, 1250–1550*. New Haven: Yale University Press.

Pagliarini, Marie Anne. 1999. "The Pure American Woman and the Wicked Catholic Priest: An Analysis of Anti-Catholic Literature in Ante-bellum America." *Religion and American Culture* 9, no. 1 (Winter):98–127.

Pals, Daniel. 1996. *Seven Theories of Religion*. New York: Oxford.

Pantoja, Segundo S. 2001. "Religious Diversity and Ethnicity Among Latinos." In *New York Glory: Religions in the City*, ed. Tony Carnes and Anna Karpathakis, 162–173. New York: New York University Press.

Paredes, Américo. 1958. *With a Pistol in His Hand: A Border Ballad & Its Hero*. Austin: University of Texas Press.

Paredes, Raymund. 1982. "The Evolution of Chicano Literature." In *Three American Literatures: Essays in Chicano, Native American, and Asian-American Literature for Teachers of American Literature*. In Baker, Houston A. ed., 33–79. New York: The Modern Language Association.

———. 1993. "Mexican American Literature: An Overview." In *Recovering the U.S. Hispanic Literary Heritage*, ed. Ramón Gutierrez and Genaro Padilla, 31–51. Houston: Arte Público Press.

Parrinder, Patrick, ed. 1979. *Science Fiction: A Critical Guide*. London: Longman.

Parrington, Vernon L. 1927. *Main Currents in American Thought: An Interpretation of American Literature from the Beginning to 1920*. New York: Harcourt, Brace, and Co.

Paz, Octavio. 1986. *El laberinto de la soledad*. México: Fondo de cultura económica. First published in 1950.

———. 1988. *Sor Juana*. Cambridge: Harvard University Press.

Peña, Milagros. 1997. "Border Crossings: Sociological Analysis and the Latina and Latino Religious Experience." *Journal of Hispanic/ Latino Theology* 4, no. 3 (February):13–27.

Pérez, Lisandro. 1994. "Cuban Catholics in the United States." In *Puerto Rican and Cuban Catholics in the U.S. 1900–1965*, ed. Jay P. Dolan and Jaime R. Vidal, 147–208. Notre Dame History of Hispanic Catholics in the U.S. Volume 2. Notre Dame: University of Notre Dame Press.

Pérez y Mena, Andrés Isidoro. 1991. *Speaking with the Dead: Development of Afro-Latin Religion Among Puerto Ricans in the United States*. New York: AMS Press.

———. 2000. "Understanding Religiosity in Cuba." *Journal of Hispanic/ Latino Theology* 7, no. 3 (February):6–34.

Pinn, Anthony. 1999. *Why Lord? Suffering and Evil in Black Theology*. New York: Continuum Press.

Poey, Delia. 2002. *Latino American Literature in the Classroom: The Politics of Transformation*. Gainesville: University Press of Florida.

Poliakov, Léon. 1974. *The Aryan Myth; A History of Racist and Nationalist Ideas in Europe*. New York: Basic Books.

Pollack, Sandra and Denise D. Knight. 1993. *Contemporary Lesbian Writers of the United States: A Bio-Bibliographical Critical Sourcebook*. Westport, Connecticut: Greenwood Press.

Poole, Stafford. 1995. *Our Lady of Guadalupe: The Origins and Sources of a Mexican National Symbol, 1531–1797*. Tucson: University of Arizona Press.

Porter, Stanley E. and Brook W. R. Pearson, eds. 2000. *Christian-Jewish Relations through the Centuries*. Sheffield: Sheffield Academic Press.

Portillo-Orozco, Febe. 1981. "Rudolfo Anaya's Use of History, Myth, and Legend in his Novels: *Bless Me, Ultima* and *Heart of Aztlán*, Master's Thesis, San Francisco State University, San Francisco, California.

Poyatos, Fernando, ed. 1988. *Literary Anthropology: A New Interdisciplinary Approach to People, Signs and Literature*. Amsterdam: John Benjamins Publishing Company.

Pratt, Annis, with Barbara White, Andrea Lowenstein and Mary Wyer. 1981. *Archetypal Patterns in Women's Fiction*. Bloomington: Indiana University Press.

Pratte, Trish. 1993. "A Comparative Study of Attitudes toward Homosexuality: 1986 and 1991." *Journal of Homosexuality* 26, no. 1:77–83.

Prem, Hanns. 1997. *The Ancient Americas: A Brief History and Guide to Research*. Translated by Kornelia Kurbjuhn. Salt Lake City: University of Utah Press.

Quiñones Keber, Eloise. 1992. "Rediscovering Aztec Images." In *Amerindian Images and the Legacy of Columbus*, ed. Rene Jará and Nicholas Spadaccini, 132–162. Minneapolis: University of Minnesota Press.

Ramos, Juanita. 1993. "Gloria E. Anzaldúa (1942–)." In *Contemporary Lesbian Writers of the United States: A Bio-Bibliographical Critical Sourcebook*, ed. Sandra Pollack and Denise D. Knight, 19–25. Westport, Connecticut: Greenwood Press.

Ramos, Marcos Antonio. 1986. *Panorama del protestantismo en Cuba*. San Jose, Costa Rica: Editorial Caribe.

Ramsey, Paul and John F. Wilson, eds. 1970. *The Study of Religion in Colleges and Universities*. Princeton: Princeton University Press.

Ray, J. Karen. 1978. "Cultural and Mythical Archetypes in Rudolfo Anaya's *Bless Me, Ultima*." *New Mexico Humanities Review* 50, no. 3:23–28.

Rebolledo, Tey Diana. 1995. *Women Singing in the Snow: A Cultural Analysis of Chicana Literature*. Tucson: University of Arizona Press.

——— and Eliana S. Rivero. 1993. *Infinite Divisions: An Anthology of Chicana Literature*. Tucson: University of Arizona Press.

Reilly, Robert, ed. 1985. *The Transcendent Adventure: Studies of Religion in Science Fiction Fantasy*. Westport, Connecticut: Greenwood Press.

Rivera, Tomás. 1975. "Remembering, Discovery, and Volition in the Literary Imaginative Process." In *Tomás Rivera: The Complete Works*, ed. Julián Olivares, 365–370. Houston: Arte Público Press. First published in *Atisbos: Journal of Chicano Research* 1 (1975):66–77. Rivera-Pagán, Luis N. 1996. *Mito, exilio y demonios. literatura y teología en América Latina*. Río Piedras, Puerto Rico: Publicaciones Puertorriqueñas.

———. 2000. "Theology and Literature in Latin America: John A. Mackay and *The Other Spanish Christ*." *Journal of Hispanic/Latino Theology* 7, no. 4 (May):7–25.

Roberts, Jon H. and James Turner. 2000. *The Sacred and the Secular University*. Princeton: Princeton University Press.

Rodriguez, Jeanette. 1994. *Our Lady of Guadalupe: Faith and Empowerment among Mexican-American Women*. Austin: University of Texas Press.

Roeder, Beatrice A. 1988. *Chicano Folk Medicine from Los Angeles, California*. University of California Publications: Folklore and Mythology 34. Berkeley: University of California.

Rogers, Jane. 1977. "The Function of the La Llorona Motif in Rudolfo Anaya's *Bless Me, Ultima*. *Latin American Literary Review* 5, no. 10 (Spring-Summer):65–69.

Roof, Wade Clark and Jennifer L. Roof. 1984. "Review of Polls: Images of God among Americans." *Journal for the Scientific Study of Religion* 23, no. 2:201–205.

Rosario-Sievert, Heather. 1997. "Conversation with Julia Alvarez." *Review: Latin American Literature and Arts*, 54 (Spring):31–37.

Rouët de Journel, M. J. 1922. *Enchiridion patristicum: Loci SS. patrum doctorum, scriptorum ecclesiasticorum*. Berlin: Herder and Company.

Rubio Goldsmith, Raquel. 1987. "Shipwrecked in the Desert: A Short History of the Mexican Sisters of the House of Providence in Douglas, Arizona, 1927–1949. In *Women on the U.S.-Mexico Border: Responses to Change*. ed, Vicki Ruiz and Susan Tiano, 177–195. Boston: Allen and Unwin.

Ruether, Rosemary. 1974. *Faith and Fratricide: The Theological Roots of Anti-Semitism*. New York: Seabury Press.

Ruiz, Jean-Pierre. 1996. "Naming the Other: U.S. Hispanic Catholics, the So-Called 'Sects,' and the 'New Evangelization.'" *Journal of Latino/Hispanic Theology* 4, no. 2 (November): 34–59.

Ruiz, Ronald. 2000. *http://www.smartvoter. org/ 2000/11/07/ca/scz/ vote/ruiz_r/* viewed March 14, 2002.

Ruiz, Vicki and Susan Tiano, eds. 1987. *Women on the U.S.-Mexico Border: Responses to Change*. Boston: Allen and Unwin.

Russell, Bertrand. 1957. *Why I Am Not a Christian and Other Essays on Religion and Related Subjects*. New York; Simon and Schuster.

Russell, James W. 1994. *After the Fifth Sun: Class and Race in North America*. New York: Prentice Hall.

Ryckman, Richard M. 1982. *Theories of Personality*. 2nd ed.. Belmont, California: Wadsworth.

Saldívar, José David. 1991. "Chicano Border Narratives as Cultural Critique." In *Criticism in the Borderlands: Studies in Chicano Literature, Culture, and Ideology*, ed. Héctor Calderón and José David Saldívar, 167–180. Durham: Duke University Press.

Samarin, William. 1972. *Tongues of Men and Angels: The Religious Language of Pentecostalism*. New York: The Macmillan Company.

Samuelson, Norbert M. 2002. "The Death and Revival of Jewish Philosophy." *Journal of the American Academy of Religion* 70, no. 1 (March):117–134.

Sánchez, Marta Ester. 1985. *Contemporary Chicana Poetry: A Critical Approach to an Emerging Literature*. Berkeley: University of California Press.

Sánchez Cardenas, Julio. 1993. "Santería or Orisha Religion: An Old Religion in a New World." Pages 474–495 in *South and Meso-American Native Spirituality: From the Cult of the Feathered Serpent to the Theology of Liberation*. Gary H. Gossen and Miguel Leon Portilla, eds.; New York: Crossroad.

Sánchez Korrol, Virginia E. 1994. *From Colonia to Community: The History of Puerto Ricans in New York City*. Berkeley: University of California.

Sánchez Mayers, Raymond. 1989. "The Use of Folk Medicine by Elderly Mexican-American Women." *Journal of Drug Issues* 19, no. 2:283–295.

Sandmel, Samuel. 1978. *Anti-Semitism in the New Testament*. Philadelphia: Fortress.

Sandoval, Moises. 1990. *On the Move: A History of the Hispanic Church in the United States*. Maryknoll, New York: Orbis.

Schiefelbein, Michael E. *The Lure of Babylon: Seven Protestant Novelists and Britain's Roman Catholic Revival*. Macon, Georgia: Mercer University Press, 2001.

Schuyler, Jane. 1990. "Michelangelo's Serpent with Two Tails." In *The Sistine Chapel*, ed. William E. Wallace, 405–411. New York: Garland. Reprint of original in *Source: Notes on the History of Art* 9 (1990):23–29.

Sen, K.M. 1984. *Hinduism*. Harmondsworth, UK: Penguin.

Shadow, Robert D. 1987. "Production, Social Identity, and Agrarian Struggle Among the Tepecano Indians of Northern Jalisco." In *Ejidos and Regions of Refuge in Northwestern Mexico*, ed. Crumrine, N. Ross and Phil C. Weigand. Anthropological Papers of the University of Arizona, no. 46. Tucson: University of Arizona Press.

Shamdasani, Sonu. 1998. *Cult Fictions: C. G. Jung and the Founding of Analytical Psychology*. London: Routledge.

Sharer, Robert J. *The Ancient Maya*. 1994. 5th ed. Stanford: Stanford University Press.

Sharpe, Eric. 1985. *The Universal Gita: Western Images of the Bhagavad Gita, a Bicentennary Survey*. La Salle, Illinois: Open Court.

Shea, Maureen E. 1993. "Latin American Women and the Oral Tradition: Voice to the Voiceless." *Critique* 34, no. 3 (Spring):139–153.

Shorris, Earl. 1992. *Latinos: A Biography of a People*. New York: W. W. Norton and Company.

Short, Margaret. 1993. *Law and Religion in Marxist Cuba*. New Brunswick, New Jersey: Transaction Publishers.

Shumway, David R. 1994. *Creating American Civilization: A Genealogy of American Literature as an Academic Discipline*. Minneapolis: University of Minnesota Press.

Sigmund, Paul E. 1990. *Liberation Theology at the Crossroads: Democracy or Revolution?* New York: Oxford.

Silva Gotay, Samuel. 1998. *Protestantismo y política en Puerto Rico 1898–1930*. 2nd ed.. San Juan: Editorial de la Universidad de Puerto Rico.

Sizer, Theodore R. 1967. *Religion and Public Education*. Boston: Houghton Mifflin.

Slade, Carole. 1995. *St. Teresa of Avila: Author of a Heroic Life*. Berkeley: University of California Press.

Smith, Jane I. *Islam in America*. New York: Columbia University Press.

Smith, Jonathan Z. 1987. *To Take Place: Toward Theory in Ritual*. Chicago: University of Chicago Press.

———. 1990. *Drudgery Divine: On the Comparison of Early Christianities and the Religions of Late Antiquity*. Chicago: University of Chicago Pres. Smith, Michael E. 1996. *The Aztecs*. Malden, Masssachusetts: Blackwell Publishers.

Smith, Richard L. 1994. *AIDS, Gays, and the American Catholic Church*. Cleveland: The Pilgrim Press.

Smith, Wilfred Cantwell. 1963. *The Meaning and End of Religion: A New Approach to the Religions of Mankind*. New York: Macmillan.

Socolovsky, Maya. 2003. "Narrative and Traumatic Memory in Denise Chávez's Face of an Angel," *MELUS* 28.4: 187–205.

———. 2003. "Deconstructing a Secret History: Trace, Translation, and Crypto-Judaism in Achy Obejas' *Days of Awe*" *Contemporary Literature* 44.2: 225–249.

Soden, Wolfram von. 1994. *The Ancient Near East: An Introduction to the Study of the Ancient Near East*. Translated by Donald Schley. Grand Rapids, Michigan: W.B. Eerdmans Publishing Company.

Soldatenko, Michael. 1998. "The Genesis of Academic Chicano Studies, 1967–1970: The Emergence of Perspectivist and Empirical Chicano Studies. *Latino Studies Journal* 9, no. 2 (Spring):3–25.

Sow, Alfa I. and Mohamed H. Abdulaziz. 1999. "Language and Social Change." In *Africa since 1935*, ed. Ali A. Mazrui, 522–552. General History of Africa 8. Paris: UNESCO.

Spicer, Edward H. 1980. *The Yaquis: A Cultural History*. Tucson: University of Arizona Press.

Stanford, Peter. 1999. *The Legend of Pope Joan: In Search of the Truth*. New York: Berkley Books.

Stavans, Ilan. 2000. *The Essential Ilan Stavans*. New York: Routledge.

———, ed. 1996. *Oscar "Zeta" Acosta: The Uncollected Works*. Houston: Arte Público Press.

Sternberg, Meir. 1987. *The Poetics of Biblical Narrative: Ideological Literature and the Drama of Reading*. Bloomington: Indiana University Press.

Stevens-Arroyo, Anthony M. and Ana Marìa Dìaz-Stevens. 1994. *An Enduring Flame: Studies on Latino Popular Religiosity*. PARAL Studies Series Volume I. New York; The Bildner Center for Western Hemisphere Studies Graduate School and University Center City University of New York.

———— and Gilbert R. Cadena. 1995. *Old Masks, New Faces: Religion and Latino Identities*. PARAL Studies Series Volume II. New York: The Bildner Center for Western Hemisphere Studies Graduate School and University Center City University of New York.

———— and Andrés Perez y Mena. 1995. *Enigmatic Powers: Syncretism with African and Indigenous Peoples' Religions Among Latinos*. PARAL Studies Series Volume III. The Bildner Center for Western Hemisphere Studies Graduate School and University Center City University of New York.

———— and Segundo Pantoja. 1995. *Discovering Latino Religion: A Comprehensive Social Science Bibliography*. PARAL Studies Series Volume IV. New York; The Bildner Center for Western Hemisphere Studies Graduate School and University Center: City University of New York.

Stoll, David. 1990. *Is Latin America Turning Protestant? The Politics of Evangelical Growth*. Berkeley: University of California Press.

Stuckrad, Kocku von. 2002. "Reenchanting Nature: Modern Western Shamanism and Nineteenth Century Thought." *JAAR* 70, no. 4:771–799.

Sullivan, Lawrence. E. ed. 2000. *Native Religions and Cultures of North America: Anthropology of the Sacred*. New York: Continuum.

Tamez, Elsa. 1997. "Quetzalcoatl Challenges the Christian Bible." *Journal of Hispanic/Latino Theology* 4, no. 4 (May):5–20.

Taylor, William B. 1987. "The Virgin of Guadalupe in New Spain: An Inquiry into the Social History of Marian Devotion." *American Ethnologist* 14, no. 1 (February):9–33.

Tedlock, Dennis, ed. 1991. *Popol Vuh: The Mayan Book of the Dawn of Life*. New York: Touchstone.

Thomas, Denis. 1979. *The Face of Christ*. Garden City, New York: Doubleday.

Thompson, Bard. 1964. *Liturgies of the Western Church*. Cleveland: The World Publishing.

Tombs, David. 2002. *Latin American Liberation Theology*. Boston: Brill.

Trejo, Arnulfo, ed. 1979. *The Chicanos: As We See Ourselves*. Tucson: University of Arizona Press.

Trotter, R. T. II. 1985. "Greta and Azarcon: A Survey of Episodic Lead Poisoning from a Folk Remedy." *Human Organization* 44:64–72.

————. 1991. "A Survey of Four Illnesses and Their Relationship to Intracultural Variation in a Mexican-American Community." *American Anthropologist* 93:115–125.

Turner, Frederick Jackson. 1996. *The Frontier in American History*. New York: Dover Publications. Reprint of 1920 edition.

Turner, James. 1985. *Without God, Without Creed: The Origins of Unbelief in America*. Baltimore: The Johns Hopkins University Press.

Turner, Richard Brent. 1997. *Islam in the African American Experience*. Bloomington: Indiana University Press.

Tweed, Thomas A. 1996. "Identity and Authority at a Cuban Shrine in Miami: Santería, Catholicism, and Struggles for Religious Identity." *Journal of Hispanic/Latino Theology* 4, no. 1 (August):27–48.

————. 2002. "On Moving Across: Translocative Religion and the Interpreter's Position." *Journal of the American Academy of Religion* 70, no 2 (June):253–277.

Vanderbilt, Kermit. 1986. *American Literature and the Academy: The Roots, Growth and Maturity of a Profession*. Philadelphia: University of Pennsylvania Press.

Vasconcelos, José, *La raza cósmica:Misión de la raza iberoamericana* (Mexico City: Coleccion Austral, 1948). First published 1925.

228

Vélez-Ibáñez, Carlos. G. 1996. *Border Visions: Mexican Cultures of the Southwest United States.* Tucson: University of Arizona Press.

Vidal, Jaime. 2004. "The Puerto Rican Religious Experience." In *Introduction to the U.S. Latina and Latino Religious Experience*, ed. Hector Avalos, 42–65. Boston: Brill.

———. 1994. "Citizens Yet Strangers: The Puerto Rican Experience." In *Puerto Rican and Cuban Catholics in the U.S. 1900–1965*, ed. Jay P. Dolan and Jaime R. Vidal, 11–143. Notre Dame History of Hispanic Catholics in the U.S. Volume 2. Notre Dame: University of Notre Dame Press.

Vuola, Elina. 2001. "Sor Juana Inés de la Cruz: Rationality, Gender, and Power." *Journal of Hispanic/Latino Theology* 9, no. 1 (August):27–45.

Wallace, William E. 1990. *The Sistine Chapel*, New York: Garland.

Wansbrough, John. 1978. *The Sectarian Milieu: Content and Composition of Islamic Salvation History.* London.

———. 1977. *Quranic Studies:Sources and Methods of Scriptural Interpretation.* Oxford: Oxford University Press.

Warhol, Robyn R. and Diane Price Herndl. 1991. *Feminisms: An Anthology of Literary Theory and Criticism.* New Brunswick, New Jersey: Rutgers University Press.

Weigle, Marta. 1976. *Brothers of Light, Brothers of Blood: The Penitentes of the Southwest.* Santa Fe: Ancient City Press

Weiss-Rosmarin, Trude. 1993. *Judaism and Christianity: The Differences.* New York: Jonathan David. First published in 1943.

Westhelle, Vítor and Hanna Betina Götz. 1995. "In Quest of a Myth: Latin American Literature and Theology." *Journal of Hispanic/ Latino Theology* 3, no. 1(August):5–22.

Whitelam, Keith W. 1996. *The Invention of Ancient Israel: The Silencing of Palestinian History.* New York: Routledge.

Wiebe, Donald. 1999. *The Politics of Religious Studies.* New York: St. Martin's Press.

Williams, Norma. 1987. "Changes in Funeral Patterns and Gender Roles among Mexican Americans." In *Women on the U.S-Mexico Border: Responses to Change*, ed. Vicki Ruiz and Susan Tiano, 197–217. Boston: Allen and Unwin.

Winner, Thomas G. 1988. "Literature as a Source for Anthropological Research The Case of Jaroslav Hašek's Good Soldier Švejk." In *Literary Anthropology:A New Interdisciplinary Approach to People, Signs, and Literature*, ed. Fernando Poyatos, 51–71. Amsterdam: John Benjamins Publishing Company.

The World Almanac and Book of Facts 2002. New York: World Almanac Education Group.

Wuthnow, Robert. 1988. *The Restructuring of American Religion. Princeton*: Princeton University Press.

———. 1989. *The Struggle for America's Soul: Evangelicals, Liberals, and Secularism.* Grand Rapids, Michigan. W. B. Eerdmans Publishing Company.

X, Malcolm [with the assistance of Alex Haley]. 1966. *The Autobiography of Malcolm X.* New York: Grove Press. First published in 1964.

Zamora, Lois Parkinson and Wendy B. Faris, eds. 1995. *Magical Realism Theory, History, Community.* Durham: Duke University Press.

Zimmerman, Marc. 1992. *U.S. Latino Literature: An Essay and Annotated Bibliography.* Chicago: March/Abrazo Press.